POLITICS AND GLOBALISATION

Globalisation is widely understood as a set of processes driven by technological, economic and cultural change. Few have successfully defined the changing character and role of politics in global change. Political institutions such as the nation-state have been seen as 'undermined' by globalisation, or needing to 'respond' to it.

This book clarifies the tensions which global change has provoked in our understanding of politics. *Politics and Globalisation* suggests that globalisation is a process which is politically contested and even politically constituted. The volume presents five key intellectual and political contests in globalisation:

- the extent and political significance of globalising changes in economy and society
- how and how far the relations and forms of nation-state organisation are transformed
- whether the given concepts and methods of political science as a discipline can be applied to global and regional politics, or whether they require radical reformulation
- the role and significance of ethical questions in global change
- whether global change is constituted by, or denies, radical political agency.

Politics and Globalisation brings together scholars in the fields of political science and international relations. Revealing divergences over globalisation, as well as common ground, between these two fields, this book addresses the gaps in existing literature on the global challenge to politics.

Martin Shaw is Professor of International Relations and Politics at the University of Sussex. His many previous publications include *Dialectics of War, Post Military Society, Global Society and International Relations*, and *Civil Society and Media in Global Crises*.

ROUTLEDGE ADVANCES IN INTERNATIONAL RELATIONS AND POLITICS

1 FOREIGN POLICY AND DISCOURSE ANALYSIS
France, Britain and Europe
Henrik Larsen

2 AGENCY, STRUCTURE AND INTERNATIONAL POLITICS
From ontology to empirical enquiry
Gil Friedman and Harvey Starr

3 THE POLITICAL ECONOMY OF REGIONAL CO-OPERATION IN THE MIDDLE EAST
Ali Carkoglu, Mine Eder and Kemal Kirisci

4 PEACE MAINTENANCE
The Evolution of International Political Authority
Jarat Chopra

5 INTERNATIONAL RELATIONS AND HISTORICAL SOCIOLOGY
Breaking down Boundaries
Stephen Hobden

6 EQUIVALENCE IN COMPARATIVE POLITICS
Edited by Jan W. van Deth

7 THE POLITICS OF CENTRAL BANKS
Robert Elgie and Helen Thompson

8 POLITICS AND GLOBALISATION
Edited by Martin Shaw

9 HISTORY AND INTERNATIONAL RELATIONS
Thomas W. Smith

10 IDEALISM AND REALISM IN INTERNATIONAL RELATIONS
Robert M. A. Crawford

POLITICS AND GLOBALISATION

Knowledge, ethics and agency

Edited by Martin Shaw

London and New York

First published 1999
by Routledge
11 New Fetter Lane, London EC4P 4EE

Simultaneously published in the USA and Canada
by Routledge
29 West 35th Street, New York, NY 10001

Typeset in Sabon by
MHL Typesetting Limited, Coventry
Printed and bound in Great Britain by
St Edmundsbury Press, Bury St Edmunds, Suffolk

British Library Cataloguing in Publication Data
A catalogue record for this book is available from the British Library

Library of Congress Cataloging-in-Publication Data
A catalogue record for this book has been requested

ISBN 0-415-20698-7

CONTENTS

FIGURES AND TABLES

Figures

Tables

NOTES ON CONTRIBUTORS

Martin Shaw is Professor of International Relations and Politics at the University of Sussex. His books include *Post-Military Society* (1991), *Global Society and International Relations* (1994) and *Civil Society and Media in Global Crises* (1996).

Jan Aart Scholte is Reader in International Studies at the University of Warwick, and was formerly at Sussex University. He has published *The International Relations of Social Change* (1993).

Michael Nicholson is Professor Emeritus of International Relations at the University of Sussex. His books include *Rationality and the Analysis of International Conflict* (1992) and *Causes and Consequences in International Relations* (1996).

Angus Cameron, a former coordinator of the *Review of International Political Economy*, is a Research Officer in the Department of Geography at the University of Durham, and is completing a thesis at the University of Sussex.

Ronen Palan is a Lecturer in International Relations at the University of Sussex and an editor of the *Review of International Political Economy*. He is the author (with Jason Abbott) of *State Strategies in the Global Political Economy* (1996).

Francis McGowan is a Lecturer in Politics at the University of Sussex and author of *The Struggle for Power in Europe* (1993), and editor of *European energy policy in a changing environment* (1996).

Neil Stammers is a Lecturer in Politics at the University of Sussex and author of *Civil Liberties in Britain During the Second World War* (1983). He has written recently on human rights in *Political Studies* and *Human Rights Quarterly*.

Paul Taggart is a Lecturer in Politics at the University of Sussex and author of *The New Populism and the New Politics* (1996).

Stephanie Hoopes was a Lecturer in Politics at the University of Sussex until 1999. She is the author of *Privatisation, Public Choice and International Forces* (1996).

Zdenek Kavan is a Lecturer in International Relations at the University of Sussex. He co-edited (with Mary Kaldor and Barbara Einhorn) *Citizenship and Democratic Control in Contemporary Europe* (1996).

Christien van den Anker is a Lecturer in International Relations at the University of Sussex. She is preparing her thesis on *Global Justice* for publication.

Fiona Robinson is an Assistant Professor of Political Science at Carleton University, Canada, and was formerly a Lecturer in International Relations at the University of Sussex; she is the author of *Globalizing Care: Ethics, Feminist Theory and International Relations* (1999).

John MacLean is a Senior Lecturer in International Relations at the University of Sussex. He has written on Marxism, Critical Theory and international relations in *Millenium* and various edited volumes.

ACKNOWLEDGEMENTS

My thanks and those of the contributors go to the International Relations and Politics Group at the University of Sussex, which supported the research workshops in 1997 and 1998 which produced this book, to the Group's administrator, Shirley Stay, for her invaluable support at all stages, and to Yoram Allon for compiling the Bibliography.

Martin Shaw
Brighton

INTRODUCTION

Martin Shaw

> In major transitions the fundamental interrelations, and very identities, of organisations such as 'economies' or 'states' become metamorphosed. Even the very definition of 'society' may change.
> (Mann, 1993: 9)

In the theoretical world of the social sciences, as in the practical world of social action, ideas are changing rapidly at the turn of the twenty-first century. The discourse of globalisation rose swiftly to primacy among both academics and practitioners in the last decade of the old century. Reflecting the new world-market era which seemed to open up following the fall of Communism, the simple hegemony of this discourse peaked, perhaps, in the middle of the 1990s. The idea attracted increased criticism as the end of the decade beckoned – not least because of the crises of globalised financial markets, in which the problems of post-Communist Russia loomed large.

The end of the first post-Cold War decade is therefore an appropriate point at which to take stock of 'global' change. While the concept of globalisation has become as current in academia as in popular debates, here it is always viewed at least somewhat critically. The crises of a globalising world are not as surprising to most scholarly writers as they have been to some pundits. Nevertheless, there are profound differences among academic social scientists on the meaning and significance of 'global' change – over both the extent to which globalisation is occurring, and its meaning and effects.

However, academic writers have tended to accept the wider consensus that – to the extent that it is a reality – the main loci of globalisation are in technology, economy, communications and culture. In other words, politics has been seen as secondary to globalisation; political institutions, forces and ideas are generally believed to be responding to phenomena which are located primarily in other social realms. Where political theorists have entered the fray, it is often with dire warnings of the social and political effects of unbridled globalisation (Gray 1998) or at least serious reminders of the continuing salience of nation-states and other political institutions (Hirst and Thompson 1996).

Political scientists have been tempted therefore to accept the terms of the debate as it has been posed in the other social sciences, as well as in popular discourse. According to these, the question is whether globalisation undermines political institutions, above all the nation-state, and indeed politics itself. Some credence, at least, has been given to the idea that in a globalising world, states may be stripped of their functions and politics dissolved into the common sense of universal markets. Of course, critics of globalisation theses argue that these claims are exaggerated but they often concede that they have some degree of truth.

There have moreover been divergent responses to 'global' change between the fields of politics and international relations. Globalisation theory has made more headway among international scholars than among political scientists in general. The former have faced a much more direct challenge than students of domestic politics to established assumptions about the world they study. The year 1989 signalled a veritable *bouleversement* of the Cold War certainties which had been at the centre of the international field.

The other reason why international relations has evidently been particularly affected is more fundamental. It reflects the different ways in which the fields have been constituted within the national–international political structure of the modern world. In politics and other core social sciences what Scholte (1993) called 'methodological nationalism' (a concept he extends here in the idea of 'territorialism') was for the most part implicit. Although society, state, economy, etc., were mostly operationalised in national terms – and the 'comparative method' assumed such units – these disciplines oscillated, as Mann (1993) argues in the case of sociology, between narrow national and broad civilisational meanings of such terms. The possibility of generalisation beyond the national was always present.

The international relations field, on the other hand, has been constituted in a most direct way by the national-and-international division of the world. This structure of thought is not merely a tendency or operational practice, but the very definition of the field. Moreover, the international relations mainstream adopted the most conflictual understanding of 'international' – as necessarily anarchic – as paradigmatic. Even the view that interstate relations involve cooperation and consensus as well as coercion and war was a subordinate theme.

It is not surprising therefore that as world realities change, international relations should have become a major fulcrum of critical global theorising – reflected in this book in the predominance of international relationists among the contributors who give the greatest weight to globalisation. International relations has responded with a radical diversification of its subject-matter and intellectual traditions. These changes have involved, however, some movement away from international politics, in the sense that this has been understood traditionally, and towards political economy, sociology and culture, as well as philosophy and method. Because of these changes, much critical international theory has challenged the viability of separating 'politics' from economic and social relations. Some international theorists even define away a specifically political content to global change.

It is evident that international relations and political science, while commonly still sharing institutional space in university departments, have had increasingly contrasting intellectual trajectories. One purpose of this volume is therefore to develop a dialogue between the two fields, of a kind which is all too rare in British and North American academia. In bringing together reflections on politics in a globalising world from both political science and international relations perspectives, we aimed to see what shared ground there might be. It seemed most likely to be constituted by re-examining the meaning of the political, as well as of the global. Even if some international scholarship disputes the primacy of the political – which the discipline originally inherited from political theory – it is clear that any viable international conception must still attempt to grasp politics in some way.

Moreover, this book represents as much a debate within and across each of the disciplines as between them. Precisely because global change brings into question the national-and-international structure of the world which has constituted both fields, globalisation presents challenges to all political and international scholars (indeed all social scientists). However we generalise about responses within disciplines, in reality individual scholars respond in distinctive ways, and there are major differences among scholars within each subject. In this book, therefore, international relations and political science chapters are not categorically separated. There is instead a common agenda which individuals from both groups address, although there are clusterings of the fields around different parts of the agenda.

The book originated in debates within the International Relations and Politics subject group at the University of Sussex, and contributors are all past or present members of the group. The juxtaposition of international relations and politics in the Sussex context raised the contradictions between the fields particularly sharply. Sussex international relations has been particularly historical and sociological in its approach, in the forefront of critical work on global political economy, and known for an emphasis on critical theory. Politics in the university, on the other hand, has been definitely political science, more or less in the comparative sense which Paul Taggart emphasises here. This book was based on a series of workshops in which we came together, to clarify as well as to resolve our differences.

Five contests in the politics of globalisation

This book represents, therefore, a view of politics in globalisation as complexly contested. To order the parameters of contestation, the debates are organised around five major issues, around which each part is formed. Each part contains two or three chapters, representing different positions in relation to a broad question which defines it. The chapters do not, for the most part, respond directly to each other (although contributors sometimes comment on each other's previous work), but in developing contrasting approaches emphasise the contested nature of the politics of globalisation.

The first part of the book, 'Contesting globalisation', centres on the question: 'How fundamental is the change in social and political relations represented by globalisation?' For Jan Aart Scholte the phenomenon represents a broad and deep change signifying the need for a paradigm shift in the social sciences, but for Michael Nicholson the novelty of globalising trends appears overstated. The contrasting answers of these two international relations scholars offer an introduction to the book which is itself contested – thus signalling that there is no full consensus over globalisation's meaning or historical significance, and that the contest over these issues is a part of the meaning of politics in a globalising era.

The second part, 'State and economy', takes us into the area most commonly fought over in the politics of globalisation, with the question: 'How has globalisation affected the relationships between the nation-state and the economy?' However, the contributors eschew the sterile debate between naive globalising concepts of the undermining of the state and simple global-sceptic reassertions of the nation-state's power. Adopting instead variants of a third, transformational approach to state forms, Angus Cameron and Ronen Palan examine how the 'national' economy is being reconstituted, while Francis McGowan examines the significance of regional integration to understanding the state in globalisation.

The third part, 'Power and knowledge', deals with the question: 'How far does globalisation involve reconceptualising the nature of politics and the structures of political knowledge?' The authors – all political scientists – examine both major explanatory concepts of politics and the rationale of the discipline itself. They offer radically different answers. Neil Stammers sees the understanding of social movements in a global context as requiring a reconceptualisation of power itself. On the other hand, Paul Taggart sees the politics of the European Union as fully comprehensible through the comparative method and concepts (cleavages, cycles, etc.), established at other levels of political analysis. Finally, Stephanie Hoopes offers a more broadly based political science response to a 'global politics' agenda but like Taggart, emphasises conceptual, methodological and empirical continuities in the understanding of change.

The fourth part, 'Ethics and politics', extends this discussion by asking: 'Does global change involve reconceptualising the relations of ethics and politics?' Zdenek Kavan's chapter discusses the role of a new, ethical 'anti-politics' of civil society in the transformation in central Europe, and its fate in the region's incorporation into market-led globalising processes. Christien van den Anker, while accepting that the cosmopolitan argument about ethical universality is valid independently of contemporary global change, argues that globalisation does have ethical implications. Fiona Robinson, in contrast, examines the globalisation of liberal values which she sees as deeply problematic.

The final part of the book, 'Agency and globality', addresses the question: 'How should we understand agency in global change, and globalisation itself as a contested process?' Here the contest *about* globalisation, with which we began the book, turns directly to historically informed understanding of the contest *within* globalisation, which was anticipated in the discussion of ethics and politics. Here, in place of a conclusion to the volume, two chapters offer radically divergent, although tantalisingly overlapping, readings of the role of agency in global change. My own partly polemical chapter counterposes globality – constituted by political meaning – to globalisation, and sees the global transition as an unfinished revolution located in popular struggle, in tension with the politics of Western elites. John MacLean's extended chapter, in contrast, sees emancipatory political *and* economic agency – he disputes the possibility of categorically separating these – as still to be constituted, and emphasises how much globalisation is constituted within dominant agency.

Towards a critical reading of this collection

By opening and closing this book with pairs of chapters, between which there are important divergences, I have tried to emphasise the multiple contestations of politics in globalisation and avoid any premature closure. Nevertheless, some comments seem in order about the shape of the debate which ensues. The editor is privileged to have the last word within the volume, although readers and reviewers will (I hope) have more to say about its arguments.

As to the relationship between international relations and political science, it could be argued that the initial critical thrust, defining globalisation in terms of a paradigm shift (Scholte) – although important historical caveats are entered by Nicholson – is largely bypassed by some of the political scientists (Taggart, Hoopes) who contend that political theory and research can comfortably incorporate global phenomena. How successful this move is judged to be depends, it seems to me, on two things. One is the question of how far political science has actually been implicated in a national-and-international framework of thought. If the complicity is deep, then how plausible is it to escape from it without actually confronting the problems of this framework and the historical challenge to it? The second issue is the fundamental question of how far political studies are necessarily historical, not simply in the conventional sense of being informed by detailed historical knowledge, but in the broader sense of being concerned with historically changeable realities?

If political science is more concerned to identify relatively timeless patterns in political behaviour than to grapple with contemporary (or past) structural change, it is in tension with the more historical concepts of social knowledge argued for in some international relations contributions. Clearly, the relatively ahistorical approach has counterparts in a certain kind of 'scientific' concept of international relations (e.g., Waltz 1979) but this is little defended these days in the European international relations literature, and finds little favour with contributors here. (The difference is clarified in the interview with Waltz carried out by Fred Halliday and Justin Rosenberg 1998.) In a historical approach to politics and international relations, the timelessness of categories such as 'national', 'international' and of course 'global', as well as 'power', 'state' and 'politics' is precisely what is in question.

However, other political science contributors adopt partially different strategies from those of Taggart and Hoopes. Stammers sees global change entering into domestic as well as international politics, and social movements as a type of collective actor particularly representative of global conditions. McGowan sees the global and regional as specific levels or spatial dimensions of contemporary politics. There is a recognition of change in these chapters, which is more congruent with the international relations debate, although in the latter MacLean defines its terms in such a way as to limit the significance of these kinds of political thought.

Where new trends in political studies and international relations strikingly converge in this volume is in the discussion of normative political theory. The chapters by Robinson and van den Anker, although partially differing about the contemporary relevance of liberalism, nevertheless show how the methods of political theory can be applied in globalisation. My chapter and Kavan's also imply significant roles for ethically informed politics in global change although, once again, MacLean is more critical.

This book therefore brings to the fore certain contradictions in both political and international studies in the current period. The contrasting intellectual trends in it represent clearly divergent estimates not only of contemporary change but of the intellectual challenges to existing social-scientific understanding. This suggests that the gulf between the poles of international relations and political science may actually be increasing. Clearly no simple reconciliation of opposed positions is possible – but in a period of fundamental political change such differences are unavoidable.

Upheaval challenges us to define both the specificity of our times and the fundamentals which may guide us through them. Each of these is complexly contested in this book. Those of us who emphasise history and change still differ about its character; those who lay more stress on timeless concepts, explanatory or normative, do so in very different ways. Moreover academic differences over the significance of globalisation may themselves be highly political; the pairing of my chapter and MacLean's suggests a contest between different paradigms of emancipatory politics in global change, arising from different understandings of the relations between emancipatory and dominant politics. In this book we have opened up the debate about politics in globalisation; we cannot close it because it is central to questions which are deeply contested in practice as well as in theory.

Part I

CONTESTING GLOBALISATION

1

GLOBALISATION: PROSPECTS FOR A PARADIGM SHIFT

Jan Aart Scholte

Globalisation calls into question the adequacy of comparative politics and international relations as methods to understand the organisation and exercise of power in social life. The growth of a global dimension of social relations can even cast doubt on the very project of political science and the academy's practice of disciplinary divisions more generally. Contemporary accelerated globalisation gives ample cause for a paradigm shift in social analysis toward what might be called 'world system studies'. That said, entrenched intellectual traditions and institutional forces exert substantial resistance to such a change.

This argument is elaborated below in seven steps. The first section distinguishes three common but redundant notions of 'the global'. The second elaborates a distinctive conception, namely, globality as supraterritoriality. The third locates the rise of supraterritoriality in (mainly recent) history, while the fourth stresses that this trend brings with it continuities as well as changes. The fifth section suggests that contemporary globalisation (as deterritorialisation) requires us to abandon the methodological territorialism that has underlain conventional social science. The sixth section proposes an alternative methodology of world system studies. The seventh identifies some of the intellectual and institutional forces that stand in the way of this reorientation.

Globalisation as old hat

The vocabulary of 'globalisation' is quite new. Not until the 1890s did English speakers begin regularly to use the adjective 'global' to designate 'the whole world' in addition to its earlier meaning of 'spherical' (OED 1989: VI, 582). The terms 'globalise' and 'globalism' were introduced in a treatise published fifty years later (Reiser and Davies 1944: 212, 219). Before the 1980s, no one spoke of 'global governance', 'global political economy', 'global environmental change', and so on. The noun 'globalisation' first appeared in a dictionary (of American English) in 1961 (Webster 1961: 965). Subsequently, similar words have surfaced in many other languages: e.g., *globalización* in

Spanish; *globalizare* in Romanian; *globalisaatio* in Finnish; *globalisasi* in Indonesian; *bishwavyapikaran* in Nepali; *Quan Qiu Hua* in Chinese; and so on.

Yet what core idea do these new words capture? The implications of 'globe talk' for social knowledge hinge very much on how one conceives of the central notion 'global'. Approached in certain senses, 'globality' and 'globalisation' open no insights that have not been available through pre-existent terminology and methodology. Sceptics (such as Michael Nicholson in this volume) can with good reason reject such usages as jargon. However, other constructions of 'global-ness' offer a qualitatively different understanding of social relations and cannot be so readily dismissed as old hat. The following paragraphs identify three redundant notions of 'the global'. The next section then advances an alternative conception which can prompt a paradigm shift in social enquiry.

One common conception has equated globalisation with universalisation. In this usage, a 'global' phenomenon is one that is found all over the world, and 'globalisation' is the process of spreading various objects and experiences worldwide. We could in this sense have a 'globalisation' of asphalt roads, decolonisation, Disney films, and much more.

Globalisation of this kind has certainly transpired in the late twentieth century, and on quite a substantial scale; however, impulses toward universalisation are hardly new to the present day. Indeed, the prehistoric transplanetary spread of the human species could be seen as the initial instance of this sort of 'globalisation' (Gamble 1994). Several world religions, too, have for a thousand years and more extended across large tracts of the earth. Transoceanic trade has for centuries distributed various goods in 'global' (read world-scale) markets. Yet the pre-existent vocabulary of 'universality' and 'universalisation' is quite adequate to describe these age-old trends. This first formulation of 'globalisation' offers nothing distinctive and new.

A second common usage has equated globalisation with internationalisation. From this perspective, 'global' is simply another adjective to describe cross-border activity between countries, and 'globalisation' designates a growth of international interaction and interdependence. Evidence of such 'globalisation' is purportedly to be found in enlarged movements between countries of people, goods, money, messages, ideas, etc.

Globalisation of this second kind has indeed occurred on a substantial scale in the late twentieth century; however, exchanges between country units have also increased in various earlier periods during the 500-year history of the modern states-system. In particular, as many analysts have noted, the late nineteenth century witnessed levels of cross-border migration, direct investment, finance and trade that, proportionately, are broadly comparable with those of the present (Hirst and Thompson 1996; Wade 1996). No vocabulary of 'globalisation' was needed on previous occasions of internationalisation, and the terminology of 'international relations' arguably remains quite sufficient to examine contemporary transactions and interlinkages between countries.

A third widely employed conception has equated globalisation with liberalisation. Used in this sense, 'globalisation' refers to a process of removing officially imposed restrictions on movements between countries in order to create an 'open' and 'integrated' world. Contemporary evidence for such a trend can be found in the widespread and large-scale reduction or even abolition of regulatory trade barriers, foreign-exchange restrictions, capital controls, and (for citizens of certain states) visas.

Yet, like the first and second conceptions, notions of globalisation as liberalisation are redundant. The long-established liberal discourse of 'open' markets and 'free' trade is already available to convey these ideas. 'Global-speak' was not needed in earlier times of widespread liberalisation like the third quarter of the nineteenth century, and there seems little need now to invent a new vocabulary for an old story.

The remarks in this first section endorse the sceptics' position that 'globalisation' tends to be a social scientist's jargon, a journalist's catchphrase, a publisher's sales pitch, a politician's slogan, and a businessperson's fetish. Indeed, the three understandings outlined above between them cover most academic, official, corporate and popular discussion of things 'global'. Critics are right to assail the conceptual imprecision, historical illiteracy and empirical shallowness that mark most claims of novelty associated with globality.

Globalisation as new idea

However, should we dismiss as fad and hype *all* talk of 'global' governance, ecology, gender relations, communications, trade, finance, consciousness and the like? Are ideas of globalisation *always* reducible to universalisation, internationalisation and/or liberalisation? Should we not ponder why a new terminology would spread so far and stick for so long if it did not reflect an appreciation (perhaps still largely inchoate) of some kind of unprecedented change?

Important new insight into relatively new circumstances is available from a fourth perspective which identifies globalisation as deterritorialisation. Each of the three conceptions of globality discussed above assume a world of territorialist geography, where macro-level social space is wholly a question of territorial locations, territorial distances, and territorial borders. (I specify 'macro-level' insofar as the present discussion concerns large-scale social contexts rather than micro-level spaces such as buildings and views.) Territoriality involves tracts on the earth's surface separated by distance and (in many cases) borders. In a territorialist world, the length of territorial distances between locations and the presence or absence of territorial (especially state) borders between places generally determines the possibility, frequency and significance of contacts between people at the different sites.

Yet current history has witnessed a proliferation of social connections which are at least partly – and often quite substantially – detached from territorial space. Take, for instance, telephone networks, electronic finance, multilateral institutions, the depletion of atmospheric ozone, markets for many pharmaceuticals, and much contemporary textile production. Such phenomena cannot be situated at a fixed and limited territorial location. They operate largely without regard to territorial distance. They substantially bypass territorial borders. The geography of these global conditions cannot be understood in terms of territoriality alone; they also reside in the world as a single place.

Globality thereby marks a distinct kind of space–time compression, and one that is more or less unique to contemporary history. To be sure, the world has long been 'shrinking', as territorial distances have been covered in progressively shorter time intervals. Whereas Marco Polo took years to complete his journey across Eurasia in the thirteenth century, by 1850 a sea voyage from south-east Asia to north-west Europe could be completed in 59 days. In the late twentieth century, motorised ships and land vehicles take much less time again to link places. Nevertheless, such transport still requires measurable time spans to cross territorial distances, and these movements still face substantial controls at territorial frontiers. Although speed has markedly increased, proximity in these cases remains a function of distance (as measured using euclidean geometry on a three-dimensional grid) and borders.

For global transactions, in contrast, territorial locations are not fixed, territorial boundaries present no particular impediment, and territorial distance is covered in effectively no time. Satellite television, the United States dollar, the women's movement, the anthropogenic greenhouse effect, and many other contemporary conditions all have a pronounced *supraterritorial* quality. Globality (as supraterritoriality) describes circumstances where territorial space is substantially transcended. Phenomena like Coca-Cola and faxes are 'global' in this sense because they can extend anywhere in the world at the same time and can unite locations anywhere in effectively no time. The geography of, for instance, Visa credit cards and world service broadcasts has little to do with territorial distances and substantially transcends territorial borders. Likewise, using specific and fixed territorial coordinates, where could we situate Special Drawing Rights, the Rushdie affair, the magazine *Elle*, the debt of the Brazilian government, karaoke, the production of a Ford automobile, and the law firm Clifford Chance?

All such circumstances reside at least partly in the world as one more or less seamless sphere. Global conditions can and do surface simultaneously at any point on earth that is equipped to host them, e.g. Internet connections. Global phenomena can and do move almost instantaneously across any distance on the planet, e.g. a news flash.

Place, distance and borders only retrieve vital significance in respect of global activity when the earth is contrasted to extraterrestrial domains. Thus, for example, the 'border' of the New York Stock Exchange lies at the earth's outer atmosphere, and time again becomes a significant factor in respect of radio signals when they have to cross the solar system. However, within the domain of our planet, location, distance and borders place no insurmountable constraints on global relations.

Various social researchers across a range of academic disciplines have discerned a rise of supraterritoriality in contemporary history. Already at mid-century, for example, the philosopher Martin Heidegger proclaimed the advent of 'distancelessness' and an 'abolition of every possibility of remoteness' (1950: 165–6). More recently, the geographer David Harvey has described 'processes that so revolutionise the objective qualities of space and time that we are forced to alter, sometimes in quite radical ways, how we represent the world to ourselves (1989: 240). The sociologist Manuel Castells has distinguished a 'network society', in which a new 'space of flows' exists alongside the old 'space of places' (1989: 348; 1996). The international relationist John Ruggie has written of a 'nonterritorial region' in contemporary world affairs (1993a: 172).

Hence globality in the sense of transworld simultaneity and instantaneity – in the sense of the singularity of the world – refers to something distinctive that other vocabulary does not cover. The difference between globality and internationality needs in particular to be stressed. Whereas international relations are *inter*territorial relations, global relations are *supra*territorial relations. International relations are *cross*-border exchanges *over* distance, while global relations are *trans*border exchanges *without* distance. Thus global economics is different from international economics, global politics is different from international politics, and so on. Internationality is embedded in territorial space; globality transcends that geography.

In addition, global (as *trans*border) relations are not the same as *open*-border transactions. Contemporary liberalisation has often occurred in tandem with globalisation. This large-scale removal of statutory restrictions on transactions between countries has both responded to and facilitated the rise of supraterritoriality. However, the two trends remain distinct. Liberalisation is a question of regulation, whereas globalisation (as deterritorialisation) is a question of geography.

Global events are also distinct from universal circumstances. Universality means being spread worldwide, while globality implies qualities of transworld concurrence and coordination. Universalisation has sometimes transpired in tandem with globalisation, both encouraging and being encouraged by the growth of supraterritoriality. However, the two trends remain distinct. Universality says something about extent, whereas globality says something about space–time relations.

To stress this key point once more: globalisation as understood here is *not* the same thing as universalisation, internationalisation or liberalisation. It is crucial to note that analysts who reject the transformative character of 'globalisation' have almost invariably conflated the term with internationalisation, liberalisation and/or universalisation. Yet the potential for a paradigm shift lies in the idea and practice of deterritorialisation, not in the other three notions. To appreciate the present argument in its own terms, the logic and the evidence must be assessed in the light of a fourth, different definition.

Globalisation in history

Like universalisation, internationalisation and liberalisation, the spread of supraterritoriality has some antecedents in earlier times. For example, we can trace intimations of global consciousness – i.e., conceptions of the earthly world as a single place – back half a millennium. From the fourteenth century onwards, certain intellectuals contemplated the possibility of transborder government (cf. Hinsley 1963: ch. 1). In literature, Shakespeare's Puck thought to 'put a girdle round about the earth in forty minutes' (1595–6: 38). During the eighteenth century a number of London-based transatlantic traders considered themselves to be 'citizens of the world' (Hancock 1995). Roland Robertson has suitably characterised such developments as the 'germination phase' of globalisation (1992: 58).

Globality began to take more material form in the second half of the nineteenth century. These decades saw the early development of telecommunications, including intercontinental telegraph cables. The first overseas plant of a manufacturing enterprise appeared in 1852. A few products like Remington typewriters and Campbell tinned soups began to acquire global markets in the late nineteenth century. The same period witnessed the creation of the first regulatory agencies with a worldwide remit, such as the International Telegraph (now Telecommunication) Union in 1865 and the General (now Universal) Postal Union in 1874. Transborder peace, labour, anarchist and women's movements also became active at this time. Further growth of global consciousness was encouraged with events such as world fairs, first staged in 1851, and the modern Olympic Games, first held in 1896.

That said, on the whole the scale of nineteenth-century globalisation was vastly smaller than that of the present day. The thousands of telegraph messages that moved between countries each year a hundred years ago cannot be compared in scale or consequence with the millions of telecommunications signals that transcend territorial geography each day in the 1990s. In the late nineteenth century only a tiny proportion of the world's population purchased globally marketed products. With staffs of less than twenty persons each, the handful of global governance bodies of the 1890s can scarcely be likened to the several hundred multilateral institutions of the 1990s, some of them with payrolls running into the thousands. Many other major forms of globality did not exist at all in the nineteenth century, e.g. electronic transworld finance, transborder production chains, electronic mass media, computer networks, liquid-fuel rocketry, global ecological problems, and so on. Hence, although globalisation has a longer history, the antecedents must not be exaggerated. In particular, the precursors of contemporary globalisation are nowhere near as great as the earlier instances of internationalisation.

When conceived as deterritorialisation, globalisation has unfolded mainly in the late twentieth century. In 1950, the vast majority of the world's population never made telephone calls, watched television or boarded an aircraft. The loss of global biodiversity began to increase exponentially around mid-century, while significant ozone depletion started in the 1960s. Satellites, intercontinental missiles and transoceanic telephone cables date from the mid-1950s. The count of transborder companies (i.e. firms operating in several countries at once) multiplied sixfold between the late 1960s and the late 1990s (UNCTAD 1994: 131; UNCTAD 1997: 6–7). Since the 1960s global governance agencies and transborder civic associations have likewise proliferated and grown at unprecedented rates (cf. UIA 1997: 1763). All but four of the dozens of offshore financial centres currently in operation have been created since 1950. The first eurocurrency deposits appeared in the early 1950s, the first euromarket loan in 1957, the first eurobond in 1963, and the first transborder electronic link between stock exchanges in 1985. In earlier times, only a narrow circle of intellectuals and businesspeople thought globally, and then usually only fleetingly; however, today globality is widely embedded in everyday popular consciousness.

To be sure, supraterritorial spaces have involved different countries, classes, nationalities and other social groupings to uneven extents. For instance, global relations have been more concentrated in the North relative to the South and the East. The rise of supraterritoriality has touched urban centres (especially so-called 'global cities') more than rural areas. The trend has involved propertied and professional classes more than poorer and less literate circles. Women and people of colour have generally had less access to global spaces than men and white people. That said, accelerated globalisation of the late twentieth century has left almost no one and no locale completely untouched.

Nothing in the above remarks is meant to suggest that globalisation is inevitable or irreversible. However, global spaces have become large and significant in the late twentieth century, and most current signs point to further rather than less globalisation during the foreseeable future. For the time being, to take a phrase from the *Wall Street Journal*, globalisation 'is one buzzword that's here to stay' (26 September, 1996: R2).

Change/continuity

To stress these changes in world social geography is by no means to disregard the existence of significant continuities. As always, continuity and change are interrelated and mutually defining in social relations (Scholte 1993). It is simplistic to understand globalisation with either a change thesis or a continuity thesis, and it is regrettable that debates on this subject tend to be set up in unhelpful polarised terms of continuity versus change. The challenge for research is to trace the complex interplay of continuities and changes.

The transformative aspect of contemporary accelerated globalisation is important; the trend has brought an end to territorialism. As a result, macro-level social space can no longer be mapped completely on the three axes of latitude, longitude and altitude. Territorial concepts of place, distance and borders are inadequate by themselves to describe the geography of cyberspace, global warming, offshore banking, export processing zones, structural adjustment policies, human rights advocacy, and so on. A further, supra-territorial aspect exists in respect of such phenomena, and this move from three- to four-dimensional geography fundamentally changes the map of social relations.

That said, the rise of a fourth dimension of social space of course does not mean a disappearance of the other three. The rise of supraterritoriality has not marked, and in all likelihood will not produce, an end to territoriality. Globality does not suppress and replace territoriality; the two types of space coexist and interrelate. Hence the wider social developments associated with contemporary globalisation show a blend of change and continuity. For example, large-scale deterritorialisation has brought an end to territorialist governance, where regulatory activity was concentrated almost entirely in the (territorial) state. However, this move has in no way meant an end to the state which, on the contrary, remains a crucial part of a new post-sovereign politics (Scholte 1997, 1999). In relation to collective identities, large-scale globalisation of the late twentieth century has broken the previous near-monopoly of the (territorially centred) nationality principle. However, the nation remains a key form of community (amongst others) in the contemporary globalising world (Scholte 1996b). Likewise, more territorial forms of capitalist production (e.g. agriculture and mining) have persisted while new nonterritorial commodities (e.g. information and communications) have risen to prominence in recent decades. Similarly, territorial ecologies have not become irrelevant with the growth of supra-territorial environmental issues, although a local problem (e.g. of deforestation) has often acquired a different significance with the rise of global concerns (e.g. of climate change).

In short, to highlight the importance of globalisation is not necessarily to subscribe to globalism. We live in a globalis*ing* rather than a totally globalis*ed* circumstance. Indeed, it seems unlikely that the foreseeable future will bring a fully deterritorialised social world. On the other hand, we no longer inhabit a territorialist world either, and this change requires shifts in the ways that we theorise and practise politics.

Farewell to methodological territorialism?

A transformation of social space requires adjustments to the ways that we conceive of social relations and pursue social enquiry. Since methodological territorialism has had such a pervasive and deep hold on conventional social science, globalisation (as deterritorialisation) implies a major reorientation of approach.

Methodological territorialism refers here to the practice of understanding the social world and conducting research about it through the lens of territorial geography. Territorialist method means formulating concepts and questions, constructing hypotheses, gathering and interpreting empirical evidence, and drawing conclusions all in a territorial spatial framework. These habits are so engrained in prevailing methodology that most social researchers reproduce them unconsciously. Methodological territorialism lies at the heart of mainstream conceptions of geography, economy, governance, community and society. Thus geographers have traditionally conceived of the world in terms of bordered territorial (especially country) units. Likewise, macroeconomists have normally studied production and distribution in relation to national (read territorial) and international (read interterritorial) activity. Students of politics have automatically treated governance as a territorial question (i.e., of local and national governments, with the latter sometimes meeting in 'international' organisations). Similarly, anthropologists have usually conceived of culture and community with reference to territorial units (i.e., local and national peoples). Finally, territorialist habits have had sociologists presume that 'society' takes a territorial form: 'Chilean society', 'Iranian society', 'British society', etc.

Like any analytical device, methodological territorialism involves simplification; indeed, it offered a broadly viable intellectual shortcut in an earlier day of social enquiry. After all, the Westphalian states-system that arose in the seventeenth century and spread worldwide by the middle of the twentieth century was quintessentially territorial. Likewise, the mercantile and industrial activity that dominated capitalism during this period operated almost exclusively in territorial space. Similarly, the main forms of collective identities during these times (namely, ethnic groups and state-nations) had pronounced territorial referents. Nor did anthropogenic global ecological changes occur on any significant scale prior to the mid-twentieth century. Hence methodological territorialism reflected the social conditions of a particular epoch when bordered territorial units, separated by distance, formed far and away the overriding framework for macro-level social organisation.

However, territorialist analysis is not a timeless method. On the contrary, no scholarly research was undertaken five hundred years ago with reference to bounded territorial spaces. After all, countries, states, nations and societies did not in that earlier epoch exist as clearly delineated territorial forms. World maps showing the continents in anything like the territorial shape that we would recognise today were not drawn before the late fifteenth century. It took a further two hundred years before the first maps depicting bordered country units appeared (Campbell 1987; Whitfield 1994). Not until the high tide of colonialism in the late nineteenth and early twentieth centuries did a territorialist logic extend across all regions of human habitation on earth.

If methodological territorialism is a historical phenomenon, then it has an end as well as a beginning. There is no reason why, once installed, territorialist assumptions should last in perpetuity. The emergence of the states-system, the growth of mercantile and industrial capitalism, and the rise of national identities all understandably prompted the development of methodological territorialism several centuries ago. However, today widespread and accelerated globalisation may stimulate another reconceptualisation. If contemporary human circumstances have gained a substantial global dimension, then we need to develop an alternative, non-territorialist cartography of social life.

To put the point starkly, how can territorialist thinking possibly be applied to the present-day world, given that it contains:

- nearly 900 million telephone lines
- 1.8 billion radio sets
- a billion television receivers
- tens of millions of Internet users
- 44,500 transborder companies with collective annual sales of $7 trillion
- over 250 multilateral regulatory institutions
- some 16,000 noncommercial, nonofficial transborder associations
- thousands of globally marketed products
- $635 trillion in annual transborder movements of securitised funds
- several trillion dollars' worth of offshore bank deposits
- yearly foreign-exchange turnover of $450 trillion
- a billion commercial airline passengers per annum
- thousands of strategic warheads for missile delivery
- accelerated global warming
- enormous reductions in biological diversity.

This list could be substantially lengthened, and most of the numbers currently show notable upward tendencies. None of the above phenomena existed to a remotely comparable extent in 1960 or at any earlier juncture in history. Of course, as statistics, each of the various indicators can be queried in one way or another. However, such a large accumulation of data surely suggests a significant trend away from territorialist social organisation.

Indeed, it is arguably dangerous to give methodological territorialism further lease on life in a globalising world. For one thing, these assumptions about space and space–time relations are obviously unsuitable in respect of global ecological problems. Likewise, if significant parts of capitalism now operate with relative autonomy from territorial space, then old intellectual frameworks cannot adequately address the issues of distributive justice which have always accompanied processes of surplus accumulation. Similarly, political theory that offers a post-Westphalian world only territorialist constructions of democracy and community is not only obsolete, but also positively hazardous. Evidence now abounds that contemporary globalisation poses far-reaching challenges to ecological sustainability, social equity, democracy and community (Scholte, forthcoming). Hence the stakes in the call for the construction of a post-territorialist methodology go far beyond academic point scoring.

On to a world system perspective?

Contemporary social enquiry needs a methodology that is appropriate to a globalising world. Such an approach should be neither territorialist nor globalist. A geography centred on the concept of 'world system' offers such an alternative.

The notion 'world' is particularly suitable, since it privileges neither territoriality nor globality and indeed readily encompasses both. 'World' social relations may have a global, regional, international, national, local and/or other spatial character. The term 'world' does not prejudge what kinds of domains will be relevant in a given situation. A world system methodology requires only that a researcher considers a variety of possible geographical contexts and does not assume in advance any particular spatial framework.

The notion 'system' conveys the premise that social geography in practice involves an interrelation of spaces. In other words, the distinction of the local, the national, the international, the regional, the global and so on is an analytical exercise. In concrete social experience these domains are not separate, but interconnected dimensions of 'world' space. A social researcher should therefore never treat a 'level' of geography in isolation. Localism, statism, regionalism and globalism are all equally misguided abstractions.

Before proceeding further, the present argument for a world system methodology needs to be sharply distinguished from the particular sort of world-system analysis pursued by Immanuel Wallerstein (1979), Christopher Chase-Dunn (1989), Peter Taylor (1996a) and others. The (unhyphenated) world system method advocated in the present writing is different from (hyphenated) world-system theory. The former offers a starting premise for social enquiry; the latter elaborates this general principle in a specific way. A researcher can adopt a world system methodology without necessarily endorsing a Wallersteinian analysis of the modern capitalist world-economy.

Indeed, most world-system theory has had a territorialist character. True, researchers in this school have taken the welcome step of abandoning methodological nationalism (i.e., enquiry in terms of discrete country units) and associated endogenous models of development. Few statements have captured this issue so well as Wallerstein's pointed question: 'societal development, or development of the world-system?' (Wallerstein 1986). Yet world-system theory has replaced a primary focus on nation-state-societies with a primary focus on groups of countries (or 'zones') under the labels of 'core', 'periphery' and 'semiperiphery'.

In short, world-system theory has supplanted one type of territorialism with another. The approach has barely begun to address the question of globality (in the sense of supraterritoriality) (see Hopkins and Wallerstein 1996). In contrast, the world system concept advocated here abandons not only methological nationalism, but also methodological territorialism more generally.

A world system methodology has far-reaching implications for political studies. For example, this approach calls the conventions of comparative politics fundamentally into question. Comparative analysis has traditionally entailed a presumption of distinct state apparatuses and separate national polities, i.e., assumptions of methodological nationalism. In contrast, a world system concept suggests that, on the one hand, local relations deeply divide nation-state-country-societies while, on the other hand, international, regional and global relations deeply interconnect nation-state-country-societies. These internal divisions and external interlinkages render meaningless any notion of a discrete 'Canadian' politics that might be compared with a discrete 'Chinese' politics. To be sure, a researcher today might wish to compare, say, the responses of the Ugandan and Romanian states to ethnonationalism, taking into account similarities and differences in the local, national, international, regional and global forces that affect the respective situations. However, such a comparison is qualitatively different from traditional comparative politics.

A similar critique applies to so-called 'area studies', with their presumption of separate regional units. Internal divisions (local and national) and external interconnections (international and global) make the notion of discrete regional politics unsustainable. There is no 'Latin America', 'South East Asia', 'Africa' or 'Western Europe' which exists outside a complex multidimensional geography in which the regional context plays only a (often perhaps quite limited) part.

World system methodology is also irreconcilable with the conventions of international relations and associated subfields such as international political economy. Inherent in the concept 'inter-national' are territorialist assumptions: (a) that world politics is a question of interactions and interdependence between countries (especially their 'sovereign' governments); and (b) that state borders always delineate the foremost social unit. International relations and international political economy arbitrarily place the primary emphasis on international space, giving only secondary if any attention to globality, regionality, nationality and locality. Differently named :ises of 'world politics' and 'world political economy' would impose no such rigid hierarchy. (The alternative disciplinary labels of 'global politics' and 'global political economy' seem objectionable insofar as they appear to privilege supraterritorial spaces over other domains.) The shift in vocabulary from 'international' to 'world' would reflect a full-scale methodological reorientation. Indeed, a number of researchers in 'international relations' and 'international political economy' have since the 1980s already taken considerable steps in this direction, even though they have not shed the old terminology.

A world system perspective likewise implies a methodological reconstruction of other fields of social enquiry. For example, geographers would with this approach attend to the mutual determination of local, regional, national, international, global and other social spaces, always understanding one abstracted sphere in the context of the others. Similarly, sociologists would examine world social relations rather than national and/or local societies. As for anthropologists, they would study culture and community as a product of interconnecting supraterritorial, national, local and other networks. For their part, macroeconomists would abandon the traditional *a priori* fixation on national economies, e.g. in terms of gross national products, national price indices, national money supplies, national balance of payments, and so on. Instead, economists would explore questions of employment, inflation, exchange rates, income distribution, etc. as a product of intersecting spatial domains, where global, regional and local aspects could in principle exert as great an influence as national and international dimensions.

The adoption of a world system approach might also provide an occasion for other methodological transformations in addition to the abandonment of territorialism. For example, world-system theorists have also defined their project in terms of a transcendence of disciplinary divides (cf. Wallerstein 1991; Taylor 1996a). Indeed, in respect of globalisation it is difficult to see how global ecology, global governance, global production, global culture and the like can be adequately understood through isolated disciplinary enquiries. However, the creation of inter-, trans-, anti- and post-disciplinarity is logically a different exercise from the deconstruction of methodological territorialism. It might (as the present author indeed believes) be desirable for the two changes to be pursued in tandem, but they are not co-dependent.

Likewise, the shift from methodological territorialism to world system studies can provide an occasion to reiterate and expand critiques of positivism, of individualism and structuralism, of eurocentrism and of other purported shortfalls of mainstream social science. Indeed, I have elsewhere advocated a more comprehensive methodological reconstruction of this kind (Scholte 1993). Once more, however, the adoption of the world system principle does not in itself necessitate such wider reorientations.

Challenges ahead

This chapter has advanced an argument that 'globalisation' can be formulated as a distinct concept that designates an extensive, significant and historically mainly recent transformation of social geography. An end to territorialism in concrete social relations implies a need also to end methodological territorialism in social enquiry. A world system perspective provides an alternative approach that is suitable to the contemporary globalising human circumstance.

The logic and evidence presented above to elaborate this argument appear compelling. Indeed, taken on its own terms the case that globalisation warrants a paradigm shift would seem to be incontrovertible. To be sure, alternative accounts of contemporary politics can be made internally coherent on the basis of different starting assumptions. However, as stressed earlier, territorialist conceptions seem wholly unsuited to address current challenges to democracy, social justice, social cohesion and ecological integrity. These policy grounds make the choice of definitions and methodologies more than a question of intellectual preference.

Nevertheless, the urgency of concrete world problems runs against the considerable inertia of established academic cultures and institutional interests. It demands great mental energy of social researchers to reconstruct their starting premises and work through alternative lines of analysis. Indeed, by questioning orthodoxies, PhD completion might well be delayed, academic jobs might become harder to secure, and the flow of publications might slow. By now, in the late 1990s, institutions of higher learning, journals and publishers are more ready than before to hear the sorts of arguments articulated in this chapter. However, intellectual change continues to lag behind social and political need.

2

HOW NOVEL IS GLOBALISATION?

Michael Nicholson

Some sceptics have wondered whether globalisation is really as new as is claimed. Undeniably there is a greater degree of interaction between different parts of the world than there used to be a century ago. Further, this interaction is very much quicker both in the ability of human beings to travel quickly and in the way information can be conveyed instantaneously. However, is there anything qualitatively different about the globalising trends in the world from those operating before, say, the Second World War? In the intermittently more liberal economic system of the early part of the twentieth century, there was great inter-penetration of the various developed economies with each other. Hirst and Thompson (1996) claim that the penetration of the British economy in the period immediately before the First World War was as great as it is today. It can plausibly be argued that what we are witnessing is not so very different from what went on before – except that it is more intensive. In this chapter, I consider this question. I also consider whether the increased interactions and their effects are due to something inherent in the process of globalisation or due to the increased liberalisation of both national economies and the international economy. Though often presented as such, there seems no reason to suppose that this liberalisation is, in itself, inevitable. I shall conclude with some comments about the benefits and drawbacks of globalisation.

Initially I shall use 'globalisation' to mean that there is a high level of interaction between people in very distant locations. This is usually used to mean geographically distant but it can also be used to mean socially and politically distant. I use 'people' meaning 'individuals' deliberately, though if it is true of people as individuals it is also likely to be true of organisations such as firms. On this definition it is not difficult to show that there has been a high degree of interaction over very large parts of the globe for many centuries. Thus, from the beginning of the sixteenth century onwards there were big population moves from Europe to America, both North and South, followed by the equally large but involuntary movements of Africans to the Americas (prior to 1770, more African slaves than Europeans went to the Americas (Curtain 1969)). Around the same time, Europeans opened up sea routes to

India and interactions began even if they were not always welcome. The incorporation of China into the global network came later. While there may not have been much reciprocal interaction between individuals in those days, clearly different societies influenced each other a great deal. In the eighteenth century the Americas were governed from London, Madrid and Lisbon. By the later part of the nineteenth century, this had altered, but many parts of the world were directly governed from London, Paris, The Hague and other European capitals. Business firms based in the West were vastly influential on the economies of the world, whether ostensibly independent, as in Latin America, or overtly colonial, as in most of Africa. This surely indicates a very high degree of interaction and, on this definition, globalisation. (The interaction was asymmetric, of course – but so is a lot of it today.) Diseases passed round the globe then as now even if the spread of them was slower. The various episodes of the Black Death started in India and traversed the world.

This is not to deny that the degree of interaction has increased steadily over time, though the time involved has been centuries rather than the last few decades. The various industrial revolutions speeded this up. Basically, once two societies trade, they become interdependent. The stock market collapse in New York in 1929 triggered the Great Depression in all parts of the world with any significant economic relationships with the United States. Interactions were quicker than they had been previously and they were to become even faster. The advanced capitalist economies were tied closely together in the long run even if short-term fluctuations were less quickly passed on. However, is speed of such enormous importance? Thus, there is a global stock market today in that information from a stock market in one part of the world is transmitted instantaneously to those in others; ever since the start of electronic communication this has been the case. In practice, information in London about the New York market passed more slowly before 1939 and even more slowly before 1914. It was slower in spreading around and was far less detailed than now. Nevertheless, big movements in the stock markets were known and mirrored in the stock markets of the world. Short-term and smallish fluctuations are reflected throughout world markets today more quickly than they were in the 1930s, but big and long-term fluctuations always were mirrored around the world once markets had become interconnected.

We can go even further back and argue that globalisation, in the sense of a growth in interconnectedness between members of different states, is itself only a special case of something more general. In medieval Europe most people for most of the time stayed close to where they were born. They consumed mainly local goods and, for the most part, produced either for themselves or for a very local market. Economies were largely local. Trade over significant distances took place on water either by sea or river, which accounts for the disproportionate number of towns and villages which were either by the sea or on rivers. Human beings seem to have had a constant urge to detach themselves from the locality as much as the technology of the day permitted. Of course there have always been big movements, sometimes of populations looking for better conditions and of conquerors building empires. Under the Roman Empire, large parts of Europe were 'globalised' in this sense – and the degree of globalisation declined with the Empire's retreat. The medieval Church could be seen as some form of globalising force but the degrees of interaction and interdependence were much reduced in the so-called Dark Ages.

Communications are also of significance in considering the 'nationalisation' of various states. As communications improved (which before electronic communication meant, in practice, how fast people could travel), states had much more practical unity. This was particularly true of large states such as Canada and the United States where the railroad meant that people could travel between the major population centres, and many of the minor population centres, within two or three days as opposed to weeks. Markets then became national as an immediate precursor to becoming international. These changes can all be considered parts of the same process.

On this view, globalisation is a trend which has been going on for centuries, which is undeniably continuing and may be accelerating. In this sense, the present period is not in itself novel. However, Scholte (1997, and Chapter 1) argues that there is more to globalisation than this. For him globalisation is not just interaction on a global scale but deterritorialisation or super-territorialisation of many activities which formerly were tied to some territory, not as a matter of accident but as a matter of necessity. Thus, there is effectively a global stock market. There is twenty-four hour trading in the world as a whole and traders in, say, the Tokyo market keep a close eye on the London market on a real-time basis. There are differences. Tokyo is not just a postal (or e-mail) address of no significance but these differences are minor compared with the similarities or with the differences that existed even thirty years ago. It would presumably be possible to locate all the world's stock markets in a single place – say on a South Sea island – and it would make very little difference. It would probably make even less difference if this were to be done in twenty years' time. (It might be an improvement. The traders might be so tempted by the sun and the good life that they would spend less time trading, thus trade less frenetically, and calm the often totally unnecessary fluctuations in the various financial markets.) Conversely, of course, all the traders could work from home. This is the point. The actual geographical location is unimportant.

Scholte argues that this is different from just interaction, that it is novel, at least in its extent, and that significant moves to deterritorialisation represent something fundamentally new in global relations. (That it is largely new, and new in its extent, is fairly readily acceptable but one could argue that the medieval Catholic Church contained some elements of globalisation in

Scholte's sense of going beyond internationalisation.) This is to be distinguished from internationalisation which is the continuance of interactions which are, nevertheless, located in a geographical place and where it is significant where that place is. Unfortunately 'globalisation' is often used loosely to refer to both. Even though they may overlap, there is a clear analytical distinction which needs to be made.

I shall now discuss these issues in the context of the various changes in the global system which are usually associated with globalisation in the more ordinary sense with which I started. We cannot seriously doubt that there has been a great increase in the quantity of interactions over vast geographical distances in recent decades. There might, however, be debate about the nature and novelty of these interactions; in the next section, I examine these issues. To do so, I shall now narrow the usage of the word 'globalisation' to Scholte's sense of deterritorialisation. 'Internationalisation' I shall use to mean the degree of interaction between different parts of the world in which, in contrast, the location of the various activities is significant. Both require a high degree of interaction over geographical space. In principle, it is possible to have globalisation without internationalisation and likewise internationalisation without globalisation. However, there is a supposition that internationalisation would precede globalisation and we would be unlikely to have globalisation without it. Further, there need not be a clear dichotomy between the two. Thus in some cases – as with many financial markets – location might matter but not very much, making them 'largely globalised but a bit internationalised'. I argue that this is a meaningful phrase.

Information and travel

One of the most obvious differences between the world of today and the world of 1930 is the immense increase in the speed of communications. We should distinguish, moreover, the speed with which people can travel around from the speed with which information can travel. The facts concerning travel are well known so I shall comment only briefly. In 1930, the fastest time from London to New York was just over five days (Hyde and Hyde 1975). It was also quite expensive. (To Tokyo it took a small number of weeks, and was very expensive.) Even for organisations such as commercial firms where money was no object, face-to-face meetings of people based on opposite sides of the Atlantic, let alone the Pacific, were rare.

In these circumstances, it was a matter of great significance whether a business executive was based in New York or London, let alone Tokyo. It is now no longer of anything like so much significance where an executive is based. If people are temporarily in the wrong place for a meeting, they can be moved to the right place in any part of the globe in a matter of hours. In interstate politics it has also made a difference. Prime ministers, foreign secretaries and the like did not meet each other very often if indeed at all.

Chamberlain in 1938 was probably the first state leader to fly to a summit meeting to try to settle a problem (providing an unhappy precedent). For migrants too, time and expense were also of significance. Once someone had left Europe for Australia, they rarely returned. The pattern of migration now often includes an expectation of holidays back in the home country. Long-distance aircraft, which really came into their own with the jet engine, have altered patterns of movement fundamentally. Further, such movements can be inexpensive.

All this is added to by the speed of the communication of information. For the normal forms of information-passing, such as speech, there is always the telephone. This has been around, even in its intercontinental form, for many years. However, it is now much more convenient and cheap. This means that meetings, though possible, are often less necessary. Added to this are devices such as teleconferencing, which gives the illusion of direct meeting even if the people are at the opposite ends of the world. This sort of thing can be expected to get still cheaper and more convenient. It is possible that despite its increasing cheapness transport may become more and more redundant as actual physical movement becomes less necessary. Perhaps the present heyday of the international academic conference may pass. The complex forms of data which cannot be readily handled by speech can be conveyed directly from computer screen to computer screen anywhere in the world. For technophobes, there is always the fax.

The changes over the last ten years have been remarkable. We can only speculate, perhaps rather nervously, about what the next ten or twenty years may have in store. We will want to know how much human beings, as deeply social animals, will still want and need direct human contact with those with whom they interact. The simulations of contact, however close, may lead to some form of destructive isolation and impede the very processes they are meant to help (Giddens 1990). The social nature of human beings might put some limit on the degree of deterritorialisation which is possible.

These issues are consistent with the Scholte version of globalisation, at least for certain purposes. If we consider international decision-making groups such as those controlling a firm, their geographical location is not of great importance. If they need to be together, they can get together quickly. If they are not together, they can talk or otherwise share information without difficulty. The problems are low-level practical issues such as time differences when people are situated at significantly different longitudes. There is also the problem of language which is a barrier to smooth global communication. English is often a lingua franca (convenient for those of us who are native English speakers), but it cannot be assumed. Its widespread use in international exchanges might become more problematic as China plays a more significant role.

As far as population migration is concerned, the nonterritoriality of the issue cannot be dismissed so lightly. Clearly a person migrates because it makes a difference where they are. People move from Pakistan to Britain for the most part because incomes are higher, even though they may be coming to a culture which is not always welcoming. However, they may be readier to move in the first place because it is easier to travel and return. Migration, though a geographically relevant activity, is not as committing as it was in the nineteenth century, or even a few decades ago. Thus migration is more a part of internationalisation than of globalisation.

For rather different reasons we can argue that the interactions between senior statespeople are a part of internationalisation. From a purely practical point of view it may not matter where they meet and getting there is not a problem. The hotels and meeting rooms are all virtually interchangeable. Thus it might look like globalisation, since the location is accidental. However, where statespeople meet is often significant symbolically. Further, they are meeting as representatives of states which are still as territorially defined as ever. Of course, the nature of international transactions at the political level has been very significantly affected by the frequency of contact. The role of diplomats has declined when they can get instructions quickly from home and when their political bosses meet if there is any issue of significance. However, the style of the interactions is very different from the content. The discussions are still about state issues and could, in principle, strengthen the state basis of it all.

The international economy

Over the last few decades the international economy has grown together with the degree of interaction. This can be construed as an increase in internationalisation, and possibly globalisation. However, some deny it. Although both trade and capital movements flourish today, it is easy to point out they have done so for a long time. There are fewer impediments to both than before, but this is because most governments today embrace the general economic liberal view that impediments to economic activity as dictated by the market are a bad thing. In the late nineteenth century, the leaders of most states, apart from the UK, thought that the economy was subordinate to the interests of the state. It was deemed appropriate for governments to intervene in trade issues and economic issues in general if this strengthened the state.

This view is now completely out of fashion, at least since the demise of the Soviet Union. There has been a greater degree of internationalisation/globalisation (I leave it open as to which until it has been discussed in greater detail) as a consequence of this liberalisation. However, while the developments in technology were not the result of a planned decision but the largely unforeseen consequences of a lot of decisions, liberalisation has been a policy explicitly adopted by most governments.

The general argument for the liberalisation of economic transactions follows from considerations of economic efficiency. However, it is important to see what this argument consists of. An economically efficient position in this sense is one where it is impossible to increase one person's well-being without decreasing another's. This is known as 'Pareto optimality'. There are clearly innumerable positions which are Pareto-optimal and thus efficient in this sense. It can be looked at as a position where there is no waste. However, a position can be efficient without being fair. Nothing in Pareto optimality has anything to do with fairness. As it stands, it is a very abstract concept of efficiency according to which, as new resources become available, they are used where they can produce goods most cheaply. If lampshades are best made in Argentina, resources should flow there, while the erstwhile lampshade makers of, say France, produce Citroen cars or whatever they are good at. What matters is relative cost not absolute cost. The arguments for trade and the arguments for capital flows are similar in that it is argued that capital should go where the returns are highest, though bearing in mind risk which is important in international capital movements. However, there is one major qualification of this model as providing a goal to aim for. What is most profitable to produce depends on the income distribution of the buyers. Rich people, and hence rich groups, have much more influence over what is produced than poor ones. Hence, though this might result in an efficient distribution of resources, there is no reason to suppose that it produces a fair distribution. Nevertheless, it is this principle which lies behind the general notion that free markets are the best economic arrangement. This is now a widespread ideology within governments. No doubt it has been strengthened by the abysmal performance of the planned economies of the former Soviet Union and other communist countries, most of whom managed to be inefficient by any criterion, as well as unfair.

However, let us consider the way in which the world economy is becoming more internationalised and globalised. Trade barriers are lower than ever before and will probably get lower. This story is often told so I will not go further with it. There are also some technological factors which increased the volume of trade in recent years. First, the vast amounts of data which can be kept on computers and communicated instantly mean that the knowledge of traders of what is available at what prices around the world is widespread. It was less likely, fifty years ago, that the seller of lampshades would have known the price of Argentinian products and so trade might not have taken place. Not only is the flow of information much greater than it used to be, but the ability to handle the large amounts of information provided is much greater, courtesy of the computer. A global market-place in this sense can be a reality. Secondly, the weight to value ratio of many goods is probably much lower than it was. Computers are rather expensive per kilo. This knowledge is not very relevant to the user of a computer but it is very relevant to the transporter. Thus the value added to a computer because of transportation costs is a small fraction of the overall costs and makes the location of its manufacture less important. Thirdly, cheap air transport means that perishable commodities like strawberries and flowers can be carried quickly and, again because of a low weight/value ratio, are worth transporting all around the globe. Daffodils in Jersey and in Chile are in direct competition in a way which would have been inconceivable until recently when the daffodil market was narrow both regionally and in time. Fourthly, containerisation makes even the trading of heavy commodities by sea much cheaper than it was. Most importantly, the shifting of goods from ships to lorries to trains and so on, which is a very expensive aspect of transportation, is vastly simplified. Finally, the instantaneous movement of information makes it possible to trade services between countries which would have simply been untradeable before. The often quoted case of airline booking in Britain being done by workers in India is a classic example of this. The transport costs are almost zero. Thus for these technological reasons trade would be more extensive than it was even if there had been no increase in the liberalisation of international markets.

Now let us turn to capital movements. We can usefully distinguish three sorts of capital movements which are all rather different things. First are movements of capital across state boundaries which are for ‘real investment’. Second are exports of capital goods where the commodities used to make further commodities are exported. Third are speculative moves of capital. The first and second need not be particularly closely correlated. Capital goods may be purchased with money provided internally or by a third party. Conversely loans might be made by one country (that is, capital exports) which are used for consumption purchases in another. Notoriously, loans can be used for military purposes which are not, of course, expanding the productive capacity of the recipient country.

Both capital movements and the movement of capital goods are likely to be increased rather than decreased by the same factors as related to trade in general. The wider the knowledge of opportunities – which is very wide today – the more trading is likely to take place. In addition, the nature of capital goods is altering so that, like consumer goods, they are easier to transport. Thus the machines in light engineering are fairly easy to move, making the location of such factories much more dependent on factors such as relative labour costs and regulatory regimes.

Speculative capital is rather different. The liberalisation of capital markets in the 1980s has led to vast flows of capital around the world. The ratio of capital movements to ‘real’ movements of either capital or current trade is around 20 to 1. That is, only about 5 per cent of financial transactions are to finance real movements of resources whether capital or consumption (Gray 1998). A justification of speculative markets is that they induce stability by ironing out peaks and troughs unjustified by the underlying economic circumstances. It is hard to see how this argument can be applied to the speculative moves in the financial markets of the last decade or so. One would not expect such a low proportion of real transactions to speculative ones in a stabilising market. It seems much more plausible that the masses of speculative capital have increased the volatility of the markets in which, of course, the real transactions have to operate. The uncertainty caused by the volatile international financial markets may be one reason why the rate of growth of the world economy has not been impressive during the days of liberalism which was supposed to be so good for our economies.

The general phenomena described above are widely accepted except, perhaps, that some neoliberals might object to my description of the adverse effects of speculative markets. However, are these developments internationalisation or globalisation? I have argued above that the speculative markets are becoming globalised in the sense of deterritorialised. However, the movements of productive resources and trade are less obviously so. They move precisely because there are differences in different parts of the world; where they are is central.

Unlike the volatile speculative markets which could be regarded as globalised in the Scholte sense, the movement of real economic resources is an issue of internationalisation on his definitions. Movement between places is a crucial issue but the movement comes about because of the relevance not the irrelevance of the geographical position. They are perhaps globalised in the sense that there is global, or near global, information about the conditions in different parts of the world and thus are rather like different parts of a national economy. However, they are international in that national governments still have control over some of the variables and sometimes compete with each other for the favours of global capital. This has always been the case and what we have is a more extensive version of a much longer historical process.

Problems for the state

The new liberal economic order has made it harder for the state to carry out its activities. This is true of the activities which traditionally have been associated with states, even with the pared-down 'night-watchman' state of the classical liberal. It is even more true of the activities which states running mixed economies did quite well in the decades after the Second World War. Thus, the much improved provision of a broad range of collective goods such as health care and the provision of a relatively stable economy with low levels of unemployment seem to be fond dreams of the past which, we are assured, are now impossible in the bracing global economy of the present. The willingness of capital to move makes such activities very difficult. As the capital is largely in the control of people who are averse to collective goods anyway, as they are well enough provided with private ones, the whole situation is very difficult. I shall look at the problem of taxation in particular.

Quite apart from its role in issues of macroeconomic stability, taxation is central for the provision of collective goods. This includes the collective of military defence which is, of course, central in the real international relations and is thought of more fondly by conservative economic liberals than are self-indulgent matters such as health and education. Taxation is more difficult to raise in connection with capital than it is in connection with personal taxation. Though there is a lot of international labour movement, not many people move because of taxes. Pop stars, tennis stars, possibly some business people and other very rich people may do so, but few of even the moderately wealthy follow them. The main reason some governments – such as the Blair administration in the United Kingdom – are reluctant to raise taxes is the belief (for which the evidence seems thin) that people are very resistant to high taxes. They do not really expect the middle class to emigrate *en masse* though they might vote the government out of office.

However, when it comes to capital or business, worries about the consequences of high tax rates are more serious simply because capital is more mobile. These issues are well known. Tax rates are one reason why businesses may locate in one place rather than another – which can lead to low-tax competition between states, tax holidays, the provision of 'offshore' facilities and the like (see Chapter 3). Poor countries, anxious for capital imports to get the economy growing, are faced with effective auctions to keep tax rates down. Even where firms are in supposedly high-tax countries, any competent accountant employed by a multinational can make sure that profits are allocated to low-tax countries rather than high-tax countries. There are several notorious examples of this. Successful monitoring of transactions is, of course, central to any tax collecting programme, but electronic movement of money and information make monitoring very difficult. The Russian government is experiencing this problem acutely; tax avoidance is widespread, but this is due more to internal state failure than to Russia's role in the global system.

Taxation is a central issue for governments. Without the ability to tax, they are unable to do anything very much. The problems of the provision of collective goods are obvious. Issues such as redistribution in an unequal society are others. I am not suggesting that governments are helpless but they do have much less control over their economies than they used to and not just with respect to taxation issues. This is true at both the micro and macro levels. At the micro-level, it is not just low wage-rates and other costs which the entrepreneur will seek out. They will also seek weak regulatory regimes concerning safety and environmental issues. A nicely disciplined labour force, with a pliant police force to guard against agitators, is much to be preferred to a unionised and aggressive labour force. This means that a government concerned with health and safety regulations and other such impediments to change might find capital moving away and be unable to attract foreign investment.

Governments are faced with difficulties, not only in keeping economic activity in their countries but also in controlling major economic variables such as unemployment and inflation. This has always been the case. For example, all post-war British governments – in particular Labour governments – have had to battle with threatened foreign exchange reserves and with the general problem of keeping the economy on a balanced international keel. The problem is aggravated now by the various liberal money-market regimes which came into being in the 1980s and which reduced the degree of control of governments over the macro-economic variables.

Post-war governments in the so-called 'mixed economies' succeeded in achieving a number of important social goals which more recent governments have failed in, notably in keeping levels of unemployment low. Jobless levels which would have been regarded as disastrous in the 1950s are now regarded as issues for congratulation in both the US and the UK. Some of this may be due to structural factors in the economy, perhaps involving the nature of technological innovation. However, some is due to the openness of the economies meaning that they are subject to the vagaries of the speculative money economy. This is arguably much more the problem than the competition of genuinely cheaper products or than higher real rates of return on productive capital in other parts of the world. Basically people have given up on the idea that there can be full employment in the sense in which it was known until the early 1970s.

We are thus faced with an ironic dilemma. Economic life is much less secure than it was. The lower down in the economic hierarchy one is, the greater the uncertainty and insecurity. This is true both within states and over the world as a whole. However, the scope of the government in protecting us is much less than it was, partly due to the lack of control but also, as is becoming increasingly clear, to the lack of will of governments, even those of the supposedly political left. In an uncertain, internationalised economy, we need stronger, not weaker welfare states. The nature of an insecure society is that there are more casualties and hence a greater need for secure social defences.

These reductions in the powers of government are not necessarily because they have been ceded to anyone else. The multinational corporations (MNCs) which have great power in directing economic flows nevertheless are not particularly interested in taking over the issues of governance which the state can no longer cope with. Susan Strange (1996) argues that the processes of globalisation and internationalisation have produced not just a shift in governance, but a decline in governance.

Are globalisation and internationalisation inevitable or desirable?

Many of the characteristics of globalisation are determined by the development of technology and in particular computers and electronic communication. Future developments in technology are likely to increase this tendency rather than otherwise. I have argued that trade involves a process of internationalisation rather than globalisation but that this is also partly brought about by technological factors. Cautiously, at least, we could predict that the same directions will be followed. Whether one likes or loathes them, these processes are likely to continue. In the case of the processes of internationalisation, it is just a case of developing that which has characterised most of human history, the continuous expansion from the local. However, the move beyond this to the irrelevance of geographical location has become more significant in recent years and in its significance, if not in its origins, is something novel.

All other things being equal, the growth of interactions, whether globalising or internationalising, is to be commended. Being rich is better than being poor and, broadly speaking, trade makes people richer. However, there are three serious issues about the ways in which both globalisation and internationalisation are going on today. First is the high levels of uncertainty brought about by the financial markets. Some of this is a likely consequence of speculative markets divorced from any real economic processes. It is also partly due to the corruption of some of the financial organisations. However, such enormous opportunities for vast wealth are likely to bring corruption with them so we should not be too surprised. Secondly, the increases in efficiency in the economic sense, assuming that they exist, say nothing about the distribution of wealth. Within a state which is not too exposed to the world economy, such redistribution can take place. However, in the world as a whole there is no mechanism except the goodwill of the rich which will ensure such redistribution. There is nothing in the free-market mechanism which will automatically bring it about. Thirdly, economic actors have great power and their relative power over states it increasing. Lord Acton's aphorism applies to economic actors as well as any other: 'Power corrupts and absolute power corrupts absolutely'. One weakness of the classical economic liberal position is its neglect of power in its analysis of economic actors.

These difficulties come because, though we have a high level of internationalisation and globalisation, international governance is weak. This is, of course, a classical problem of international relations. However, the willingness of many governments to abandon the idea of international economic governance is worrying. An uncritical acceptance of the free market, without a consciousness of its deficiencies, is disturbing. Thus, while some aspects of globalisation and internationalisation are nearly inevitable and probably desirable, the perversions of the processes and the extreme *laissez-faire* ideology which seems to have accompanied them are open to objection. However, governments acting in concert are not powerless. A more pragmatic attitude to both markets and the accompanying internationalisation and globalisation can have great merits. Thus I do not want to decry these processes but, in a way abominated by the Critical Theorists, I want to tinker with the system and solve problems, to release the benefits of globalisation while minimising its drawbacks.

Part II

STATE AND ECONOMY

3

THE NATIONAL ECONOMY IN THE CONTEMPORARY GLOBAL SYSTEM

Angus Cameron and Ronen Palan

The idea of the nation-state is bound up today in a curious process. On the one hand the state is assumed to be diminishing in importance (if not actually disappearing) in the face of economic, political and cultural globalisation. On the other hand the state seems to be enjoying something of a revival. Not surprisingly, this 'revivalist' tendency consists largely of long-standing critics of globalisation, who always maintained that the claims for globalisation were overblown. They have been joined, however, by an increasing body of opinion that takes the idea of globalisation seriously yet looks to the state to offer continuity and security.

Such positions are not, of course, without their contradictions. National governments can be actively involved in the creation of transnational currencies, such as the current moves towards monetary union in Europe, whilst treating monetary sovereignty as 'a richly, almost superstitiously cherished component of government' (Dodd 1995). At the other end of the scale the World Bank, which is responsible in part for the way that globalisation has been conceived and encouraged, recently warned of 'a crisis of statehood' that must be overcome because 'the state is essential for putting in place the appropriate institutional foundations for markets' (World Bank 1997; *Financial Times* 1997). This is a significant deviation from the neo-liberal orthodoxy that has hitherto dominated the discourse of globalisation in multilateral institutions. Suddenly, it seems, the self-regulating market that was so trammelled by the existence of borders and the interfering governments that upheld them has need of the state after all. The problem with understanding these apparently contradictory positions on the part of national governments and the likes of the World Bank, of course, is the meaning of state itself and, in particular, the meaning and content of the *national economy*.

Assuming that policy and practice is generated in response to conceptions of reality, the concept of the nation-state, whether imaginary or not, has had a specific material impact on the practice of politics and policy. It follows that current and changing conceptualisations of the nation-state are equally significant and worth exploring on their own merits. The object of this chapter is to explore and to map out the dimensions of the national economy that have emerged in the context of contemporary political and economic processes. Our purpose in doing so is not to propose an alternative to current concepts of the state, but to map out the subtle forms by which the traditional concept of a national economy is being transformed, scripting a radically different set of spatial, temporal and institutional relations from those commonly assumed in the social sciences.

The chapter starts from the basic observation that for all its contradictions and, for some, obsolescence in the face of globalisation, the idea of a national economy retains a powerful function in the contemporary world.[1] Politicians of all hues fight and win or lose elections on their policies towards it, journalists and statisticians plot its ups and downs on an hourly basis, economists formulate theories about its past and future, and academics throughout the social sciences simply take it for granted. In spite of the popularity of the concept, however, the actual dimensions and dynamics of the national economy are far from self-evident. In practice the national economy has no fixed or definite boundaries and no permanent form or function – indeed the national economy is neither particularly national nor particularly economic and, moreover, never has been.

There is, of course, no fundamental reason why the economy should correspond to the state. There is ample historical evidence to demonstrate that the notion of a 'national system of political economy' (as promoted by Friedrich List in the 1830s) is of relatively recent vintage and what is meant by the 'national economy' changes considerably in form and function over time. Fernand Braudel (1979) argued that there was only a short period between about 1860 and 1870 that European economies even approximated national boundaries and even then there were barely a handful of them. The national economy, therefore, has always been a construct, forming an imaginary link between territorial, political, social, cultural and economic aspects of states (Castoriadis 1987). It is a compromise vital to the capitalist state since it maintains a fiction of coherence and unity whilst undergoing a continuous (if not constant) process of change.

The argument presented here draws on the post-rationalist tradition that has developed over the past two decades in international political economy, critical theory, institutional and evolutionary economics, critical sociology and human geography. In rejecting rationalist, progressivist and crude materialist accounts of social reality, such approaches present historicised, non-disciplinary explanations of social processes and practices (Amin, Palan and Taylor 1994; Amin and Palan 2000). The materiality of social institutions and their dynamics are understood to be produced within evolving and interrelated systems of institutions and discourses rather than as grounded in externalised and objective social realities. This chapter attempts to map the dimensions of the contemporary 'reality' of the national economy, therefore, in terms of the hermeneutics that it represents. This is not a rejection of the materiality of the national economy, but a historicised reconceptualisation of the dynamics (historical, conceptual and practical) of that materiality. As we argue below, the content of the contemporary configuration of the national economy can no longer be reduced to descriptive accounts of self-identifying institutions but must also account for the political, cultural, social and ethical norms embedded within them and the processes of their development. Inevitably, since these are discourses dominated by a European and North American ideology of the nation-state, the remarks made here correspond most closely to the socio-spatial configurations of northern, post-Fordist states than to those of the South.[2] That said, there are clear resonances for states of all kinds that are based, however loosely, on the European model whereby the national economy is understood to be coextensive with and subordinate to the state.

The argument is divided in the following way. First, there is a short, historical and theoretical analysis of the ways in which the relationship between the state, the national economy and, latterly, the 'global' economy have been articulated. Second, we briefly analyse the ways in which the problematic concept of the national economy has been sidelined by much globalisation literature. Third, we present an image of the contemporary national economy as a tripartite system of overlapping sub-economies, each marked by a characteristic set of institutions and processes – the *offshore economy*, the *private economy* and the *anti-economy*. These three combine to form a more complex image of the national economy than that which is assumed by orthodox, state-centred accounts. Finally, we offer some concluding remarks regarding the implications of the restructuring of relationships between state and national economy that this tripartite schema implies.

Under this tripartite schema, the national economy is seen to be stretched both across space and time. It is stretched over space in that there is a differentiated economic geography for those with access to the institutions and processes of each sub-economy; a geography that does not correspond to the territory of the state. It is stretched across time because there is a normative historical dynamic, implied by the different relationships of these three elements of the national economy, that 'pulls' towards and privileges the 'global'. These processes of stretching are not new, but have particular contemporary configurations that have a direct impact on the nature of policy-making and, more broadly, on the nature of social and economic identity.

The 'imagined' economy

The idea of a territorially embedded national economy is, for all its evident power and currency, profoundly contradictory. There is a strong implication contained within it that the national economy fits into a progressive hierarchy of material and objective geographical economies, ranging from small-scale settlements, through increasingly large urban spaces, up to and including the global, understood here in the literal sense of one single economy encompassing the entire planet. This linear spatial hierarchy is derived from and indeed legitimises orthodox developmental histories of the global economy which see a progressive expansion of the territorial extension of economic spaces resulting, inevitably, in the 'global'.[3]

This easy progression is deceptive, however, since unlike all other forms of territorial economy, the national economy is not essentially definable in relation to identifiable, non-contingent economic spaces. All other territorially defined economies have in common the fact that they constitute identifiable networks of economic interactions of particular types and/or centred on particular places. Although they can be distinguished from each other in terms of qualitative differences in their function and content, they have in common the fact that they are embedded territorially and spatially. As such they describe centred systems of economic interaction which, for all that they are not exclusively bound to territory, at least share a common spatial reference point such as a city or a particular market.

The national economy differs fundamentally in that whilst it may include economic centres and even entire local economies, it is characterised by being bounded. The national economy is not centred in the way that other spatial economies are, but is by definition extended evenly over a particular two-dimensional space described by conventional geographical mapping, demarcated by a border. This border is developed historically not as a consequence of economic activity (though this clearly plays a part) but primarily through the extension of political and juridical control over populations and territories. Rejection of progressivist and rationalist accounts of the territorial national economy points to the need for alternative, hermeneutic, explanations of the concept.

In his account of the development of the 'imagined community' of the western nation-state Benedict Anderson cites the census, the map and the museum as crucial facilitating elements of western imperialism. He maintains that in combination they allowed a 'totalising classificatory grid which could be applied with endless flexibility to anything under the state's real or contemplated control,' and 'serialisation: the assumption that the world was made up of replicable plurals' (Anderson 1991: 184). To extend Anderson's list of institutions, we might also add the national currency and the national central bank both as crucial instruments in the psychology of the state and as functional tools in the maintenance of the claimed coherence of the national economy (Dodd 1995). Just as the framework of thought supported by the census, the map and the museum enabled the imagination of the state as a national community, so they – in combination with institutional demonstrations of economic sovereignty – also made possible the concept of the state as coextensive with a national economy.

Such a reading suggests that the strongly territorial idea of the nation-state was from the outset closely bound up with the extension of regulatory control over the assets and transactions of the national population and the emergent institutions of the private and public sectors. At the same time, the state border as an economic boundary serves to separate and create the 'domestic' and the 'international' economies as discrete spaces. A bounded political economy was, for example, a prerequisite for the regulation of all forms of international trade, a concept that has no meaning except in a world economy divided by national borders. Regulation and taxation within the political jurisdiction of the state are likewise dependent on the notion of the national economy as a bounded and homogenous unit.

Prior to the nation-state becoming the norm of socio-economic organisation during this century, 'national' economies were essentially located in urban centres of cities like London or Paris and could encompass imperial territories far beyond the territorial boundaries of the metropolis (Jacobs 1985). The spatial configuration of the national economy, therefore, was not essentially embedded in or constrained by territoriality. It is only in the twentieth century – when the 'national economy' has been defined by various configurations of Fordism and post-Fordism or the autarkic visions of fascist and state socialist economies – that the concept of the bounded, territorial economy has become the norm.

Whereas the national economy was understood in the latter part of the nineteenth century as the material base for the spiritual pursuits of the (European) nation, the same national economy in the twentieth century has come to imply something very different; the primacy of national state forms of regulation in support of capitalist accumulation. An imaginary vision of a coherent national economy served to legitimise the shared political and economic goals of the modern, corporate, interventionist state. The Bretton Woods agreement, for instance, imposed strict limitations on international movements of capital in order to protect the new national macroeconomic planning measures of the 1930s (Helleiner 1994: chapter 2).

Notwithstanding its contradictions, the relationship of spatial correlation and subordination fundamental to the concept of the national economy is commonplace throughout the social sciences. Among sociologists it is represented most clearly in the work of the structural functionalists. Talcott Parsons (1952), for instance, viewed the economy and politics as two functional sub-systems of the 'social system'. Similarly Easton (1953) defines the political system as an alternative to the economy as a mode of 'resource allocation' (the marginalists in the nineteenth century defined the economy in terms of efficiency of resource allocation).

These ideas were then echoed in the first wave of development theory, namely modernisation theory, which is predicated on the assumption that the world is divided into discrete politico-economic entities, nation-states. Probably the best known and in policy terms most notorious such theory, is Rostow's (1971) account of stages of political development against which the economic capacities of each nation-state can be evaluated. Since politics defines economic goals, the theory suggests an intimate correspondence between the political system and the economic system. The combination of a 'proper' political system with an appropriate personality system within the state was believed to be fundamental to the generation of economic growth (Pieterse 1996).

But in advocating a particular political system, modernisation theorists and liberal economists, together with the rest of the literature predicated on the concept of a 'national economy', were already implicitly acknowledging the centrality of political choice. The notion of the national economy as consisting of both the 'political' and the 'economic' systems, implied not only separation from the wider environment, but also a self-organising, self-producing (according to Maturana and Varela 1980, *autopoietic*) capacity of the nation-state (see also Jessop 1990). National economic policy is, after all, a matter of choice, a choice which is, ostensibly at least, open to 'the nation'. The nation may choose to adopt open borders and a free trade policy, or it may choose instead varying degree of protectionism. Economists as a whole argued in favour of the former and against the latter, but the issue of choice, and hence the ideological debate surrounding national choices was central to the political debate.

The golden years of the national economy concept, from 1940 to 1980, saw therefore impassioned debates as to which 'national' economic policy should be adopted. It was a period characterised throughout the world in a battle between 'isolationists' and 'universalists', between advocates of protectionist, nationalist and socialist policies and of free trade and open borders. In this ideological guise, national political parties presented their voters with an apparently simple choice of either 'going it alone' or submerging the national economy in an increasingly transnationalised economy – as though these were mutually exclusive options.

These sorts of political debate were predicated on a central assumption, namely, the idea that the state mediates between the demands of international markets and the demands of its citizens for social and economic equality and other social goals. It is our contention that the erosion of the second part of the equation, and its replacement by an ideology that places the emphasis on the state as supporting, sustaining, and introducing international goals within a domestic context, works within a changing perception of the nature of the national economy. The rule of the market and transnational capital is actively being legitimised through a reconceptualisation and mapping of the 'national economy'.

The offshore, private and anti-economies of the state

It appears to us that the ostensibly homogenous space of the national economy is currently fragmenting into three types of spatial-temporal economy: the offshore economy, the private economy and the anti-economy. These are not wholly separate or fixed categories but are, nonetheless, marked by different institutional, spatial and economic relationships and processes. All are, however, present in the contemporary idea of a 'national economy' and all are, to a greater or lesser extent, embedded within a reconceptualisation of the state. Of the three only the private economy can be said to even approximate the boundaries of the state, but this should not be understood as a rejection of the concept of the national economy in relation to the state. As stated above there is not, and never has been, any essential relation between the territory of the state and the space of the national economy. The temporal and spatial stretching of the economic space of the state implied by the scheme presented below, therefore, is not intended to 'discover' that state and economy do not correspond, rather it is to explain some of the current dimensions of what correspondence there is.

In this new imagery those occupying the offshore economy are able by and large to escape the controls imposed by national regulatory frameworks resulting in a growing scale and velocity of particular types of market integration; in short, globalisation. The image is of a new economic space spanning the globe, a space of 'flows', transcending and penetrating all national boundaries without let or hindrance (Castells 1989, 1996; Lash and Urry 1994).

The private economy, supported by the state, responds to these changes by increasingly attempting to accommodate the needs of the offshore economy to attract and protect investment. Unlike the offshore economy, the private economy's globalising tendencies manifest themselves not directly as a new spatial terrain, but indirectly, through the notion of competitiveness. The private economy is increasingly linked globally as a competitive node within one, overwhelming market-place (McMichael 1996: 1).

The third economy under this scheme, the anti-economy, is that most often left out of the global versus national debate, except when it is wheeled on as evidence in support of one side or the other. The anti-economy consists of various sections of hitherto national economies that are now presented as the 'left out' and 'left over'. The concepts of the underclass and of social exclusion that have developed in policy circles and academia in the past twenty years are the clearest statements of this. The task of the state with regard to such groups is to 'reintegrate' them into the private economy as though they had somehow departed from it. These three elements of the national economy are presented schematically in Table 3.1.

The national offshore economy

That the 'offshore' economy should constitute a significant element of a national economy is, at first sight, a flat contradiction in terms. The image conjured by the concept of offshore is, after all, one of exotic island tax havens

Table 3.1

Private sector		*Public sector* / *Third sector/ social economy*
Offshore	*Private*	*Anti*
Institutions	*Institutions*	*Institutions*
World/global economy	National economy	Local/peripheral economy
Global markets	National state bodies	Community
Global firms	Local state bodies	Family
Merchant banks	Domestic firms	Household
Global cities	Borders	Welfare state
Media corps.	Domestic market	
'Global' organisations (WTO, etc.)	Retail banking	
TNCs		
Processes	*Processes*	*Processes*
Globalisation	Privatisation	Dependency
Technicisation	Liberalisation	Stagnation
Securitisation	Deregulation	Decline
	Enabling	Exclusion
	Modernisation	Marginalisation
	Globalisation	Obsolescence
Normative characteristics	*Normative characteristics*	*Normative characteristics*
Economic	Political	Static
Dynamic	Dynamic	Uncompetitive
Site of competition	Competitive	Inflexible
Impersonal	Flexible	Pre-global
Apolitical	Globalising	Residual
Economic	Privatising	Dependent (aid or welfare)
Future-oriented	Enabling (business)	Un- or de-skilled
Developing	Modernising	Outmoded
Expanding	Open to trade	Third World
World market	Market led	Unemployed
Technological	Employed	Underclass
'Real'	Onshore	
'Mainstream' economy ('social inclusion')		*'Welfare' and/or 'informal' economy ('social exclusion')*
		Potential change in status available only through: flexibilisation, retraining, reskilling, 'insertion', 'integration', modernisation, development, formalisation

somewhere in mid-Pacific, populated by a heady combination of the super rich, arms dealers and representatives of drug cartels. Whilst such places and their inhabitants exist and are undoubtedly very significant, the majority of institutions and individuals that together form the world of offshore are very firmly 'onshore' and much more mundane.

Offshore is a paradoxical realm that exists within the physical boundaries of states, is sanctioned and encouraged by national governments and yet represents the creation of a regulatory environment that seems to both contradict and undermine the very idea of a national economy and a coherent national space. Above all, offshore represents a radical disjuncture between economic activity and physical space, since fundamental to the idea of offshore is that it is 'placeless' (hence the possibly apocryphal proposal that the Moon could be used as the ideal offshore 'location'). However, the relationship between offshore and national economy is inherently contradictory only if we start from the assumption that the national economy is entirely homogenous and entirely 'onshore'. The main impact that the development of offshore has had for the state and national economy since its inception in the 1950s is the disruption of conventional notions of regulation and sovereignty over the economy (Palan 1998).

That offshore might be situated within the state, and even within the same national institutions, is crucial to understanding the effect that it has had on the territorial embeddedness of capital. Whilst, as we shall demonstrate, offshore has by no means removed the significance of territoriality from capital, it has transformed the relationship between capital and state by altering the spatial configuration of national economies (Roberts 1994). Offshore has allowed those with access to its institutions and processes a choice of economic spaces, within which they are able to circumvent the exigencies of territoriality. Offshore is not, however, a homogenous phenomenon, nor is it wholly disengaged from the national economy. Rather, offshore develops new (and not so new) sets of regulatory boundaries that, whilst different from the conventionally understood territorial boundaries of the state, are nonetheless real. These boundaries create spaces of differential regulation within and across states that add to the functionality of the border as much as they might seem to contradict it. Offshore creates a 'third space' consisting of three main institutional elements: Euromarkets, Export Processing Zones and tax havens (Palan 1997, 1998).

Euromarkets, by definition, operate beyond the regulatory control of states; indeed this was precisely why they were established in the first instance. However, the apparent anarchy of offshore belies its origins in conscious policy decisions taken by, amongst others, the Bank of England in the 1950s (Burn 1997). The Euromarket freed up the flow of international capital during the post-war reconstruction, by providing mechanisms by which the American dollar could be traded by banks outside of the jurisdiction of the United States.

Such transactions were, therefore, not subject to the constraints of national taxation, reserve requirements, reporting or capital controls.

Export Processing Zones represent the extension of the domain of offshore to manufacturing and trade by creating spaces within the boundaries of the state but which benefit from greatly reduced or wholly removed taxation, import duties and more general regulations. Approximately one-quarter of the world's manufacturing currently takes place in Export Processing Zones and free trade zones, the majority of which consist of assembly plants for components made elsewhere, all of whose products are then re-exported.

Tax havens offer a variety of specific services to their clients – such as shipping registration, discrete and secure banking and, of increasing importance, corporate citizenship. Tax havens 'sell' sovereign citizenship to the private firms of other states, thus allowing them to be incorporated 'offshore' and, therefore not subject to the juridical and fiscal requirements of those places within which its operations are physically located.

These three together seem to many to represent a terminal dislocation of the national economy – its fragmentation prior to absorption by the global. However, as has been argued elsewhere (Palan 1998), the power of Euromarkets to circumvent national economic regulations does not, as many assume, mean that they are the antithesis of national economies. Euromarkets still deal, after all, in currencies and other forms of securitised instruments, that are still formulated, regulated and supported within the context of the national political and juridical space. Whilst there is little doubt that the dynamics of offshore have altered the nature of money itself by delinking it radically from any notional materiality and territoriality it once had (and as monetary theorists since Simmel have amply demonstrated, this is hardly new: Simmel 1997; Dodd 1994), this does not remove the function of the national economic space. The sovereign space of the state retains a very powerful mediating function, delivering the variety of regulatory spaces that is so important for the lubrication of capital flows. These may be 'economies of signs and space' but they are still embedded in the concept of national sovereignty over economic activity.

The national private economy

The national private economy that we have identified has already found expression in a number of different concepts. The 'competition' state and the 'enabling' state both present images of the interaction between state and economy whereby the state is seen to withdraw to a much diminished role (Cerny 1990). The Fordist or corporatist idea of the state as operating a managerial role with regard to the national economy, including a fairly high degree of direct capitalist ownership and production is long recognised to have passed (Amin 1994). The post-Fordist state that has replaced it was a product partly of conscious policy, most obviously by 'privatisation', and partly as a consequence of wider structural changes in the world economy. The ongoing process of privatisation throughout the world was itself a response both to the emerging fiscal crisis of the state during the mid-1970s and the reconfiguration of the world economy following the collapse of Bretton Woods. The internationalisation of production during these years, which many regard as the first phase of globalisation, saw the first tangible delinking of systems of finance and manufacturing from traditional locations, particularly the industrial regions of Europe and North America.

The consequences of these changes have largely been analysed in relation to emerging space economies at the global and local levels. A commonly cited feature of the highly mobile capital of the emerging global economy is its capacity to circumvent the national level altogether. Whilst the most marked expressions of this are found in those parts of the state designated (by the state itself) as 'offshore', this is also true of the rest of the national economy. A considerable literature has developed to explore the dimensions of the relations between global capital and local places, which tends to assume that the institutions of the national economy are wholly circumvented. In the new 'economy of flows' or the 'economies of signs and space' what matters is the 'glocal' (Robertson 1995). National economic policies have become geared towards promoting internal competition between different industrial regions for investment. Competition is engendered by a combination of spatial and fiscal policies such as regional development agencies, 'pre-competitive' infrastructural improvements, tax holidays and all manner of financial 'sweeteners'. As a consequence, transnational capital is seen to negotiate directly with regional authorities – over the terms and conditions of their investment, including labour conditions, levels of service provision and infrastructure – as much if not more than they do with national government.[4] It is as though local and regional economies have ceased to be embedded in a national economic space, but now compete directly with other similar places in other states in a global space.

Not surprisingly the centrality of national economy is obscured by this new configuration, not least because, as suggested above, the national economy is not primarily a spatial category. The global and the local as, respectively, all-inclusive economic space and production 'node' or 'growth pole' are far more convincing spatial configurations (Amin and Thrift 1994). The role of the state faced with this new reality is to withdraw and to enable private capital to exploit the potential of the new competition.

The 'hollowing-out' of the state entailed in these processes of privatisation and globalisation/localisation is, however, much overstated. The presentation of the role of the state as progressively 'deregulating' economic space obscures the extent of *re*regulation that is taking place (Dodd 1994: 90). In many ways even that is an overstatement since the core function of the state with respect to the economy has not in fact changed all that much. Rather than be constrained by an external force of globalisation across the board, as the cruder versions of that theory tend to claim, the state has created conditions whereby it must remake the normative differentiation drawn between different aspects of its 'national' economy with respect to the global. The state has not retreated but has reconfigured the way it applies its regulations so that they are no longer national, in the sense of being universally and evenly applied throughout the territory of the state. The 'reality' of the global economy is, therefore, routinely marshalled in defence of the orthodox econocentric solutions to national social and economic problems (Peck 1998). So, for example, the European Commission's 1993 White Paper on Employment, Growth and Competitiveness has four objectives to aid competitiveness in the global economy. These are

- helping European firms to adapt to the new globalised and interdependent competitive situation
- exploiting the competitive advantages associated with the gradual shift to a knowledge-based economy
- promoting a sustainable development of industry
- reducing the time-lag between the pace of change in supply and the corresponding adjustments in demand (European Commission 1993).

All of these objectives are dictated '*in the wake of* the globalisation of economies and markets' (emphasis added). The state has created a market for sovereignty and regulation for capital external to its boundaries in order to attract it and has likewise created a space of differential accumulation within the state to ensure that it stays.

The national private economy is a normatively created regulatory space in which the state retains the function of law-maker and law-enforcer, a role which has, if anything, been strengthened by globalisation/localisation. Membership of the global trade regime administered by the World Trade Organisation, for example, entails the adoption of standard measurement and reporting procedures by member-states which they in turn must enforce on their national economies. A considerable proportion of the agreement that forms the Organisation's constitution comprises these rules for accounting and reporting. Intriguingly, much of this reporting is itself privatised, being factored out to private accountancy or trade surveillance firms. However, whether carried out by state agencies directly or through proxies, the surveillance function of the state remains a national obligation and continues to define national economic space. In similar ways, the World Trade Organisation's 'rules of origin' regulations are explicitly designed to establish criteria for the identification of the national content of goods and services being exported. That national law might be being defined in relation to external authorities, and therefore represent a diminution of sovereignty, ignores the extent to which this has happened at least since the sixteenth century and the beginnings of the *lex mercatoria*, the 'law merchant' (Cutler 1995; Teubner 1997; Palan 1997).

The conventional image of the enabling state is one that is essentially withdrawn from the economy. The state no longer replaces entrepreneurship through public ownership but enables it through a combination of privatisation, 'pre-competitive' measures and structural adaptation. The imagery and practices of the corporatist and/or Fordist state have been replaced by a much more fragmentary and fluid conception of national economic space, which although still bounded and regulated, is beyond the capacities of the state to control. This is both a deliberate policy fostered by national governments anxious to resolve balance of payments and fiscal problems, and a product of the massive expansion of the financial and securities sector.

The state may have withdrawn to some extent as an owner of capital (though of course in most cases states retain considerable asset portfolios and direct capital investments), but the state's role as regulator of capital relations and as provider of currency and security remains. Privatisation has often been misrepresented as a process of deregulation, particularly by those with a political interest in claiming state withdrawal as a virtue, whereas it is more properly seen as a process of reregulation.

As such the involvement of the state with its territorial economy has not diminished, rather, its emphasis has changed. The private national economy is concerned to attune national economic policy to the realities of the global economy and, even more vaguely, to the exigencies of the process of globalisation. This in itself does not represent as much of a difference as is often claimed since the global economy is an extension of the long-established concept of the 'world economy'. Indeed, it is worth recalling that the concept of a world economy was coeval with that of the national economy and has always lent the national economic boundary a dual role. The boundary operates both as a territorial delimitation of one state from another, but at the same time has always operated as a line drawn between the territorial space of the state and the virtual space of the 'world'. The world economy, like its global successor, occupies a space that is variously above and between national economies. It functions as a neutral space that provides a benchmark, arrived at through the aggregation of national economic statistics, to generate world prices. Everything has a world market price against which national (or regional in the case of the European Union and North American Free Trade Association) prices are gauged.

The concept of the global economy greatly extends this concept, not least by giving it a powerful institutional framework, but does not significantly alter its function. The global economy does, however, stand in a different relation to the state since it is no longer neutral. It is still presented as apolitical, and is therefore still understood to be 'economic', but it has also become a normative and, indeed, normalising, reality. The global economy functions differently with regard to the state; whilst movements in the world economy have long influenced economic policy within the state, the global economy presented as a new reality forces changes in national policy as a whole. This has the further consequence, as we shall see below, of forcing the state to differentiate between its proper function with regard to the global future and its function with regard to a sub-national, local past.

Through the creation of the competition state, the homogeneity of the national economy although assumed in theory is compromised in practice. The national private economy ceases to be conceivable as an homogenous unity and becomes a single but differentiated space. This has, of course, always been the case, but the mobility of capital and the collapse of the labour-intensive fordist production systems in the North has sharpened the differences between regions of the same state.

The national anti-economy

The various aspects of the national economy represented above as offshore and private national economies will be fairly familiar to students of international relations and international political economy. Whilst the treatment of these issues we have suggested is often poorly understood, the rise of offshore and some of its effects on the state are fairly widely explored. Less familiar to the student of globalisation will be the third of our sub-economies, the anti-economy.[5]

The anti-economy is so designated, not because it is in any way 'uneconomic' but because, in breaking the normative rules of the new global reality, it is set aside from 'proper' or mainstream economic activity. As much as globalisation implies the creation of new spaces, structures and relationships, it also implies the redundancy (often literally) of older forms of organisation and those members of the population dependent upon them.

The meaning of the anti-economy is best illustrated by consideration of the extensive and often problematic debate concerning 'social exclusion' that has emerged in Europe in recent years. Exclusion generally refers to those sections of the population that do not 'fit' with the emerging order – who for a variety of reasons cannot respond to the exigencies of the globalising world. It is among the socially excluded that we find the long-term consequences of the disaggregation of the national economy from national space (geography) and the national population (including immigrant populations and refugees). These groups are, of course, still contained physically within the national economy, but that part of it which remains rooted in territory, rather than in new global economies of flows. These people do not live beyond the global and nor are they separate from it, but they are conceptually excluded from it by virtue of existing only on the margins of the new centres and processes of economic activity.

Social exclusion is, like globalisation, a vague and ambiguous term. It is used to refer to chronic, multiple deprivation through discrimination, displacement, unemployment, disability and ill-health – problems which conspire to isolate individuals and communities physically, socially and economically from the basic standards expected by the rest of society. Whilst the concept of exclusion convincingly describes the lived experience of many people it is a term which functions very differently in other contexts. In particular, as the concept of exclusion has been adopted both by increasing numbers of national governments and international agencies in recent years, it has been progressively removed from its material and descriptive roots.[6] As it has been internationalised, social exclusion has become a normative category which is defined ultimately (though never explicitly) in relation to the global economy (Levitas 1996; Cameron 1997). Although other causes for exclusion are commonly acknowledged, unemployment is routinely paraded as the single greatest cause of exclusion worldwide – to which the automatic solution is assumed to be employment or reinsertion into the labour market (Clasen, Gould and Vincent 1998).[7] The essence of the concept of exclusion in common usage therefore replaces descriptive complexity with a single, blanket category.

Social exclusion as a normative category is an important element in a prescriptive remapping and reinscribing of the social world, particularly in redefining the function of the state with regard both to its 'citizenry' and the global system. Exclusion implies a radical disjuncture in the conventional equation of state and society. The two are no longer coextensive since the state itself administers an internal 'border' between the included (those in employment and therefore active in the private or offshore economies), and the excluded. Despite this distinction, the task of resolving the problem of social exclusion is still the responsibility of the state. Social exclusion may have been caused by the vagaries of the global economy but responsibility for it still ends at the border. Social exclusion, therefore, denotes a space of exclusion within a society, a normative separation that places certain individuals and communities into a discrete non-territorial space, simultaneously *within* the state but *beyond* the society.

We have chosen to call this space of the excluded the anti-economy, because its normative construction implies not just a different space but a definite movement away from the new ideals of economic reality. Those occupying the anti-economy are seen, albeit through no fault of their own, as a brake on globalisation and as representing its antithesis. If globalisation is characterised by movement, placelessness, simultaneity and universality, the anti-economy consists of categories of economic activity which are static, place-dependent and particular. This signifies an extra dimension to our tripartite structure of the national economy, namely a normative historical motion from the local to the private and offshore worlds. In other words there is a quasi-moral dimension to globality whereby to be socially excluded and economically marginal is, to put it bluntly, to fail to be global enough.

These three elements of the national economy can also be interpreted, therefore, as developmental phases extending across time – time defined according to the standard teleology of globalisation. This is expressed most clearly by the limited number of options available to national governments to bring those occupying the anti-economy into the mainstream categories of the private and offshore economies. Since they must, it seems, be brought into the formal labour market, they must be made more 'employable' (Layard 1996). The list of transitional processes from exclusion to globality is as familiar as it is limited – 'flexibilisation', 'reskilling', 'retraining', 'integration', 'insertion', 'modernisation', etc. All these transformative process are geared towards making the socially excluded better equipped for the global economy – not the other way round. If we were to plot motion onto this it would be in one direction only, from right to left. This is clearly expressed in current policy terms by the growing interest in the so-called 'third sector' as a solution to problems of unemployment and exclusion. Our schematic relates the three elements of this social hierarchy to various economic 'sectors'. The classical distinction between 'public' and 'private' sectors, although contestable, is well enough known not to need much elucidation. The idea of a third sector – understood to be located 'between' the state and the market and/or the public and the private – has been around for a very long time, but is enjoying a renaissance together with interest in social exclusion. The third sector is seen as a way of circumventing the contraction of the public sector and the welfare state, by acting as a bridge between public and private sectors. Third-sector organisations include, for example, Intermediate Labour Markets, certain types of cooperative, many voluntary organisations, community enterprises, housing associations and alternative currencies (such as Local Exchange Trading Systems and 'time dollars').

The role of the third sector is promoted in two main ways. First it is seen as a temporary, transitional arrangement between old corporate welfare-based solutions and a new, market-based solution to poverty and disadvantage. The third sector in this sense performs a specific function and then is effectively absorbed into the private sector. All that is left of the public sector after this process is a 'safety net' for those who cannot work. Second, the third sector has been seen as a permanent addition to the other two sectors, providing a lasting route for the disadvantaged into the private world of employment.

Whichever of these definitions is used, the ideology of the third sector contributes to the construction of normative historical motion. The third sector is commonly seen as the natural home of the socially excluded and, increasingly, is their only option as public services are increasingly shifted into the voluntary sector or privatised. Conceptually, since it is by definition not part of the private sector, the third sector actively contributes also to the notion that the private sector is sacrosanct and operates according to a set of internal, immutable rules. Much of what the third sector does is to emulate conditions in the private sector, as preparation for future employment in the 'mainstream' (private) labour market. The evidence that it actually does so is at best very ambiguous.

The most striking consequence of the evolving discourse of social exclusion and the third sector is that together they serve to absolve the processes and institutions of globalisation from responsibility for its consequences. By contributing to the normative spatial and historical stretching described here, they create a new pathology of poverty not dissimilar to nineteenth-century distinctions between the 'deserving' and the 'undeserving' poor. The deserving poor in the contemporary national economy conform to the exigencies of globality either by choice or, as the increasing use of coercive 'workfare' schemes bears witness, by force. Increasingly the only people seen to have a responsibility for resolving the problems of social exclusion are the socially excluded themselves.

Conclusion

The debate that has raged around the theory and practice of globalisation in recent years has been dominated by a single theme – whether globalisation is seen to be antithetical to the state, a product of it or a figment of the intellectual imagination. The terms of its examination have been founded on a set of firm assumptions about the nature of the nation-state and its homogenous national economy. It is the sovereign state, after all, that globalisation is supposed to be departing from.

The paradox of this is that the concepts of nation-state and national economy have never been so widely and uncritically accepted as at the time of their (alleged) passing. What we have tried to demonstrate here is that much of this debate is being conducted wholly within the terms of the hermeneutic system of the state itself. If the global and the state are constructed, as they so often are, using the tools of rationalist thought, as being distinct and even mutually exclusive entities, both spatially and temporally, then we should not perhaps be surpised to find the debate about their interrelationship riddled with inconsistencies. If, however, we incorporate the knowledge that our understandings of the global, the local and the national (and, for that matter, all other forms of social categorisation) are being produced within the same evolving hermeneutic system, then we begin to be able to understand the structural connections between institutions and processes that seem on the face of it to be wholly distinct.

This is not, however, simply a matter of finding better (i.e. more complete) descriptions of a complex reality. Rather it represents the beginning of an exploration of how material existence is embedded in systems and practices of meaning, which we both reproduce and are subject to. The 'autopoiesis' that has been attributed to 'the social system' is only possible because each individual within that system plays by similar hermeneutic rules and thus lends that system the appearance of autonomous dynamism. Paradoxically it is only by removing the crude materiality of rationalism and pursuing ideas that have long been considered esoteric by the mainstream social sciences, that we can reinvest our comprehension of the contemporary world with a material and human scale.

This is because, ultimately, the abstract schematic that we have introduced above offers a picture of different levels of access to the resources of power. By this we do not simply refer to material resources, as in traditional conceptions of the class system for example, but more importantly to resources of meaning, language and history that are crucial to the realisation of political and economic power at any level.

Notes

1 For a useful review of approaches to globalisation in relation to national autonomy see Martin (1994).
2 This is also a product of the fact that much of the empirical research, particularly that concerning the issue of social exclusion, has been carried out with regard to Europe.
3 See, for example, the progressivist accounts in Dicken (1992), Trebilcock and Howse (1995) and Cameron (1989).
4 In recognition of this possibility, the new South African constitution expressly prohibits the competitive undercutting of wages, safety and environmental standards by regional authorities in pursuit of inward foreign investment.
5 See Saurin (1996) and Tooze and Murphy (1996) for two very powerful statements concerning the absence of adequate accounts of poverty from international relations and international political economy in general and the globalisation debate in particular.
6 The first Council of Ministers resolution to deal explicitly with the problem of exclusion came in 1989, to be followed by a strong policy statement, the 1994 White Paper on Growth, Competitiveness and Employment. Since then the European Commission has been developing an extensive research programme to assess the problem of social exclusion and to find ways of tackling it. UNESCO cites social exclusion as one of the main targets of the Management of Social Transformation (MOST) programme.
7 See also several of the essays in Gual (1996) (particularly Gual, Drèze and Layard), which are predicated on the assumption that the only solution to unemployment is 'job creation'.

4

GLOBALISATION, REGIONAL INTEGRATION AND THE STATE

Francis McGowan

This chapter explores the position of regional integration in a globalising world, considering it as not only *intermediary* but also *intermediating* between national and global levels. The processes of state development, regional integration and globalisation are clearly interrelated, at times reinforcing, at others conflictual. In recent times many have argued that the balance has shifted away from the national towards the regional and increasingly the global. Yet these shifts appear to be partly results of the actions (or inactions) of governments themselves. While global processes are often seen as beyond the control of nation-states, able to constrain or transform those traditional authority structures most clearly vested at the national level, these changes are due at least partly to state preferences. Nation-states remain reluctant to engage collectively at the appropriate level, in responding to or regulating globalising forces: the level of global governance (in terms of states cooperating and sharing sovereignty within global authority structures) is generally low. By contrast, states have been willing to transfer or share sovereignty in regional settings. Can regional integration serve to intermediate between the global and the national and, if so, to what ends? Does regionalism reconfigure national sovereignty or does it hasten its demise? What lessons can be drawn from regional experiences which could be applicable in global settings?

Much depends on whether one views regionalist projects as buffers against globalisation or as catalysts for it (Lawrence 1996). Regional blocs could arguably serve as a shelter from, or a constraint upon, globalisation as governments and others seek to retain a collective space for autonomy, insulating themselves through more or less explicitly protectionist schemes (Cable and Henderson 1994; Mittelman 1996; Tussie 1998). The catalytic role, by contrast, is best understood as an extension of 'open regionalism', where integration is encouraged as a conduit to global competitiveness, enhancing interactions at the regional level but not exclusively so (Bergsten 1997).

The contentious role of regionalism as both strategy and concept, and our understanding of it, are at the core of this chapter. It therefore focuses on the interaction of the national, the regional and the global in terms of both 'actually existing conditions' and changing analytical perspectives. After a brief review of the categories of the nation-state, regionalism and globalisation, it examines their changing inter-relationships from the vantage point of 'embedded liberalism' (Ruggie 1982). Three phases of the post-war political economy are identified, reflecting shifts in the balance of power between the global, regional and national. In the early post-war period, a relatively reinforcing dynamic between the national, regional and global is seen. This is contrasted with the crises of the 1970s, when governments appeared intent on defending their autonomy against regional and global integration – a period of embattled liberalism, or 'the crisis of embedded liberalism' (Keohane 1982). This in turn changes in the more recent period when globalisation has been in the ascendant – requiring a redefinition of the state and the expansion of open regionalism as 'disembedded liberalism' (Ruggie 1995). Over this period, moreover, there have been changing conceptions of the balance of power between national, regional and global, and it is instructive to put our current concerns into that historical context. The chapter thus concentrates on the pivotal role of regionalism and considers how its analysis might inform our understanding of the globalisation process and offer strategies for more effective governance.

A number of questions of approach, biases and categorisation are begged by the analysis in this chapter. I address the issues primarily from a traditional political economy perspective, embracing political science and economics. This is because I am mainly concerned with questions of economic governance and the challenge that globalisation presents to nation-states and regional blocs in this domain. Arguably this is where the impact of globalisation is most acute (particularly *vis à vis* states) and the intermediary role of regional integration is most obvious. However it is clear that economic globalisation and regionalism cannot be examined in a vacuum – indeed the wider literature on globalisation notes its consequences for identity, culture, etc., and for some authors at least these effects may be a reaction to, or associated with, the transformation of the economic (Mittelman 1996; Shaw 1997; Scholte 1997). Moreover, the success of European regionalism seems both to be rooted in a wider political and cultural context and to beg questions about how non-economic aspects of public life are addressed, as evidenced in debates on the democratic deficit and Social Europe (Williams 1990; Garcia 1993; Neunreither 1994; Wallace and Smith 1995). Towards the end of the chapter, I return to this aspect in setting out the relationship between globalisation and regionalism.

One might also object that both the historical narrative and the theoretical approaches identified in this chapter are too Eurocentric in their focus. However, a methodological Eurocentrism is to some extent inevitable. It is clearly the case that much of normative political thought on the supranational (whether regional or global) has been Eurocentric not just in the sense of the thinkers' physical and intellectual roots but also in their territorial and political concerns; for them all the world was Europe.[1] Most blueprints for world government before the post-war era were designed to address problems of international relations in Europe. Although pan-American and pan-African ideas have emerged over the last two hundred years, most of these were conceived in colonial times as emancipatory in nature and 'continentalist' sentiment withered after independence (Carter 1966; Cervenka 1977; Castaneda 1994; Pakkasvirti 1996). Although regional integration outside Europe has been widespread, the outcomes have (so far) been relatively modest (Winters 1997; Fernandez-Jilberto and Mommen 1997). Thus in dealing with regionalism the chapter concentrates on the European Union as the most extensive and evolved regionalist experiment, though it also touches on other experiences and the lessons which can be drawn from them for Europe.

Finally we should note the important practical and methodological problem of 'dissonance' – the phenomena we are addressing are intrinsically very different, functionally as well as spatially. A review of the globalisation literature would highlight the strong bias towards flows (the phenomenon as a process), whereas discussions of regional integration focus on institutional matters, particularly the interaction among states and between states and regional organisations.[2] There is a risk in other words that the respective discourses are to some extent at cross purposes; what can we expect regional integration to tell us about globalisation? Might we expect regionalism to tackle the conditions of regionalisation? Likewise should we not seek globalist solutions to globalisation? Hopefully we will demonstrate the linkages between these very different processes and the possibility of making links and applying lessons from one tier to another. Moreover, I concentrate my discussion of managing globalisation with an account both of the efforts to create global governance and of the evolution of existing multilateral institutions (Ruggie 1993b).

Multiple tiers, contrasting processes

In order to examine the relationship between national, regional and global domains, let us start by looking closely at the categories themselves. The nation-state is relatively straightforward to characterise as the focus for legitimacy and authority in internal and international affairs. While one might debate for how long this has been the case – conventional wisdom suggests that state structures have often predated national sentiment (Gellner 1983; Anderson 1991; Hobson and Weiss 1995) – the norm over the last 150 years has been an assumption of or a struggle for the trappings of autonomy and affinity which the nation-state provides.[3] Of course one can point to many examples where the fit between nation and state has been ragged at best and there have been many challenges to state structures, territorial boundaries and national identities. As Michael Mann notes, 'For much of the world a true nation-state remains more aspiration for the future than present reality. The nation-state's rise has been global but modest and very uneven' (Mann 1997: 478). Yet in both everyday and academic discourse the nation-state has been the principal focus in political and economic life, the well-spring of sovereignty or at least the formal trappings thereof. I concentrate on the role of the state as an actor, though I also touch upon aspects of state construction and nation-building.

Regionalism by contrast is an agreement by states to cooperate in some institutional arrangements for a variety of motivations, political and economic. Indeed, perhaps the most curious aspect of regionalist projects – and the analysis of them – is the confusion of means and ends. While grand political objectives have often inspired integration, the means have often been pitched in more modest terms (the use of economic mechanisms) which in turn create a distinctive system of politics. For the purposes of this chapter the defining characteristic of regionalism is that it constitutes a joint commitment on the part of states, in a few cases involving some pooling of sovereignty. It has, moreover, generally been designed as a response to and/or a means of encouraging 'regionalisation', the degree of integration within a particular space (Payne and Gamble 1996). Such integration is generally perceived as economic in nature though other social processes may be at work. Indeed there can be significant gaps between the ambitions of regionalist projects and the underlying conditions of regionalisation – a gap revealed by inertia, crises, reversals and obsolescence on the one hand and the articulation, 'rediscovery', and invention of regional affinities on the other (Smith 1992).

Moreover, the degree of regionalism and regionalisation varies over time and space. Regionalist projects outside Europe have tended to be marked by more modest ambitions, primarily economic in terms of ends as well as means. As we will see, while there is a 'demonstration effect' between regions and periods (i.e., that experiments in one place and time affect others (Baldwin 1997)), the scope of regionalisation and the impact of regionalism are quite different in their intensity. If Mann's characterisation of the nation-state is true it is even more the case for regional integration (Wallace 1997).

Globalisation is generally considered to refer to a series of social processes and therefore is not characterised by the institutional trappings which we have noted in our other two categories. In current debates, moreover, globalisation is regarded as being in the ascendancy, transforming economic, cultural and social conditions. Yet despite its fundamental effects, globalisation as a phenomenon remains largely unregulated. In contrast to the national and to some extent the regional levels, there is little equivalent global governance. Most international organisations are apparently little more than the sum of their individual members' preferences. That is not to say that there are no important multilateral activities and institutions. Given that economic and military power is concentrated, 'global orders' may emerge, broadly reflecting the interests of those most powerful (Keohane 1984). Moreover, in such conditions global institutions can constrain weaker states in both economic and security terms. Arrangements such as IMF conditionality and World Bank structural adjustment programmes give credence to the view that such organisations regulate states more than they do (Williamson 1994; Mittelman 1996; Biersteker 1998; Gray 1998). Indeed, if anything, the existing panoply of international institutions seem better designed to facilitate rather than regulate globalisation – whether in the form of investment flows, currency movements, etc., or in removing obstacles and providing infrastructure. As Murphy notes, such organisations have 'helped create international markets in industrial goods by linking communication and transportation infrastructure, protecting intellectual property and reducing legal and economic barriers to trade' (Murphy 1994: 2).

There is then a mismatch between the different levels; in the case of the nation-state we are concerned with well-established institutional arrangements which have been able to maintain considerable autonomy although perhaps the formal trappings of sovereignty are at odds with a loss of real sovereignty in some domains. In the case of globalisation we are concerned with social processes which are not effectively regulated by equivalent authorities, in part because states are unwilling to relinquish their formal sovereignty to regulate global forces through collective action. In the middle is regionalism where perhaps the fit between institutional capabilities and the processes at work is closer than in the other two cases, but where there remain significant problems of collective action, not to mention mechanisms for legitimising action and providing some sense of affinity or identity.

Mapping the relationships

What then has been the nature of the interrelationships between the global, regional and national? In some recent accounts the relationship between the global and national is seen as zero-sum, globalisation impinging upon or constraining the autonomy of states while regional integration enjoys a more ambiguous status, as catalyst or constraint. However, even if this is an accurate characterisation of the present day, it is a description of a relatively recent phenomenon. At other times the dynamic may have been very different, perhaps more reinforcing than conflictual.

It is true that many have questioned the 'newness' of globalisation, at least as an economic phenomenon, pointing to the untrammelled movement of money, trade and people in the nineteenth century (see Chapter 2; Williamson 1996; Bairoch 1996). Yet, this was also the period when nation-states consolidated their position in Europe (and some other parts of the world) as the vehicle for political and economic development and when relatively modest regionalist experiments were conducted in customs or currency unions.[4] However, in this chapter, the focus is on developments since 1945.

Embedded liberalism (1945–77)[5]

In contrast to other periods, the early post-war era has been regarded as one where nation-states, regional integration and globalisation seemed to evolve in tandem with one another; growing openness of the international economy was matched by growing governmental roles (Rodrik 1997). In some cases, an intermediary regional step was taken to reduce barriers between countries but not at the expense of state autonomy or multilateral commitments. In arguing that this relationship constituted 'embedded liberalism' Ruggie takes Polanyi's (1944) concept of embeddedness to describe the compromise between American demands for a liberal international economic order on the one hand and the desire of other states to reconstruct their economies through more interventionist polices: 'unlike the economic nationalism of the thirties, it would be multilateral in character ... [but] ... its multilateralism would be predicated upon domestic interventionism' (Ruggie 1982: 393).

For the most part embedded liberalism is usually applied to the outcomes of the economic diplomacy between the United States on the one hand and (principally) West European nation-states on the other, with the multilateral arrangements for trade and payments and the welfare state as the principal foci. However, is it not also possible to stretch this interpretation to other aspects of the international political economy and, perhaps, of internal arrangements? The concept describes the dynamic underlying integration within Europe after the war, characterising that process as a similar sort of compromise between international commitments to open up the economy on the one hand and national desires to retain autonomy in pursuing economic development and meeting domestic social needs on the other.[6] The idea seems to capture the bargain negotiated within states as well, given that domestic concerns have informed international negotiations (Gourevitch 1986; Ruggie 1995) and economic systems have been grounded in social structures and political choices (Polanyi 1944).

The era of embedded liberalism therefore is one of state reconstruction (and in the third world of state construction or 'nation building') in the context of a steadily liberalising international economy. This national-global interaction can be characterised as one of mutual reinforcement as government grows in tandem with the removal of trade and other barriers. On the one hand the openness of the economy obliges states to develop compensatory policies, on the other the state's capacity to do so is facilitated by rapid trade-led growth (Cameron 1978). Indeed, the commitment of governments to open economies is to a large extent dependent on results: 'liberalism was acceptable ... largely because of the extended period of prosperity associated with liberal policies' (Keohane 1982: 16). The period is also marked by a number of regional integration ventures, largely based on economic cooperation, but differentiated by the degree of commitment and the nature of the underlying agendas of federation, security, etc. (Deutsch 1957; Haas 1964; Haas and Schmitter

1965; Nye 1966, 1968). Such schemes were intermediary in their nature, in some cases intended as the first step towards deeper economic and political unity amongst nations; in other cases as ways of coping with multilateral liberalisation (Cooper 1986: 124–5). Though there was a debate on the contribution of regional integration to open trade – whether it created or diverted trade – the general consensus seemed to support integration as a promoter of liberalisation rather than protection.[7]

How were these relationships understood contemporaneously? For our purposes the most surprising thing to note is the extent to which the relations between the global and the national were for a long time effectively ignored. International relations approaches were still centred on the relations between nations, rooted in a realist paradigm. Political science approaches, on the other hand, largely survived in a self-contained world within the boundary, though ironically the state itself received relatively little attention.[8] What did emerge, however, were disparate accounts highlighting convergent social and political trends, identifying characteristics which were often subsumed in later globalisation analyses. Industrialism and postindustrialism literatures asserted the convergence of different polities and societies albeit on the basis of internal dynamics as much as of international pressures.[9]

Subsequently, aspects of this account were articulated in the 'transnationalist' literature, though here the main precursors were the integrationists on the one hand (Haas 1964) and international organisation theorists on the other (Claude 1965). Drawing attention to the mix of communications, investment and other factors which today constitute the dynamic of globalisation, this approach challenged state-centric approaches to international relations. It drew attention to growing interdependence between states and the growing influence of non-state actors, most notably transnational corporations (TNCs).[10] However, for all their claims of a new paradigm and the need to move away from state-centrism, the transnationalists did not call into question the primacy of the state – indeed, for them, it was partly the growing activism of governments which fostered interdependence. Only a few were ready to argue that the nation-state was 'just about through as an economic unit' (Kindleberger 1969: 207). For the most part, in any case, this debate failed to capture the public imagination in the way that possessed anything like the resonance currently enjoyed by 'globalisation'.[11] Perhaps the persistence of Cold War politics worked against any acceptance of the global–realist conceptions retained by the nation-state as the central unit of analysis (Waltz 1970).

As noted, transnationalism drew upon and owed much to an earlier wave of regional integration theory. Attempts to explain and predict the outcomes of regionalist projects had mushroomed in the late 1950s and 1960s: pluralist and neofunctionalist models associated with Deutsch and Haas spawned an extensive research agenda addressing developments in Europe and many parts of the Third World. Those approaches highlighted questions of shifting loyalties, the accumulation of responsibilities by 'spill-over' and the gradual remaking of the polity at the supranational level. We return to the debate on regional integration later but here we should note that the value of such approaches was being seriously challenged in the 1960s and apparently falsified by the early 1970s (Hoffmann 1966; Haas 1976).

Embattled liberalism (1973–84)

It could be argued that it was in the regional context that the reassertion of national autonomy became most apparent. De Gaulle's 'empty chair' policy established a veto culture in the European Community which – when combined with the economic downturn and the accession of the United Kingdom in the 1970s – contributed to a crisis of economic stagnation and institutional sclerosis (Dinan 1998). Elsewhere, the momentum behind regional integration dissipated. In all cases it was clear that the challenges of economic adjustment were to be tackled nationally not regionally. As economic problems deepened, regional blocs became at best arenas for managing trade (Curzon Price 1981).

The economic crisis of the 1970s heightened the tension between domestic social and political bargains on the one hand and the obligations of operating in an increasingly open world economy on the other (Strange and Tooze 1981). Indeed responses to openness were manifest in the efforts of governments to foster new industries and protect old ones – so-called industrial policies – as well as in various challenges from the left, notably the Alternative Economic Strategy in the UK, the Wage Earner Funds proposals in Sweden and the Mitterand experiment in France (McGowan 1994). If anything, the rhetoric and the practice of *dirigisme* was stronger in the Third World, exemplified by the emergence of the Newly Industrialised Countries (on the back of developmentalist economic strategies), by the exercise of 'commodity power' (following the example of the Organisation of Petroleum Exporting Countries) and by controls on foreign investment (Burnell 1986).[12] Internationally, this translated into an attempted interstate solidarity aimed at tackling the liberal foundations of the international order. While the sincerity of the rhetoric of many governments might be questioned, the calls for a New International Economic Order reflected 'the growing desire of countries to assert collective political authority over transnational economic forces' (Gosovic and Ruggie 1976: 344; see also Brandt *et al.* 1980; Krasner 1985). Such 'global Keynesianism' was matched by attempts in other fora (e.g. the United Nations Conference on the Law of the Sea and the United Nations Education, Science and Culture Organisation) to redefine international regimes in support of national objectives (Murphy 1994).

Against this background of state assertiveness, the state itself was 'brought back in' to the discourse of political science and the international–national interaction given greater weight by international theorists (Evans *et al.* 1985). More generally, 'economic nationalism' permeated international political economy in the form of neomercantilist and *dependencista* accounts (Krasner 1978; Evans 1978; Seers 1981). Ironically, the perception of the interconnections between the national and international and the economic and political was at the expense of the regional. The practical failure of regionalism was matched by a relative neglect of the field. To the extent that there was an account it was largely intergovernmentalist and/or policy-based – with the emphasis on explaining policy failures rather than successes (Taylor 1982; Wallace, Wallace and Webb 1983).

Disembedded liberalism (1979–)

For all the rhetoric inside as well as outside the academy, liberalism was on hold rather than in retreat; the long post-war trend to open economies was slowed but not reversed. By contrast, the lack of any significant institutional monuments to the New International Economic Order is startling, as indeed is the narrowing of policy possibilities in both North and South. In retrospect we might better define the period of embattled liberalism as a (largely failed) attempt by states to regulate intensifying global forces. By contrast, the resilience of liberalism can be seen in the elaboration of a critique of the role of the state: 'overload' highlighted the vicious circle for the state of rising expectations and limited capacities; 'sclerosis' portrayed governments as constrained by domestic pressures, preventing them from making those adjustments to labour regulation and welfare which were necessary to maintain international competitiveness; 'predation' described state bureaucracies more concerned with self-enrichment than national development (Krueger 1974; King 1975; Olson 1982; Dearlove 1989).

From the mid-1970s on, therefore, a robust political economy emerged which offered a critique of the state's failures in almost every respect. Those criticisms, moreover, found a resonance in the problems of many governments by the turn of that decade. As such, they provided a set of ideas which were to inform internal and international policy prescriptions in the 1980s (Williamson 1994). It might be argued that in this perspective the state was as much at the heart of the system as for the neo-statists, but it was more a part of the problem rather than the solution; analytically as well as practically the state's role had to be redefined. Indeed, it is ironic that, just as the state was brought back into political science discourse, the pressures for such a redefinition were intensifying (Remmer 1997).

Those pressures were particularly manifest internationally and it is in this period that we begin to encounter globalisation both as an identified phenomenon and as an analytic category. It was in the late 1980s that the most visible 'technical' features associated with globalisation (the acceleration of flows, financial, communications, investment, etc.) became most apparent.

While it is true that there is nothing new about any of these phenomena, their intensity and cumulative effect was novel. Thus while international financial markets had flourished with the creation of the Eurodollar markets from the 1960s on, the scale of currency movements by the mid-1980s was much more intense. The transformation of information technology and telecoms (one of the catalysts for the transformation of the financial sector) was accelerating in its own right in the 1980s and 1990s. Investment levels increased as did (though less dramatically) trade levels (Goldblatt *et al.* 1997; Burtless 1998). These changes were accompanied by developments in the multilateral setting. The completion of the Uruguay Round – however drawn out – signalled a renewed interest in trade liberalisation, while the Round itself had opened up hitherto closed areas to international trade (such as services). Sectoral regimes (not least in the fields of finance and communications) were also being liberalised (Nicolaides 1988; Hoekman and Sauve 1994). The creation of the World Trade Organisation in 1994 institutionalised this new determination to consolidate a global trading system.

The renewed commitment to open markets also became evident in a renewed interest in regionalist projects. The relaunch of the European Community in the mid-1980s was based on the need to deregulate and remove the remaining barriers to a single European market and secured member-state agreement to major institutional reforms (Sandholtz and Zysman 1989; Moravscik 1991). Moreover since then, the deepening of integration (as manifest in the decision to move towards Economic and Monetary Union) has imposed further constraints upon member-states' room for manoeuvre. For their part, European Union institutions have emerged as more independent actors as demonstrated by the growing activism of the European Court of Justice and the increased role of the European Parliament, in the process attempting to broaden out the European agenda beyond a narrowly-defined economic liberalism.

Yet the latter continues to be the realm where Union policy (and the Commission) has been most effective; in other areas the impact of policies has been more modest, constrained by member states and/or budgetary limits.[13] Moreover, it is that economic agenda which has informed the revival of regional integration in other parts of the world. There were 85 regional trade agreements in operation in 1998, 28 of which had been agreed since 1992. There appears to have been a 'domino effect' with key initiatives (such as the European Union revival or North American Free Trade Association) triggering agreements elsewhere in the world (Baldwin 1997). It should be noted, however, that most of these arrangements constitute 'shallow integration'. They are largely concerned with the removal of tariff and other barriers with the aim of increasing competition within the region rather than the elaboration of common policies. They are also for the most part geared towards 'open regionalism', in tune rather than at odds with a liberalising world economy. As Payne and Gamble note, these new regionalist projects 'are not intended as rivals to this globalist project but rather as a means to help achieve it' (Payne and Gamble 1996: 257).

Taken together, the increase in global economic flows and the concomitant commitment to multilateral and regional reforms appear to impose additional constraints upon the state. Yet, in many cases, such commitments have been entered into by national governments. There has been a shift in national policy priorities, initially in only some states (notably the Anglo-Saxon economies) but subsequently, and with pressure from those in the vanguard, in others. While in some cases these changes have been forced upon states (as in cases where financial crises necessitated international assistance), in many cases governments have not only acquiesced in these changes but positively embraced them (Kahler 1990; Gill 1992; Notermans 1993; Moses 1994). State strategies have been redefined towards a more regulatory rather than a redistributive or promotional role (Majone 1994; McGowan and Wallace 1996). Moreover the regulatory orientation is one designed more to facilitate global flows than to control them.

Whether one regards these developments as internally or externally driven, it is interesting to note how far 'the global' is invoked as a reason for change, as much amongst politicians as academics. Notwithstanding claims for a 'third way', the subtext of much contemporary debate is the lack of alternatives and the limited scope for autonomous development.[14] Indeed, the making of international commitments is symptomatic of a wider trend towards 'self-denial' on the part of governments, a shedding of the levers of power in order to avoid 'short-term' and 'politically-driven' decisions. Such transfer of decision-making to 'technical' agencies (the best example being that of monetary policy) is partly a way of resisting internal pressures, a development seen as economically desirable by some (Blackhurst 1997) but democratically suspect by others (Gill 1992; Scholte 1996b).

The room for manoeuvre which states enjoy has been a highly contentious part of the globalisation debate. While few serious proponents of the globalisation thesis would argue that nation-states are redundant there is nonetheless an implicit assumption that the nation-state has been transformed (Palan *et al.* 1996; Shaw 1997). Others, often drawing upon detailed empirical work cast doubt on how far the nation-state has been eroded. Such 'globo-sceptic'[15] views have sought to assert that states retain considerable autonomy, often drawing on the model of the developmental state from the 1980s (Evans 1995; Wade 1996; Hirst and Thompson 1996; Weiss 1998; Garrett 1998). Others seem to see the state role as being transformed but not necessarily because of globalisation – it may be a failure of past models (World Bank 1997; European Bank for Reconstruction and Development 1997).

What of the region? We have already noted how, in the current period, regionalism appears to work with rather than against globalisation: most blocs seem to be trade-creating rather than trade-diverting, while in practice, the regional policy makers have been highly supportive of multilateralism

(European Commission support for the World Trade Organisation being the best example). How does the region affect the state? While the impact may be relatively modest in 'shallow' integration projects, it is clear that in settings such as the European Union, the intensity and institutionalised nature of contacts not only affects the conduct of government (and non-governmental actors) but to some extent reconfigures it regionally. While the policy processes of the Union fall short of even a narrow definition of democracy, they nonetheless provide real democratic opportunities – more than exist in multilateral settings. At present regionalism predominantly operates as a means of facilitating globalisation and regulating state strategies – can it become a means of regulating globalisation and facilitating not so much the state but its citizens?

Possibilities and problems of regionalism

So far we have dealt with the shifting balance between the global, regional and national. While the role of regional integration has ebbed and flowed over the last fifty years, it appears that it now has the potential to reconcile the nation-state with globalisation. In principle, regional integration institutions should be able both to meet the requirements of accountability and participation traditionally vested at the national level and to exercise more clout in attempts to regulate global forces. Given this potentially pivotal role, we now look more closely at the regionalist perspective and consider two sets of questions. Conceptually, does the study of regionalism offer any models for understanding globalisation? More practically, can regional integration offer states a model for sharing sovereignty which can inform the debate on global governance?

Let us first consider what regional integration theory might offer to our understanding of globalisation and global governance. For many years the dominant question has been whether or not regionalism transcends or reinforces the state (Sandholtz and Zysman 1989; Moravscik 1993; Wallace 1994; Milward 1995). More recently, however, interest has shifted from the neofunctionalist/intergovernmentalist dispute to accommodate a much wider array of perspectives (Hix 1998). One of these approaches has focused upon the multiple tiers among which European policy is made. This approach does not reject the centrality of the state but it does challenge its monopoly, most notably in terms of the sharing of decision-making both above and below the nation-state. In terms of 'aboveness' it argues that supranational institutions do enjoy considerable independence and influence. In terms of 'belowness' it sees subnational actors increasingly involved in decision making and their interests and tactics may contradict those of central government. Policy becomes a matter to be discussed and resolved on a variety of interconnected tiers (Marks, Hooghe and Blank 1996).

It is this aspect which might be applied to the global level. So far, the multi-level approach has tended to concentrate on those areas of policy where 'the subnational' is most significant (most notably regional policy). In these areas it appears that the alliance between the Commission and other European institutions on the one hand and local authorities and other subnational actors on the other has been able, in certain circumstances, to set agendas, develop budgetary resources and in other ways counter the dominance of central governments in European policy making.[16] When we address global phenomena, such an approach could be used to explain the interaction between different levels of policy making, both in terms of institutions and other actors. For example, a multi-level approach would be particularly appropriate for following the evolution of global environmental regulation (from the interplay of intergovernmental, governmental and subgovernmental as well as non-governmental and social-movement actors).

Once the analysis of the process of multi-level governance is established, however, one must consider the circumstances in which it is appropriate to delegate power up or down the tiers of governance. What, in other words, are the conditions for the sharing, pooling or transferring of sovereignty? I have already noted that sovereignty is an important consideration/constraint in interaction between the national, regional and global. Any response to globalisation (practical or theoretical) must address whether and how sovereignty is affected (erosion, reconfiguration, etc.) and must also distinguish between forms of sovereignty (in particular the contrast between economic sovereignty and the formal trappings of national sovereignty). The European debate on subsidiarity is of some relevance as a focus for debates on the conditions under which states seek to pool or transfer sovereignty. Could the terms of this debate be applicable in a global context?

Put simply, the principle of subsidiarity states that governance should take place at the most appropriate level for the issue at stake (Wilke and Wallace 1990; McGowan and Seabright 1995). Thus the regulation of local transport is, in most cases, best carried out at the local level, the control of education funding at the national level, devising and implementing emission controls for problems such as acid rain at the regional level, and standardisation of computer software at the global level. It may not always be possible, however, to determine the appropriate level of governance. More importantly it may not be obvious to governments in particular when upward or downward delegation is in their interest. Upward delegation appears to take place when states require a commitment from each other to demonstrate their credibility. The institutional trappings of European Union integration are designed to reinforce that commitment. Can these structures – or those commitments – be redesigned for the global level?

The reconfiguration of regional integration at the global level, however, is fraught with difficulties. One is the question of the optimal scope of integration. Cooper suggests that 'because of organisational, managerial and information costs, the optimal jurisdiction will be well below the global level, in contrast to the optimal market area' (Cooper 1986: 135) and that for this reason regional integration is a more promising objective than global integration. Yet, while this may be right in the short term, might it not also be possible that – as regional integration evolves and engages with global problems – there may be some issues where such blocs can develop both their own strategies for dealing with globalisation, cooperating amongst themselves when necessary?

However, getting to that stage is likely to require a much deeper regional integration than has so far been achieved, even in the European Union. As we noted in the introduction, while the Union is the most successful example of an economic regional integration process – and this remains its main achievement – there is an underpinning collective identity (albeit one which generally manifests itself amongst an elite rather than more broadly) which has figured in the integration process to a greater or lesser extent (Sedelmeier 1998). Moreover, concerns over the European Union's legitimacy have prompted a number of attempts to broaden out affinity to it and to address its economic and political shortcomings (Meehan 1993; Weiler 1995). If these efforts bear fruit they may provide a model for regional integration elsewhere, though this will depend on the emergence of similar debates on democracy and accountability emerging in the affected countries.

Conclusion

This chapter has considered the role of regional integration in the evolving relationship between globalisation and nation-states. It has provided a stylised account of the dynamic between them and the ways in which that dynamic has been interpreted. More tentatively it has sought to suggest ways in which regional integration might offer practical as well as conceptual guidance on the management of that relationship. Conceptually, there are promising developments – notably around multi-level governance and subsidiarity debates – which allow a fluid approach to understanding the sharing and transfer of power and policy making from the local up to the global. The practical implications of regional integration remain for the moment modest, constrained by the limited experience of regionalism and by the paradox of sovereignty whereby states remain more concerned to maintain the trappings of formal independence than to share power to address common problems. Progress here will depend on mobilisation and pressure within and across both regions and nations, in order to overcome myopically state-centred conceits.

Notes

1 On the history of political thought concerning European and practical steps towards regional integration see Heater (1992), Henderson (1962) and Pollard (1974).
2 The distinction is most eloquently made in Gamble and Payne (1996).
3 See Chapter 3 on the failure of states to govern their economies effectively. However also note Crane (1998), on the persistence of economic nationalism.

4 Ironically it was one of the early regional integration experiments – the *Zollverein* – that paved the way for the consolidation of the Prussian state, see Henderson (1959).

5 Note that the time periods are overlapping – this reflects the variations in national and regional settings as well as of the timing of accounts of developments.

6 This is developed in McGowan (1999). See also the literature on the US role in European reconstruction to see the links between postwar multilateralism and European integration (Ikenberry 1989; Lovett 1996).

7 For a summary of the debates on integration, see Machlup (1977). Note, however, that many economists recognised that economic considerations took second place to political objectives, see Dell (1963) and Viner (1950).

8 Almond (1989) presents a review of the international-national against those who claimed this dimension was overlooked, noting in particular the work of Gourevitch (1978). On the belittling of the state in that period, see Evans, Rueschemeyer and Skocpol (1985) as well as Almond's (1988) response.

9 On aspects of postindustrialism, see Kerr (1962), Bell (1974), Aron (1967), and Brzezinski and Huntington (1964). See also Meynaud (1964) and Benveniste (1972) on technocracy and Galbraith (1967) on managerialism. As Hollingsworth *et al.* (1994b: 4) have noted, '[i]ronically . . . convergence theory was most appealing at a time when national economies were still relatively isolated from each other. As this changed with accelerating globalisation of exchanges in the 1970s and 1980s, the differences among existing capitalist systems became much more visible and more relevant.'

10 The classic account is found in Keohane and Nye (1973). Note, however, that their concern with state centrism and their perception of the need for a 'new paradigm' did not detract from the importance of the state (xxii). Indeed, it is as much the extended scope of governments which brings them into contact with the international (xxiii).

11 Amongst their other virtues, Keohane and Nye (1977: 3) provide the first reference to 'globaloney'. Interestingly, a recent collection edited by Keohane and Milner (1996) originated in a workshop on 'whatever happened to interdependence'. Even more interestingly, the book refers throughout to internationalisation and not globalisation.

12 In some developing countries, the relationship between state and market was one of leadership rather than dominance while politically, the governments involved were often authoritarian. This latter characteristic often blinded critics of the ways in which states such as S. Korea, Brazil and Taiwan were able to achieve significant state-led development. See Evans (1995) and Wade (1990).

13 This mismatch in policy was noted early on in the Community's history – see Pinder (1968) and Holland (1980).

14 Ironically in the UK, the strongest claims for the desirability and possibility of autonomous – as opposed to EU – macroeconomic policy making have come from those who had adopted a 'global' perspective on microeconomic issues.

15 Scepticism in terms of doubting the credibility rather than the outright hostility (as evidenced by Euroscepticism). Ironically, however, the claims made by globo-sceptics rested on national development strategies which have themselves been found wanting in the last year, see Wade (1996).

16 We are aware of the danger that such 'state-squeezing' perspectives overstate the influence of local government and other movements by equating activism and existence with effectiveness and influence – the long-run centralisation of local authority funds and functions witnessed in many European states (Meny and Knapp 1998).

Part III

POWER AND KNOWLEDGE

5

SOCIAL MOVEMENTS AND THE CHALLENGE TO POWER

Neil Stammers

The present intensity of globalisation processes indicate that we may be entering a period of fundamental historical transformation as significant as the industrial revolution or even the transition to modernity which began in Europe some four to five hundred years ago. By globalisation I mean multidimensional and dialectical processes of political, economic, technical and cultural change which are increasing the degree of interconnectedness and 'stretching and deepening' of all forms of social relations around the globe (Giddens 1991; Held 1995; McGrew 1997).

If such a transformation is under way, few of our traditional analytical categories and modes of analysis can be taken for granted and there is no way of predicting where we may end up. We are faced, it seems, not only with a serious threat to human existence as a consequence of the global ecological crisis, but also the 'commodification of everything' as transnational capitalist practices invade every aspect of social relations. But maybe we are also being presented – albeit much less obviously – with unparalleled opportunities to act reflexively so as to reconstruct a better, fairer, more democratic world. Perhaps, in fact, globalisation processes are opening up political, social and cultural opportunity structures – to adapt Tarrow's terminology (1994) – through which social movements might be able to make a vital and positive contribution to any such reconstruction. If this is so, how might such opportunities be grasped and understood given the failures of past attempts to actualise emancipatory projects and construct 'meta-narratives' of social change? And why, in any case, focus on social movements? What do they offer which other more institutional modes of political and social action do not?

This chapter considers the potential role of social movements in processes of global transformation, by looking at the relationship between social movements and power. In so doing, it sketches out a new analytic framework for understanding how, in general terms, social movements contribute to processes of social change. It then moves on to identify what might constitute the progressive potential of particular social movements, or radical currents within them, in contemporary conditions. While such overtly speculative and normative exercises now tend to be eschewed in the field of social movement studies, part of my purpose here is to engage critically with the explicitly normative literature in the fields of international relations and studies of global change. My concern is how these literatures connect (or fail to connect) social movements to ideas of global civil society, global democracy and global governance. I shall argue that there are systematic weaknesses in the approaches to social movements in this literature, which suggest that some writers have failed to engage fully with both the positive and negative aspects of past and current research into social movements.

The chapter is divided into three main sections. The first will focus on particular limitations in the literature on social movements in international relations and studies of global change. The second considers how we might re-think the relationship between social movements, power and social change. The third suggests how the progressive potential of social movements might be identified. The conclusion briefly summarises some key points.

Social movements and globalisation: limits of current analyses

The current explosion of literature on globalisation and global change is wide-ranging and multi-faceted. Some is entirely sceptical of the notion of globalisation, implying that previous categories and modes of analysis from both the left and the right can continue to be used to dispute the nature of capitalism, the state, power, society and social movements in their traditional ways. I do not intend to engage with this 'globalisation-sceptic' literature here because it seems to me (unlike such critics) that all sorts of social actors – corporations, financiers, politicians and social movement activists – are already busily seeking to re-constitute the social world in the light of their own understandings and constructions of globalisation. For this reason, those who characterise globalisation as just the latest in a line of bizarre intellectual fads are unlikely to see it disappear as quickly as they might expect.

The literature I focus on here acknowledges that, for good or ill, rapid political, social and economic global transformations are currently under way. Furthermore, most of the authors acknowledge the existence and possible relevance of social movements to such transformations. I shall argue, however, that their perspectives exhibit weaknesses which prevent them from fully grasping that potential. The nature of these weaknesses may be summed up as 'pessimism', 'pragmatism' and 'utopianism'. I will deal with each in turn.

Pessimism

The approaches I discuss under this heading are, as a consequence of their understandings of power, pessimistic about the capacity and potential of social movements effectively to contribute to global transformations. This is so even though they often recognise 'new social movements' as currently the most visible oppositional and critical forms of mobilisation against the relations and structures of global power. Three strands can be discerned: a relatively traditional marxist or neo-marxist approach which focuses on the 'fixity' of relations and structures of economic power; a post-modernist/ Foucauldian approach which assumes a 'fluidity' to power; and a neo-marxist hybrid of these two which sees power as both fixed and fluid at the same time.

Recent work by Leslie Sklair is representative of the first strand. In *Social Movements and Global Capitalism*, he argues that '[i]ncreasingly, as capitalism globalises, subordinate groups find difficulty in identifying their adversaries' and that, consequently, 'effective opposition to capitalist practices tends to be manifest locally' (Sklair 1995: 499, 495). While this is the central thrust of his argument, he does acknowledge at one point that local disruptions are sometimes transformed into 'global challenges to capitalist hegemony' (Sklair 1995: 502), but he clearly has no way of grasping how such shifts might occur nor what any such global challenges might achieve (see also Laxer 1995). Work by John Simpson is representative of the second strand. In an address focusing on the nature of the self, he refers to the possibilities of global action in an emerging global society and dismisses the possibility of effective self-identity being constituted in opposition to the application of power through the 'quasi-solidarities organised around causes' such as environmentalism and human rights. For Simpson, in a post-modern, globalised world no purchase on power can be found and thus '[t]he global citizen can never be more than a tourist, a consumer of partialities and surfaces' (Simpson 1996: 124).

Stephen Gill's account of what he calls the 'global panoptican' provides an interesting example of the third, hybrid, tendency. In some forty pages of close detail he describes and analyses aspects of what he calls 'disciplinary neo-liberalism' which – from his account – faces no opposition to its successful penetration of everyday life. He therefore argues that those who see a substantial democratising potential in global civil society are over-optimistic because the emergent global civil society 'is to a large degree dominated by the power and influence of the agents of transnational capital' (Gill 1995: 10). Yet if the weight of Gill's analysis points to a global and concrete realisation of the 'dystopia latent in modernity', he cannot quite bring himself to end on such a pessimistic note. So he concludes with a call for the democratisation of world fora such as the International Monetary Fund and the World Trade Organisation, suggesting that democratic oversight could be provided by elements of global civil society, including social movements. However, any sort of framework through which such possibilities could be analysed is lacking (Gill 1995: 41; see also Manzo 1992).

Pragmatism

The approaches that I focus on here are those which attempt to address how global governance might be developed and structured. They are pragmatic in the sense that they are trying to work out ways in which global politics might be *institutionally reconstructed* so as to reflect more faithfully an emerging global political community – in a way that could be more democratic than the existing United Nations and inter-state systems. Again, the relevance of social movements as social forms located within global civil society is not denied, but neither are they acknowledged in terms of having a potential capacity to generate positive social, cultural and political change 'from below'. Consequently, spaces for movements to generate such change are not contained in these institutional proposals – in sharp contrast to proposals put forward by social movement theorist Alberto Melucci (1989). Normatively, of course, these approaches are not only considering what is possible, they are also setting out a claim with respect to the limits of what is politically desirable (McGrew 1997: 241). In other words, too close an involvement and/or integration of social movements into processes of global governance is seen as problematic. Why is this?

Underlying such approaches is a top-down view of legitimate politics. In its starkest form this has been represented in national contexts by the idea that the state is necessary to 'civilise' society (Hirst 1991). At the global level, in the absence of a global state, it is argued that effective institutions of global governance need to be created that can potentially intervene to 'civilise' global society. In this sense, it appears that social movements need to be kept at arm's length from institutions of global governance precisely because they too need to be 'civilised'. The apparent necessity of such an approach is reinforced both by recent events such as the genocides in Bosnia and Rwanda and by analyses, such as those of Giddens (1991, 1994), which see the rise of fundamentalist movements as – at least in part – a consequence of processes of globalisation. Yet there is elitism at work here in the *a priori* assumption that actors within structures of global governance would necessarily be more civilised than the rest of us. There is also the danger of throwing the baby out with the bathwater in the apparent assumption that, because 'uncivil' social movements are currently flourishing, social movements cannot therefore contribute positively to social change.

The projects of global governance considered here are not predicated upon the establishment of a global state as such. Rather, they emphasise involving actors from global civil society so as to both mediate between institutionalised structures and particular communities of peoples and embed a strong element of democratic accountability within global governance. David Held's model for 'cosmopolitan democracy' is undoubtedly one of the most important and apparently radical contributions to this debate so far. Yet, interestingly and in contrast to some of his earlier work, social movements hardly appear at all in his major work, *Democracy and the Global Order*, except insofar as they take their place within 'a diversity of self-regulating associations and groups in civil society' (Held 1995: 358). As Anthony McGrew notes, the model of cosmopolitan democracy gives centrality to law and public authorities as necessary conditions for the establishment of a more democratic world but lacks a normative and moral foundation for the effective realisation of global democracy (McGrew 1997: 253). Such a foundation, I shall suggest later, could potentially be provided by certain social movements and radical currents within them.

Another important contribution to this debate is the work of the Commission on Global Governance. In its report, *Our Global Neighbourhood*, a great deal of emphasis is placed on the importance of global civil society to democratic global governance. Yet, whilst 'citizens movements' are considered alongside non-governmental organisations as 'important agents of change in civil society' (Commission 1995: 32) in their proposals for creating space for global civil society inside the United Nations system, it is non-governmental organisations alone that are specified for inclusion because, we are told, 'global civil society is best expressed in the global non-governmental movement' (Commission 1995: 254, 258–60).

To sum up, when these projects are looked at more closely, it becomes clear that what is being advocated is – at best – a form of global elite democracy in which only certain elements of global civil society would be players, presumably those which accept 'the rules of the game'. This is not a new story, but a continuation of the politics of exclusion.

Utopianism

Whereas in the field of social movements studies the concept of new social movements has been heavily criticised and its use heavily circumscribed, in some of the literature from international relations and studies of global change it has re-surfaced strongly. Here it functions both as a way of trying to link particular types of contemporary social movements to macro-level structural changes, and as a normative concept insofar as new social movements are assumed to be agents of progressive global social change. The utopianism of these approaches lies in their uncritical acceptance of the new social movements paradigm. So, for example, in a 1994 collection of articles on global transformation, Chadwick Alger (1994: 301) – citing an earlier article by Hegedus – refers to the 'planetarization' of practices formerly identified with new social movements in the West. Similarly, Bice Maiguascha (1994: 380) states:

> Today we are witnessing the proliferation of counter-hegemonic struggles at the global level, which ... are challenging the normative foundations of today's international system ... I am referring to the rise of new social movements heralding such causes as human rights, the environment, women's rights and world peace.

Interesting recent work by Dianne Otto (1996) and Elizabeth Riddell Dixon (1995) on international non-governmental organisations privileges those which they see as being closely connected to, or having emerged from, the new social movements. Finally, in *The Transformation of Democracy*, McGrew (1997: 258–9) identifies '[t]he enormous growth in progressive social movements (embracing ecological, labour, cultural, democratic, peace and feminist movements)' as one of five democratic tendencies significant to advocates of global democracy. The inclusion of labour movements notwithstanding, all the essentials of the new social movements paradigm are at work here. Citing Giddens, McGrew argues that these movements 'represent modes of radical engagement having a pervasive importance in modern social life [and that they] provide significant guidelines to potential future transformations ... glimpses of possible futures and ... in some part vehicles for their realisation' (McGrew 1997: 259).

While I am sympathetic to the thrust of this latter argument, the tendency uncritically to incorporate the concept and paradigm of new social movements into analyses of global transformation seems highly problematic given the many criticisms levelled at the paradigm. So in the next section I consider ways in which our understandings of social movements and their relation to power and social change might be re-articulated.

Social movements, social change and power

This section is necessarily exploratory and much of it is derivative. I abandon the distinction between 'old' and 'new' social movements, trying instead to think about how social movements may facilitate social change more generally. I begin, though, with some comments on the nature of social movements and their dual faces.

The dual faces of social movements

Drawing mostly on the work of Alain Touraine and Alberto Melucci, my contention is that social movements have been and remain important agents in the processes which foster or retard socio-historical change. From Touraine's earlier work (1977, 1981) on social movements and the self-production of society, I draw the idea that social movements are always engaged to some degree in a struggle for 'historicity', i.e., about the basic values, orientations and structures of a society. But in contrast to Touraine, I do not restrict the understanding of a social movement to that of a 'class actor' (one of two such actors struggling for the control of historicity in any particular epoch). Rather I adopt a broader understanding of social movements as pervasive forms of collective action and mobilisation that have existed at least throughout modernity.

From the work of Melucci (1989), I incorporate the insights that social movements have an important expressive dimension and that this dimension can be seen as embedded in everyday life through subterranean networks of

	Dual and dialectical faces		
Dimension	instrumental (*not just 'interests'*)	⟷	expressive (*not just 'identity'*)

Figure 5.1 The dual faces of social movements

contacts, affinity, identity and so on. In other words – and crucially – social movements should not be defined solely by their visibility in overtly political mobilisations. Borrowing from the work of Jean Cohen and Andrew Arato (1992), let me bring these points together by suggesting that social movements always have 'dual faces' which dialectically combine instrumental – political, economic or social – demands with an expressive dimension oriented towards norms, values, identities, lifestyles, etc. This can be represented as shown in Figure 5.1.

Whilst to talk about 'instrumental' and 'expressive' dimensions of social movements is hardly novel (see for example Melucci 1989; Scott 1992), to use such terms intentionally transcends and disrupts those analyses which have sought to explain social movements either in terms of 'interests' or in terms of 'identity', or else have attempted to look at social movements in terms of the relation between 'interests' and 'identity'. (I am also avoiding the use of the 'strategy/identity' relation as discussed by Cohen and Arato and many others because these terms seem to relate more to distinctions arising out of the *study of* social movements – i.e., resource mobilisation theory versus new social movement theory – rather than to distinctions *within* movements themselves.) The use of the term 'instrumental' here opens up the possibility of understanding that social movement actors make concrete political, economic and social demands but such demands do not necessarily serve the interests of those actors. In other words, it allows for the articulation of demands which are at the same time altruistic *and* instrumental. Similarly, the use of the term 'expressive' makes it clear that this dimension extends beyond the construction and articulation of particular identities into the broader realm of the sociocultural construction of values, norms, lifestyles, identities, symbols, discourses, etc., which are then typically articulated and projected into the wider social and cultural milieu.

The interest/identity dichotomy has been extensively used analytically to distinguish between 'old' and 'new' social movements, with 'old' movements being said to be predominantly concerned with the pursuit of material interests and 'new' movements being said to be much more concerned with identities. I do not wish to foreclose the possibility that the construction of identities is now assuming a particular importance as globalising processes detraditionalise previous patterns and structures of identity construction. However, in switching the emphasis towards an instrumental/expressive dialectic, we can recognise that, historically, social movements have always encompassed both dimensions, at least to some extent. It is clear, for example, that there was an important expressive dimension to the 'old' labour movement just as there are clear expressive dimensions to all nationalist movements – whether of the nineteenth or twentieth century varieties (on 'new' dimensions of 'old' movements, see Tucker 1991 and Calhoun 1993). I should perhaps emphasise that my propositions here are of a general nature: how this instrumental/expressive dialectic 'works out' in any particular movement will vary, and there is no necessary equivalence between instrumental and expressive dimensions in particular social movements. My point – in contrast to most previous analyses – is that this instrumental/expressive dialectic has been, and remains, a general feature of social movements while its manifestation and/or construction undoubtedly varies from movement to movement and across time and place.

Social movements and power

The idea that social movements have an orientation to power is commonplace and uncontested. At this very general level there is a consensus among analysts of social movements. But as soon as we look more closely at this issue, the consensus unravels. Unsurprisingly, the relationship of social movements to power has been analysed in a variety of ways. For example, social movements have typically and most evidently been seen as challenging particular forms of power insofar as they make instrumental demands against it. But then such analyses beg the question 'what is power?' and this is also part of the problem. So I begin by attempting to sketch out briefly how the concept of power might be re-conceptualised and how I attempt to use it here.

Over the last decade or so, analyses of power have often been mediated through interpretations of the work of Michel Foucault and, as noted above, elements of the literature in international relations and studies of global change have also sought to incorporate a Foucauldian view. While I cannot enter into detailed discussion here, it seems to me that, although Foucault's work provides crucial insights into the nature and operationalisation of power in the contemporary world, it has also generated interpretations which are highly problematic. To avoid these difficulties, I suggest that by synthesising some of Foucault's insights with the core elements of Steven Lukes' three-dimensional view of power, it is possible to see the outlines of what might be termed a 'materialist/socio-cultural' conception.

What have typically been seen as two of the strengths of Foucault's views on contemporary forms are, firstly, that power is inherently relational and 'circulates' throughout all networks of social relations and, secondly, that those subjected to power are – at least to some degree – constructed as subjects by that power. Thus, through his detailed analyses of the construction and operation of power in institutions such as prisons and clinics, Foucault (1980, 1982) draws attention both to the 'micro-physics' and 'capillary' nature of power and the extent to which subjects of power come to 'discipline' themselves. From the point of view of this chapter, what is important is that Foucault's work emphasises the importance of recognising that power is embedded in everyday life and that it cannot simply be abolished.

Whether these two aspects of Foucault's views on power are truly innovative, there can be no doubt that his work has crucially re-emphasised them. That said, many readings of Foucault's work derive these insights from a direction which negates both the possibility of grasping the material bases and concentrated nature of particular forms of power, and also any real possibility of social actors being able effectively to resist the effects of power. The heart of the problem here is the extent to which power is seen as constructed *solely* through discourse and discursive practices, and the degree to which such discourse and discursive practices can be said to *entirely constitute* the subject (of power). For example, while seeking to defend what she sees as a 'good Foucault', Sandra Lee Bartky (1995: 186) recognises the strength of interpretations which posit a 'bad Foucault', 'whose theory of the social construction of the subject within networks of power denies the possibility of agency, autonomy, and liberation from domination'. Along a related trajectory, William Carroll and Robert Ratner (1994: 14) criticise Laclau and Mouffe's 'neglect of the extra-discursive elements that constrain and enable agency' and accuse them of falling into a 'discourse reductionism', whereby (citing Rosenau) 'language becomes a world unto itself, constituting the essence of postmodern reality'.

Debates about the correct interpretation of Foucault's work will no doubt continue, but I will side-step them by suggesting that his emphasis on the socio-cultural embeddedness of power in everyday life is not only compatible with, but can be buttressed by a retrieval of Lukes' (1974) three-dimensional view of power. The strengths of Lukes' conception are that it is neither purely actor-centred nor structuralist; it recognises that power is constructed and effected materially as well as socio-culturally; and it posits that power can be constructed so as to constitute domination. That said, Lukes' focus remained on the instrumental dimensions of power.

I propose therefore that we need to see power as being held, developed and exercised consciously by individual or collective social actors – but also recognise that it manifests itself structurally through the patterning of social systems, regardless of consciousness or intent. Furthermore, power is always and necessarily embedded in a network of concrete social relations which include, but do not solely comprise, discourse. Finally, while recognising that power may be constructed so as to constitute domination, the possibility of agency – and thus effective resistance – is not negated.

Following from the above it is now possible to propose a new general analytic framework through which the relation between social movements and power may be understood in general terms. It is represented schematically in Figure 5.2.

	Dual and dialectical faces		
Dimension	instrumental	⟷	expressive
Challenge to or sustaining	existing agents, sites and structures of power	⟷	'socio-cultural' manifestations of power relations in everyday life
Conceptions of power	Lukes ⟵	materialist and socio-cultural conception of power	⟶ Foucault

Figure 5.2 Power and the dual faces of social movements

In common with most writers on social movements, I am suggesting that social movements always have orientations to extant relations and structures of power, seeking either to challenge or sustain them. To do so instrumentally, movements typically articulate specific political, economic or social demands. Expressively, movements construct or adopt, and then articulate, norms, values, lifestyles, etc., both within the movement and outwards towards the wider society. The dialectical interface between instrumental and expressive dimensions can be seen, for example, in demonstrations and other protest actions, where one aspect of the mobilisation is to make the instrumental demand, but others are to express solidarity amongst movement members and to show alternative norms, values and lifestyles to the wider society.

One point about the relationship between instrumental and expressive orientations requires further comment. It might be thought that in any particular movement there would be a necessary consonance between orientations to power across the instrumental and expressive dimensions. In other words, an instrumental challenge to a particular form of power will be paralleled by an expressive challenge to the manifestations of that form of power in everyday life. That might well be so, but cannot be assumed. It is entirely conceivable for dissonance to exist between the instrumental and expressive dimensions. In its most extreme form this could mean, say, that a particular form of power challenged in terms of its manifestations in everyday life was actually being sustained by the instrumental demands of the movement. The importance of this point will become apparent in the next section when I consider the relationship between ideology, goals and organisation in social movements. In general though, we now have an analytical framework through which the potential of social movements to foster or retard social change can be understood in terms of their orientations to extant relations and structures of power.

Such a framework could be used to analyse all forms of social movement activity. But I now turn to a question that has dogged theorists with a normative commitment to social movements' potential for fostering radical, democratic and egalitarian social change: how can any such progressive potential be identified and analysed? In the next section I examine this by considering the limits of the concept of 'new social movements' and then go on to reconstruct their progressive potential in terms of two concepts: 'radical currents' and 'critical social movements'. I shall argue that these need to be understood in terms of how they challenge extant relations and structures of power – in terms of ideology, organisation and goals.

'Radical currents' and 'critical social movements'

The concept of 'new social movements' has always had embedded within it an assumption of progressive potential. Beyond the fact that many of those who sought to theorise new social movements were themselves activists in those movements, there are two reasons for this: firstly, what may be termed the 'structural derivation' of new social movements and, secondly, what were seen as their central and defining descriptive characteristics.

Structural derivations of new social movements were rooted in analyses which claimed that there had been a qualitative or epochal structural shift in the nature of the advanced western societies: from industrial to post-industrial, capitalist to late capitalist, or – latterly – modern to post-modern. New social movements were then typically viewed 'as responses to and agents of fundamental social change' (Scott 1992: 139). 'Old' social movements – typically a euphemism for workers' movements – were similarly associated with the 'old' epoch. So, despite the fact that most theorists of new social movements eschewed the structural determinism and teleological view of historical development associated with classical marxism, the 'stagist' element of such views was not entirely abandoned. In that sense, new social movements could be seen as progressive simply in terms of the processes of historical development. Although there were variations in such approaches, one of these – mostly clearly associated with the work of Touraine (1981, 1987) – was 'post-marxist' in the specific sense that new social movements were seen as the potential transformative agent of the new epoch, taking the place that the working class occupied in the old. It is worth noting that these 'structural' analyses – developed for the most part in the 1970s – pre-dated the current debates about globalisation and were initially formulated exclusively within the context of contemporaneous developments in the advanced western societies.

These analyses also pre-dated the rise of a variety of extreme right-wing and nationalist movements in both western and eastern Europe from the late 1980s onwards. In the light of such developments it is now clear that, whatever the relationship might be between social movements and (global) structural transformation, it cannot be assumed that such transformation somehow generates only 'progressive' social movements. From this, I draw the conclusion that we cannot rely on analyses of structural change to delineate between 'progressive' and 'regressive' movements. Something else is necessary.

New social movements were also seen as 'progressive' in a more direct way – by reference to their central and defining characteristics. In terms of their ideology, goals and organisation, new social movements were typically seen as both 'new' and 'progressive' as set out in the lists below (see, for example, Dalton and Keuchler 1990: 10–16).

Ideology

- They questioned and challenged the emphasis on material wealth, growth, mass consumption and commodification within the advanced western societies.
- They advocated greater opportunities for participation in decision making whether through methods of participatory democracy and/or self-help groups and cooperative styles of social organisation.
- They typically advocated and valorised non-violent direct action, including civil disobedience, as forms of political protest.

Goals

- They sought fundamental change across a wide range of social fields.
- They eschewed the traditions of the traditional revolutionary left with its emphasis on 'seizing state power'.
- They sought to establish 'alternative' life-styles and identities as well as pursuing more immediate instrumental goals.

Organisation

- They were open and fluid networks linked to broader 'counter-cultures'.
- They sought to establish decentralised, non-hierarchical forms of organisation.
- They tended to limit engagement with political parties and the political system fearing assimilation and co-option.

The above characteristics could indeed constitute an outline framework for a 'progressive politics', a point I shall come back to shortly. But there was a major problem in seeing them as the central and defining characteristics of new social movements. This approach effectively reified the concept of new social movements so as to obscure both the diversity within them and significant continuities between supposedly 'old' and 'new' movements. Effective and substantial critiques along these lines (D'Anieri *et al.* 1990; Plotke 1990; Tucker 1991; Calhoun 1993; Beuchler 1995) have never been rebutted and are now broadly accepted amongst theorists of social movements. It was clearly wrong to assume that new social movements were necessarily 'progressive' on the basis of these characteristics, since the movements did not, in fact, conform to them. This being so, is there a way in which we can try to pin down more precisely what is 'progressive' about particular movements and/or elements within them so as to both transcend the 'old/new' dichotomy and provide a way of assessing the progressive potential of current and future movements?

As I have argued elsewhere (Stammers 1999), diversity within social movements may be re-conceptualised in terms of currents with differing orientations in terms of ideology, goals and organisation. Such currents are amenable to assessment and analysis both by scholars and social movement activists themselves. What have been claimed as central and defining characteristics of new social movements could then be understood as identifying *radical currents* within social movements. Such currents can be seen in many contemporary social movements east, west and south and are particularly apparent in those global social movements depicted as new social movements in the literature from international relations and studies of global change. But such currents were also present in the European labour and trade union movements of the nineteenth century and, from this broader perspective, we can see that what was descriptively 'new' in the Western movements from the 1960s onwards was the vibrance and strength of those radical currents. But if it is possible to assess and analyse currents in terms of their ideology, goals and organisation it should also be possible to do the same with respect to movements as such. Developing R.B.J. Walker's (1988) term, I suggest *critical social movements* can be identified as those social movements which, in terms of at least some of their predominant orientations in respect of ideology, goals and organisation, tend towards the characteristics described above.

In what sense, and why, should the characteristics listed above be seen as 'progressive'? Am I not simply making an arbitrary choice based on my own political predilections? This may be so, but such a choice is also analytically defensible in a way that most previous assertions of 'progressiveness' have not been. Let me put forward a two-step argument. Firstly, I propose that these orientations in respect of ideology, goals and organisation can be seen as 'progressive', 'radical' and 'critical' insofar as they not only seek to challenge and constrain particular relations and structures of power/domination but also because – in so doing – they seek to equalise, disperse or diffuse relations and structures of power *rather than seeking to replace one form of power with another*. For example, it is not 'progressive' to simply propose that problems of economic power can be solved by enhancing and legitimising state power (traditional socialist solutions), nor that problems of state power can be solved by enhancing and legitimising economic power (current neo-liberal solutions).

The second step of my argument is that, insofar as radical currents and critical social movements are seeking to reconstruct social relations as proposed in step one, then they are engaged in processes and strategies of *self-*

limiting transformation in the sense that they seek to combine appropriate instrumental demands with appropriate socio-cultural change. This explicitly extends Cohen and Arato's (1992) idea of 'self-limitation'; for them, progressive contemporary social movements are 'self-limiting' not only in that they eschew the revolutionary dreams of the traditional radical left but also in 'acknowledging the integrity of political and economic systems'. Thus they may continue to offer visions of emancipation, visions which are increasingly encompassing a global dimension – consequent upon, contesting, but also partially constitutive of, processes of globalisation. The two-step argument may be represented schematically as shown in Figure 5.3.

Instrumentally, radical currents and critical movements challenge existing agents, sites and structures of power by constructing and articulating political, economic or social demands which seek the democratisation, diffusion and dispersion of concentrated sites and structures of power. Expressively, currents and movements construct and articulate norms, values, lifestyles and practices with the objective of equalising, diffusing and dispersing power relations in everyday life. It is the dialectical interface between instrumental and expressive dimensions which provides the dynamic process through which the self-limiting transformation of social relations takes place. This process assumes no ultimate boundaries in terms of, say, the timeless universality of states and markets.

There are of course some huge problems in how such a general framework could capture even an element of the complexities of particular social movements, their ideologies, goals and organisation and their struggles and strategies in the context of the totality of global social relations. This clearly needs further exploration which goes far beyond the scope of this chapter. One or two points, though, stand out.

Firstly, I have already argued that the so-called new social movements are typically diverse in their ideologies, goals and organisation. Furthermore, a

Dual and dialectical faces

Dimension	instrumental	⟷	expressive
Challenge to	existing agents, sites and structures of power	⟷	'socio-cultural' manifestations of power relations in everyday life
Objective	democratisation, diffusion and dispersion of concentrated sites and structures of power	⟷	equalisation, diffusion and dispersion of socio-cultural manifestations of power relations in everyday life

Figure 5.3 The potential 'progressive' role of 'radical currents' and 'critical social movements' in the reconstruction of global social relations

case can be made that it is this very diversity which gives movements such as the green movement or the women's movement their strength and vitality. The importance of this point cannot be underestimated since movements develop and are sustained by social actors constructing collective identities in opposition to some sort of adversary. In other words, movements often coalesce and construct their unity negatively. So, even though unity may be specifically constructed against particular relations and structures of power, this does not necessarily entail the construction of a positive unity in the movement's ideologies and goals. Indeed, such diversity makes it clear that there are enormous and continuous debates and struggles within social movements over these issues and, even if any sort of consensus could be reached on ideologies and goals, huge arguments still follow about what might constitute appropriate strategies and organisational forms to achieve them. In a way, of course, these are not questions to which definitive answers can be given since this is precisely what the construction of social practices is all about. The framework offered above provides, however, a different lens through which some of these issues could be considered by movement activists and theorists of social movements.

For example, we might ask whether movement activists who argue most strongly for pursuing instrumental demands are also most likely to argue for strategies and organisational forms which 'violate' the progressive potential of movement activism, insofar as such strategies and forms could end up sustaining relations and structures of power other than those which are directly challenged by the instrumental demands. In other words, what price might be paid by trying to win specific instrumental demands through *Realpolitik*? Likewise, is it the case that to focus exclusively on the expressive dimension 'violates' the progressive potential of movement activism through a failure to grasp the need to make effective instrumental challenges to the relations and structures of power? Conversely, perhaps it is the case that activists who focus on the expressive dimension of movement activism are able to facilitate 'shifts' in the socio-cultural construction of societal norms, values, lifestyles, etc., whilst avoiding having to make instrumental challenges to particular relations and structures of power as such. Similarly, perhaps it is possible that the adoption of strategies and organisational forms inimical to the 'progressive potential' of movement activism can achieve success in their instrumental demands without those strategies and organisational forms having a deleterious effect in terms of sustaining particular forms of power.

As I have argued there are no clear answers to these sorts of questions, which have to be worked through in social relations and practices. But, it does seem to me that both analysts of social movements and activists themselves often tend to privilege either the instrumental or expressive dimensions of activism, reproducing the instrumental and expressive dimensions as *binary oppositions*. That is, they fail to grasp the complex but necessary inter-relationship between the dual faces of social movements and the *dual strategy* which they necessarily imply.

Conclusion

I have not claimed in this chapter that social movements somehow constitute the 'dynamic of history' or that they should occupy a privileged position in understanding socio-historical change. But I am arguing that historically social movements have been and continue to be deeply implicated in such processes of change. This needs to be fully recognised and analysed by those who are trying to make sense of global politics and global transformations in the contemporary period.

In particular, those approaches criticised in the first section of this chapter share a common disposition to retain modes of analysis which now need to be fundamentally reassessed. Those I described as being pessimistic about the capacity and potentials of social movements to contribute to global transformations do so from prior theoretical standpoints which generally tend to deny the possibility of social actors being able effectively to resist global relations and structures of power. Marxist and neo-marxist variants, whilst rightly pointing out the economic power of transnational capital, remain haunted by the ghost of economic reductionism, whilst those of a post-modernist bent often collapse into philosophical idealism or linguistic structuralism.

Those pragmatic approaches which focus on the practical institutionalisation of structures of global governance assume that political, social and cultural change requires management by elites. In this sense they seem to be trying to maintain the central tenets of social democracy, transposing them to the global level and seeking to limit the possibilities for a more fundamental reconstruction of social relations. Yet it is arguable that social movements culturally embed norms and values much more effectively than institutional structures, and that it is critical social movements and radical currents which could provide much of the moral foundation for an emerging global society. Finally, those approaches I described as utopian need to let go of the assumption that new social movements are necessarily progressive. The 'progressive potential' of radical currents and critical social movements is not an intrinsic quality of social movements. It has to be perpetually reconstructed and re-constituted within, between and beyond social movements. There is no pre-given way of ensuring that the 'progressive potential' of social movements will be realised. The relations and structures of power that radical currents and critical social movements face are indeed formidable, in their material resources, organisational structures and the extent to which the norms and values flowing from and to them are embedded in everyday life. But this chapter has proposed a way in which that 'progressive potential' can be more clearly seen, understood and acted upon; as challenges to existing relations and structures of power and as processes of self-limiting transformation.

6

COMPARISON, CLEAVAGES AND CYCLES: POLITICS AND THE EUROPEAN UNION

Paul Taggart

In this chapter I argue that, while there is an undoubted process of globalisation in many spheres of political and economic life, we are better equipped to deal with the changed environment if we apply the tools of comparative political analysis. Indeed, I contend that the global context offers new scope for comparative politics, which has all too often been tied too closely to national contexts. I use the example of the European Union (EU) to argue that the politics involved in global developments is comparable to politics seen at non-global levels. The development of the EU is one of the key changes in the global political context; it is without precedent or peer. As a new form of international polity, it can serve as either an indication of the process of globalisation, or a location in which we can see the possibilities of a new global politics.

One part of the scholarship on the EU has been dominated by international relations analysis. The concern is here with the phenomenon of integration, its causes, effects and characteristics. Other scholarship has often placed an emphasis on policy-making. The concern is here both with the process(es) and the output of the institutions. The particular paths that have been chosen as routes to examining the Union have both underplayed the role of politics in understanding it. Put simply the EU, as an object of study, has veered between being a macro-level phenomenon explicable in terms of larger international, transnational or global forces, or as a rather dry technical operation which invites micro-level study of its component parts.

Taking the idea of a global politics seriously means that we need to consider the politics as equal in importance to the globalisation. In considering the EU we need to consider it as a political phenomenon *par excellence*. Rather than viewing its politics as either *sui generis* or derivative of other political processes, it behoves us to understand the EU as itself an essentially political institution comparable to others. The consequence of this is not only to refocus the object of study, but also to consider the tools with which we may view the EU.

The study of political systems from a comparative perspective provides a framework for understanding the global politics of the EU (Sbragia 1992; Hix 1994). Academic discussion of the EU already makes wide use of comparative concepts such as federalism and consociationalism in describing the EU (Hix 1998) and even those concepts that are employed by those who are argue that the EU provides a *sui generis* phenomenon have their roots either explicitly or implicitly in comparisons with politics at other levels (Risse-Kappen 1996: 54; Schmitter 1996). Perhaps, just as importantly, popular discussions of the EU make extensive use of concepts that are inherently comparative, as citizens evaluate the EU in terms of its democratic deficit, or in terms of its allegedly burgeoning bureaucracy in Brussels, or as undermining national sovereignty.

In the academic realm, much has been made of the state-building comparison, but we need to think more widely than that. The emphasis here has been on comparing the growth of the EU to the establishment of nation-states, most usually the USA (e.g. McKay 1996). Reconceptualisations of the state have been part of the debate about globalisation (Shaw 1997) but it is more fruitful to conceive of the nation-state as only one institutional constellation of power and authority among many. Once we move away from fetishising the state, it is far easier to conceive of a politics that goes above and beyond national boundaries and to take in the idea of a politics of the EU.

The EU as a case of global politics

Other chapters in this book address the questions of globalisation either through wide-ranging overviews of theory or through reviews of existing literature. This chapter, in contrast, takes an explicitly empirical approach to the task of examining globalisation. Taking the EU as an example of global politics therefore requires justification, even if this argument is a clear theme of much of the academic literature on the EU (which assumes it represents part of a wider process of globalisation, e.g., Wallace and Wallace 1996) and of much of the globalisation-oriented literature (the EU represents one part of the wider phenomenon being considered, e.g., Lash and Urry 1994; Waters 1995).

If theories of globalisation can be validated only through their application to empirical phenomena, there are two particular justifications that we can consider. The first is simple; if globalisation is indeed new, or even if we are in a new stage of a longer-term process, this novelty must be identified in new phenomena. The EU represents perhaps the clearest example of a new institutional phenomenon with state-like features in European and even world politics in the second part of the twentieth century. While there are other new and important political forms in this period, European integration presents us with the clearest case of a new political system. This means that theories of globalisation must account for the EU as an example of global politics – or if it is a residual factor from politics in a non-globalised world, they must explain its persistence.

The second justification for considering the EU in the light of globalisation is that given by George Ross, who argues that the EU is not derivative or illustrative of globalisation, so much as partially constitutive of it. Adopting a largely economic conception of globalisation, Ross argues that the project of the EU involved in Economic and Monetary Union is a major contribution to the process of globalisation (Ross 1998). It is through the explicit creation of institutions and processes that are designed to counteract the costs of national structures in the face of global processes that the EU is an important source of globalisation.

Cycles of European Union politics

If these arguments amount to a *prima facie* case for considering the EU as either illustrative or constitutive of a global politics, we need to examine the nature of the politics which it involves. The argument of this section is that the emergence of the EU and its politics provide an additional intersection for different cycles of politics. Insofar as the EU represents part of the trend towards globalisation, it is indicative of a quantitative change where the number of cycles intersecting is increased. This has the effect of increasing complexity – but not necessarily of introducing qualitative change.

This argument is grounded in the idea that politics is a dynamic process. The use of the term cycles is not meant to indicate either determinism or path dependency. To posit the existence of cycles does not necessarily prejudge the question of either the duration or direction of the cycles. It does however suggest that politics moves forward in a way that is non-linear. It also suggests that momentum is unevenly distributed, so that at critical junctures small inputs can have a major impact on the direction of the cycle and that at other points it may be necessary for large-scale mobilisation to affect the direction.

In simple terms, we can identify a number of key cycles. In the following section, I illustrate the importance of cycles by examining the electoral and presidential cycles. This is by no means a comprehensive account, as it is possible to identify other important cycles that have an impact on EU politics, such as the economic cycles and cycles of legitimacy. The effects of these cycles can also be institutionally iterative. In other words the EU represents not only an arena (or set of arenas) in which cycles take place, but is also itself partially constituted through cycles as well as through other political processes.

Electoral cycles

Although the EU is associated with the identification of a democratic deficit, it is still evident that elections, both European and domestic, and referendums have important impacts on the development of the politics of the EU. The cycles associated with electoral politics at non-EU levels impinge directly on the personnel and policy agenda of EU policy-making. The European elections themselves substantially affect the composition of one branch of the EU institutional structure.

Let us first consider European elections. The attempt to provide more legitimacy for the European Parliament through the mechanism of European-wide elections for choosing the members has been in place since 1979, but this has not prevented these elections from remaining of secondary importance. The early description of elections to the European Parliament as 'second-order' elections (Reif and Schmitt 1980) has not been fundamentally changed by the recent history of European integration. Evidence shows that European elections are still used by voters to express domestic concerns (Van der Eijk *et al.* 1996). The elections are second-order in the sense that they are seen as less important than national elections and because the issue of the EU is for many a subordinate issue even in European elections.

Despite the secondary nature of European elections they serve as regular reminders of the European polity. While the causes of voting in the elections stem largely from national concerns, the very existence of an additional arena for European citizens to vote and one that occurs simultaneously across member states provides a uniquely non-national electoral outcome. This has the effect of creating a European cycle that impinges, to varying degrees, on the national electoral cycles. The extreme case is that of Luxembourg which explicitly coordinates its national electoral cycle with that of the European Parliament so that both elections occur on the same day.

A more substantive outcome of the elections is that they serve to compose the body of the European Parliament and while there are still major concerns about the limited powers of the Parliament, these are growing, and it does play a role in policy-making. Changes such as the introduction of the co-decision procedure, in which certain decisions have to incorporate the Parliament, give an illustration of this trend (Earnshaw and Judge 1995). While the Parliament has only limited budgetary and legislative powers, it has increasingly used those powers to set the EU agenda (Tsebelis 1994). Individual members of the European Parliament (MEPs) tend to build on their basis of expertise to give them access to policy-making at the EU level and there is an increasing tendency for MEPs to be in consultation with the Council and the Commission over certain matters of policy.

Both the symbolic and substantive effects of an electoral cycle for the European Parliament mean that at regular intervals there is likely to be increased concern with EU politics at the level of domestic publics and an increased focus on issues of European integration in domestic political agendas. Also changes in the membership of the Parliament can have the effect of both impinging on the process of integration and of highlighting changes in domestic political cycles.

The history of recent integration in Europe has been one in which major changes to the institutions have been the result of quasi-constitutional settlements such as the Maastricht Treaty. These settlements have been made subject to ratification by member-states. That ratification has taken the form of either parliamentary approval or referendums. Where the latter have occurred, the results have been less than ringing endorsements of the proposals. Research on the referendums has concluded that the results owe as much to support for national governments as to support for the EU (Franklin *et al.* 1994; Franklin *et al.* 1995). If we look at citizens' evaluations of the EU even at times when there is not a chance for them to express their views electorally, it is clear that national concerns remain important elements in evaluations of the EU (Gabel and Palmer 1995; Anderson 1995; Anderson and Kaltenthaler 1996). This tendency has had profound implications, most clearly seen in the Danish Referendum of June 1992 in which the Maastricht Treaty was rejected, so that it had to be renegotiated in Edinburgh in December 1992.

The effect of electoral cycles is to constrain the agenda of policy-making within the EU. This can also be seen in the case of national elections. There is a regular stalling of Union agendas before the general elections of the larger member-states. This effect is compounded when the elections are perceived as likely to result in a change of government after a period of sustained dominance by another party, or a coalition. This effect can be seen before the British election of 1997, which saw a long period of Conservative and increasingly Eurosceptical government end with the election of a more overtly Europhilic Labour Party. The situation found its equivalence in the period preceding the election in Germany in 1998, in which the perception was of a likely Social-Democratic victory ending the prolonged Christian-Democratic dominance under Helmut Kohl.

A second impact of national electoral cycles is to determine who will be important actors in the Euro-polity. Both the Council of Ministers and the Commission are composed of national politicians. In the case of the Commission, these politicians are usually but not always drawn from parties, governments or ministries. The clearest case of the national electoral cycle impacting on Union institutions is therefore the Council of Ministers, the composition of which is effectively determined through the aggregation of national electoral results. In the cases where significant changes have been made to the basis of the EU, the role of national politicians through either European Councils, the Council of Ministers or Inter-Governmental Conferences has been to the fore. Meetings at these levels and concerning fundamental quasi-constitutional questions have by no means acted as rubber stamps. Important concessions or compromises have been reached here. This has meant that specific national interests have been recognised either through national opt-outs such as those negotiated in the Social Chapter and EMU for the UK, or through more far-reaching amendments to the larger projects such as the Edinburgh amendments to the Maastricht Treaty mentioned above.

Leadership cycles

One aspect of European politics that is not the result of direct electoral cycles is the presidency of the Council of Ministers. Originally intended as the institutional embodiment of national interests, to be tempered by the non-national Commission, the Council of Ministers has grown in importance. With it, the presidency of the Council has seen a steady increase in importance. The assignation of the presidency is more akin to the Athenian use of lots to distribute key jobs than to the modern conception of representative politics. The presidency is assigned to different member-states for a six-month period in a pre-set order. The order is designed to make sure that the *troika* of the previous, present and future presidencies always includes both larger and smaller member-states.

The use of a short time-limited period, along with the centrality of the presidency, means that there is an important cycle to the presidency. It is usual for there to be a statement of the agenda from an incoming president at the beginning of the six months (sometimes termed a 'State of the Union' address) and a report to the European Parliament at the close of the presidency. More importantly, the end of each presidency is marked by a European Council that brings together Prime Ministers and foreign ministers from member-states. These Councils have often been decisive moments in the European project with initiatives such as the Single European Act, the Maastricht Treaty and European Monetary Union having much of their initial basis laid at them. This has also been the case with the recent moves to enlargement (Sedelmeier 1998). This is why Emil Kirchner has described the Councils as representing 'the main vehicle for launching new initiatives and for furthering E[uropean] C[ommunity] integration' (1992: 114).

The construction of the Council with its basis in member-state interests means that the agenda is difficult to achieve, requiring compromise and consensus among a growing number of member-states. As Hayes-Renshaw and Wallace (1997: 146) describe it, the Council 'remains an institution of diffuse consensus, not easy to manipulate or to lead by the nose, and deeply resistant to the explicit peddling of sharp national interests. Any initiative has to work with the grain of a large group of strong-minded national representatives'. Clearly then, the roles of the Committee of Permanent Representatives (COREPER) and the Secretariat of the Council become important as a means of providing continuity. In this sense they provide the basis of bureaucratic and administrative continuity that a national civil service offers between changes of government.

The success or failure of a presidency can therefore be partially dependent on using these bureaucratic resources effectively. It is by no means pre-ordained that the administrative structure is used in the same way by different presidencies. Different national norms and cultures impinge heavily on how they operate in the presidency (Wallace 1985; de Bassompierre 1988: 103–6).

Peter Ludlow (1993: 253) suggests that Danish and British under-use of the secretariat had damaging effects on their respective recent presidencies. The politics of bureaucracy, the institutional structure and agency (in terms of how political actors use those structures), are therefore as much a part of EU politics as of national and sub-national politics (Peters 1992).

The nature of the presidency means that there is a strong sense in which the early part of each period in the chair is dominated by the attempt to set the agenda, while its close sees a period in which the presidency attempts to ensure that the agenda is implemented. The agenda is pushed further through the institution of the European Council that closes the presidency. The success or failure of a particular agenda is not determined by the cycle, but the cycle provides the context in which the presidency can exercise leadership. A feature of presidentialism is that the early part of each presidency often sees a 'honeymoon' period in which agenda-setting is possible and in which this can be combined with implementation of that agenda. Presidencies try to maximise their impact during this early period through the use of informal Council meetings, both to cement good relations and as a means of reinforcing their agenda in less structured and ritualised occasions than the formal council meetings. Such active agenda-setting becomes harder as the presidential term continues.

In cases of an electoral presidential system, the honeymoon period is a period of possibility because of the explicit national and unified mandate. Mandates are less clear cut in the case of legislatively based executives because they derive their legitimacy from the legislature's composition, and the mandate is derived from a party rather than personal base, and there are usually multiple parties receiving some sort of mandate in the legislature. In the EU, however, a new presidency of the Council brings a raised climate of expectations which gives it the impetus of greater legitimacy, even though it is not elected. It is to make best use of this that incoming presidencies publicly identify clear sets of priorities.

In contrast to the early period of a presidency, the certainty that there is to be a change in regime can have a debilitating effect on the ability of the presidency to implement its agenda at the end of its term. Despite this, the short time and the use of the European Council both go some way to mitigating this effect and give a rhythm to the cycle that means that ends of presidencies are heavily evaluative and potentially effective periods. The culminating effect of the European Council can have the effect of allowing the presidency to exercise unusual leadership. In a sense it provides the presidency with some increased bargaining power towards the close of the term. The effect of the increased use of the *troika* (described above) is to increase the power of the presidency at its close, because there is still the certainty that it will be involved in close consultation with the incoming presidency.

The success or failure of a presidency depends on how far the member-state government can operate within and perhaps even manipulate the cycle of the presidency. Admittedly the scope for leadership is constrained by both the long-term continuous process of European integration (Kirchner 1992: 7) and by particular events beyond the control of the actors involved, but within those parameters member states can more or less effectively utilise the leadership capacity of the presidency. One of the factors that can impinge on a presidency may well be a national electoral cycle. In a study of the presidency in the environmental field, Rüdiger Wurzel (1996: 280) observes that recent German and French presidencies were constrained by the occurrence of national elections while the presidency was held by those countries.

The role of the presidency of the Council of Ministers illustrates two general points. The first is that the Council presidency can be compared to other presidencies. The proliferation of a literature which has debated the nature of presidentialism in comparative political science (Lijphart 1992; Riggs 1994) provides us with tools for analysing the cyclical aspects of the presidency. Although the Council presidency is not tied to an electoral cycle, it is notable that its agenda-setting capacities accord with those of presidential systems tied to electoral cycles. The presidency is also subject to being impinged upon by national electoral cycles and therefore illustrates the proliferation and increasing interlinking of different political cycles.

The second point that the Council presidency illustrates is that institutional weakness in a presidency means that leadership plays a key role. In mediating between powerful national interests and, at the same time, negotiating with the other key EU institutions (the Commission and the Parliament), the presidency faces nothing unusual for presidentialism. It is not also unusual in EU institutional politics which lacks a clear agenda-setting executive (Peters 1994). This creates structural difficulties for the other potential source of leadership, the Commission (Nugent 1995; Laffran 1997). The Council presidency faces the predicament of providing leadership in representative democratic politics. Institutions of representative democratic politics that incorporate the principle of presidentialism everywhere face the trade-off between maximising the representing interests and of providing leadership.

Cleavages in EU politics

A foundational idea of the comparative analysis of mass politics is that politics is structured through divisions that become manifest and then institutionalised as cleavages (Lipset and Rokkan 1968). If we examine how the EU is an issue in politics as well as an institutional structure, then it becomes clear that the EU is potentially very divisive. Those divisions reflect a fundamental conflict within European politics in the more general sense. The line that separates those who support and those that oppose the idea of European integration accords with a wider division in European politics. There is a fundamental cleavage between those who largely support the post-war consensus and those outside that consensus, either by identifying with the left-libertarian 'new politics' of the new social movements, or by identifying with populist politics of a revived right-wing ethnic nationalism (Taggart 1996). On these opposite sides of contemporary politics, European integration represents a dividing line.

If we examine those parties that take a Eurosceptical position, they present a strange mix. The parties range from the extreme right of the spectrum, like the French National Front through agricultural parties such as the Centre Party in Sweden, through green parties, to the extreme left such as the Portuguese and French Communist Parties. All express Euroscepticism as part of their general agenda. The constitutional challenge mounted in Germany to the ratification of the Maastricht Treaty brought together Liberals, Greens and far-right Republicans. This apparent mixture of parties conceals the fact that the real dividing line lies between the established parties of government in member-states and parties that find themselves on the periphery of their party systems (Taggart 1998). There is some Euroscepticism within governmental parties of the centre-right or centre-left but this is confined to a few parties and, more importantly, to factions within those parties. The sources of Euroscepticism reflect fundamental divisions about politics, in which European integration is treated as a second-order issue and reinforces national party-system divisions.

Insofar as mass-mobilised attitudes to the EU express a wider politics, they seem to be heavily dependent on their citizens' experiences of 'domestic politics'. Just as European elections are second-order elections, for many parties the EU represents a second-order issue. However, this does not mean that attitudes towards the EU, as expressed through political parties, are only the aggregation of several distinct member-state contexts. There is a degree of convergence among different member-states' experiences. The fact that the EU issue splits party systems along similar core-periphery lines indicates the possibility of realignment along a line created by the issue of European integration. It also illustrates the possibility that European politics may be generally facing the emergence of a new cleavage.

The line of the new cleavage is between those feeling affinity with the established form and those who express a broad rejection of the institutions and functioning of contemporary European politics. Looking at a wider European scope, Mary Kaldor (1996) describes the new cleavage in a different light, stressing the conflict between cosmopolitanism and nationalism, and this may well be the way that the reactions to politics are expressed by those on different sides of the divide. Placing the politics of the EU in a wider context, we should be careful not to over-emphasise the discontinuities. Indeed, large-scale empirical research on political attitudes in Western Europe concludes that it is the continuities that need to be explained. While new issues have emerged and there are new forms of political expression, it is clear that the institutions of government and the mechanisms for mass participation have sustained themselves remarkably well under conditions of new challenges

(Kasse and Newton 1995). The politics of the EU provide important illustrations of this finding.

Conclusion

The development of the European Union is a test case for politics in a globalised world. It demonstrates that such a politics can be *quantitatively* different. Globalisation means the proliferation of new issues and new institutional arenas for politics and the European case is a strong example of both of these tendencies. This proliferation makes, as we have seen, for more complexity. However I have shown that it does not necessarily mean a *qualitatively* different form of politics. On the contrary, the tools of comparative politics, often developed in the study of national politics, can give us useful means of analysing the politics of the EU. Concepts such as presidentialism, leadership, electoral cycles and cleavages work well as means of describing the new politics of the EU. It is therefore probable that they will be useful in analysing the wider global politics, in other regional contexts and institutional forms.

Through abandoning an over-emphasis on the nation-state, we can use the tools of comparative politics to their fullest effect. Comparative politics has come to be associated with the comparison of nation-states and proponents of comparative politics are largely responsible for that association. There is, however, nothing inherent in the comparative method that ties it to these particular institutional forms. The study of the EU has made much of the multiplication of levels of politics in Europe. Whether these are understood as two- (Putnam 1988) or three-level games (Patterson 1997) or in terms of multi-level governance (Marks *et al.* 1996), the idea persists that the same processes of governance permeate whichever and however many levels of institutional and other structures in which politics takes place. The shift to the more flexible agenda of governance allows comparative politics to make explicit the necessary break from the comparison of nation-states to which it has been mistakenly tied by both proponents and critics.

This examination of the politics of the European Union demonstrates clearly that, while there may be new arenas for the practice of politics, much of what occurs in those arenas is still reminiscent of what occurs at other levels of politics. Those elements of the politics of the EU that are not derivative of national processes, can still be analysed in comparison to national and sub-national – and indeed other supranational – political processes. The EU provides us with a context for applying the lessons of comparative politics, as well as providing us with another case to improve the empirical basis of the approach.

7

A POLITICAL SCIENCE RESPONSE TO A GLOBAL POLITICS AGENDA

Stephanie Hoopes

Has globalisation brought about such fundamental change that completely new theories of political science are needed? Is political science useful in an age when state influence is declining? Is political science a state-bound discipline? When answering these fundamental questions which this book poses for the study of politics, it is necessary to revisit the definition of political science itself.

Definitions which encompass only the study of the state or state institutions will surely render the discipline obsolete. The current definitions of the discipline, however, are more comprehensive, and, for the purpose of considering globalisation, more useful. Easton (1991: 275) defines political science as the study of the ways in which decisions are made and considered binding; while Goodin and Klingemann (1996: 7) define it as the study of the nature and sources of constraints upon social power and the techniques for the use of social power within those constraints. The 'science' dimension of the discipline, it is commonly agreed, demands from its practitioners that they produce arguments and evidence which can be made public and, therefore, subject to challenge (Stoker 1995: 5).

The range of topics covered by the subject, according to *A New Handbook of Political Science*, formally includes political institutions, political behaviour, comparative politics, international relations, political theory, public policy and administration, political economy and political methodology (Goodin and Klingemann 1996). Political scientists employ an equally important range of methodological approaches, qualitative and quantitative, including positivism, critical realism, relativism; inductive and deductive thinking. Ultimately, these are all used to develop theories, models or concepts that enable us to structure observations so that we can explain, comprehend and interpret 'reality'. These approaches enable political scientists, moreover, to evaluate and propose policies and processes.

In light of the new issues raised by globalisation, it is opportune to reassess the domain of political science. We need to consider whether the questions raised by globalisation can be addressed by the precepts of political science, and what might be the benefit of doing so. While there are many definitions of globalisation, most authors agree that it involves both a growing world-wide stretching of social relations and a compression of time and space. The growing importance of global business, trade, media, labour as political actors, challenges the traditional international relations assumption of the primacy of the state and raises questions for political science about the appropriateness of state borders as political boundaries. With access to global information instantly and most parts of the globe physically within 24 hours, as well as mobile capital, semi-mobile labour, and transnational mass production, the degree and intensity of political interactions have increased (Giddens 1990; Held 1991a; Scholte 1993; Waters 1995). It is an empirical question whether or not these circumstances have changed the nature of political actors, processes and outcomes, but one that is still under investigation. At the very least, globalisation is a subject that increasingly gains attention in both academic work and business and state strategy; perceptions are making it as important as any 'concrete' reality.

Within the discipline of political science, there are clearly a wide range of theories, methods and approaches. The purpose of this chapter is to examine whether any of these are relevant or adaptable for examining the changes being brought about by the process of globalisation. In the first section, I consider the impact of globalisation on political science's basic assumptions about individuals and groups. In the next section, I briefly set out the traditional approaches of political science and then examine the contributions they have already made towards analysing and understanding the globalisation phenomenon, and then suggest what needs to be done for these approaches to be further applied. In conclusion, I propose two future research agendas: how political science might contribute towards an eventual explanation of globalisation; and how the issues and criticism raised in the discussion of globalisation might advance the study of political science.

Fundamental assumptions about individuals and groups

The greatest threat to the existing social sciences, including political science, is whether their basic assumptions about individuals and groups remain valid in the face of globalisation. As Giddens argues, globalisation concerns 'the transformation of local, and even personal contexts of social experience' (1994: 4–5). This raises the question: have human beings and groups altered their basic characteristics and processes to such an extent that we cannot predict their actions without altering our existing behavioural assumptions? If this is the case and globalisation has changed the fundamental character of the individual or of social groups, then political science clearly needs a complete overhaul.

There is, however, little evidence of any radical transformation of the individual. The rationality assumptions at the foundation of most political theories continue to be a close enough approximation. Disputes over the degree to which individuals are rational is nothing new, and in fact continues to be one of the greatest points of debate within the social sciences. The issue of globalisation has raised, however, an interesting debate about risk and the perception of risk. Giddens (1990) and Beck (1992) have argued that there are new and different risks in a global society. People self-consciously orient themselves to the world as a whole and therefore perceive a new kind of risk. The perception of risk has long been a point of contention among political theorists, particularly public choice theorists, but this new assertion suggests that the individual's orientation and perceptions have changed. While this is also a psychological question, it is important to consider whether these changes represent a fundamental challenge to basic assumptions about human rationality and how individual preferences are aggregated.

Other writers suggest, however, that the more general characteristics of individuals seem to have remained consistent over time. Two organisational behaviourists contend that:

> One of the paradoxes of modern management [as well as politics, sociology, etc.] is that, in the midst of technical and social change so pervasive and rapid that it seems out of pace with the rhythms of nature, human personality has not altered throughout recorded history (Leonard and Straus 1997: 121).

As to groups, there are more questions. How to aggregate individuals is being hotly debated in political science. Scholars from at least Olson (1965) have been grappling with this. As Elinor Ostrom (1998) remarked in her Presidential Address to the American Political Science Association, 'the theory of collective action is *the* central subject of political science' (emphasis in original). The assumption that groups are unitary actors is assumed to be a close enough approximation to be useful; however, recent studies have shown such assumptions to be deficient for understanding policy-making (Hoopes and Nicholson 1997). Even in international relations where these assumptions seem most practical (e.g. Brams 1985), they have been under considerable attack (Keohane and Milner 1996). While not a problem created by globalisation, it is one that will surely be exacerbated by the increased number and type of groups operating in a global arena, and therefore will continue to need attention.

While some have argued that the state may be under threat and possibly losing power in relation to other actors, no one is arguing that human beings have changed in such a fundamental way as no longer to desire to be organised into groups – be they large or small – to advance common interests. From all globalisation perspectives the use of power continues to be widespread and our knowledge of the politics of individuals and groups provides a foundation for understanding its consequences – sometimes severe. In these senses, the traditional assumptions and approaches of political science remain relevant, but the issues raised by globalisation reveal that new work needs to be done.

Traditional political science

Though most political scientists like to claim Greek, Enlightenment and even great nineteenth-century thinkers as the founding fathers of political science, the discipline did not become defined and established until the mid-twentieth century (Gunnell 1991: 14–15). This self-image of political scientists is problematic because of the grandiose implication that political science is a super-discipline which encompasses economics, sociology and history. However, we can acknowledge that with its continued reliance on classic texts, there is clearly overlap between political science and other disciplines. Though human groups are inextricably linked to economic and societal organisation, there is a unique quality to the political aspect of group formation which cannot be reduced to economics or sociology.

Political science as a discipline began in the early twentieth century with the study of legal and formal laws and institutions. It was not until the 1950s, in the wake of the Second World War, that the discipline expanded and became a mainstream subject offered in most universities. What is today seen as the traditional core of political science was defined by the 'behavioural revolution' that occurred in the 1950s and 1960s, and the subsequent backlash. The basis of behaviouralism is that human actors and their behaviour are the appropriate source of information about why things happen in the world as they do, and that methodology based upon that of the natural sciences is appropriate for the study of human beings. The primary interests of behaviouralists were voting, judicial, legislative, administrative and executive behaviours as well as interest groups, parties and developing areas.

While there has been a strong reaction against behaviouralism, it has not led to an abandonment of science, but rather a substantial modification of our understanding of the nature of science (Easton 1991: 278–81). This reaction against behaviouralism has spurred the resurrection and development of new avenues of research including Marxism, political economy, cognitive political science, political philosophy, rational choice theory, and social issues such as environment, ethnic, racial, social and sexual equality and nuclear war. Easton (1991: 283–4) argues that this diversification has left political science not only without a sense of united purpose, but without a core as well, although Goodin and Klingemann (1996: 3) argue that it 'provides striking evidence of the professional maturation of political science as a discipline'. Most would agree, however, that students of political science share at least a minimal grounding in the same core literature and the same methodological techniques. In this section I consider whether this traditional core of political science, as defined by political theory, theories of the state and positive empirical methodology, is sufficient to be applied beyond the traditional state context to broader circumstances, and in particular to a globalising world.

Political theory

The core literature certainly includes classic political texts from Plato to Madison. Because these texts did not fit well with the behavioural approaches, political theory developed somewhat separately as a sub-discipline. This strand has had a re-birth in the discipline, however, during the post-behavioural backlash. Certainly, the most commonly studied political ideologies have been formulated in the context of the state – and the pursuit of democracy (Huntington 1988: 6). Despite this historical focus on the state, the study of political ideas may be the aspect of political science which is already the most successfully applied beyond the state to the global, as evidenced by other chapters on this subject in this book (e.g. Ch. 9). However, as Robinson argues in Chapter 10, the moral or political basis for applying political theory to the global level may be highly problematic. The dependence of political theories on particular cultures may limit their relevance in the global context.

Nevertheless, fundamental issues in the traditional domain of political theory, such as democracy and social justice, as well as new issues such as welfare, rights, civil society, new social movements, and racial, ethnic and gender equality, remain at the forefront of controversies associated with globalisation. There continues to be debate between established types of political theory – such as liberalism, socialism and conservatism – in the global context, as the critiques of liberalism in this book illustrate. Political theory's emphasis on the fundamentals of individuals and groups suggests some universality, or at least ability to transcend the state context (Hoffman 1995; Marquand 1997), thereby making it possible to consider new circumstances in an effective manner. If political theorists ultimately develop a particular theory of globalism – perhaps political cyberism as the successor to postmodernism – it will be rooted in classical concerns.

The normative dimension of political theory is too often overlooked by mainstream political scientists. While it is often convenient or more straightforward to focus on explaining situations and outcomes in politics, the approaches and methods devised by political theorists and philosophers to assist our questioning of the appropriateness, fairness, justness or even usefulness of pursuing particular policies or processes in politics (Rawls 1971; Walzer 1985; Rorty 1989) are at least as important to the profession. If predictions about the pace of change in globalisation are correct, explanatory analysis will be insufficient to meet the challenges of more economic and societal change. Thoughtful and thorough critiques of globalisation, from the standpoint of political theory and philosophy, will provide the necessary foundation for proposing the appropriate institutional and policy changes, which are clearly in the domain of political science.

Explanatory theories and the state context

It is impossible to deny that a key focus of political science has been theories of the state, which has been understood chiefly as the nation-state. The key question, however, is whether the applicability of the main explanatory theories is restricted to the state context in which they have tended to be developed, or whether they can be adapted or extended to the new kinds of context to which accounts of global change draw our attention. In order to examine this question from a broad point of view, I look briefly at five major theoretical approaches in turn: pluralism, elite theory, new institutionalism, public choice theory and structural theories.

The theories descending from *pluralism* are based on the importance of groups. The traditional setting for group activity, of course, has been the state – either in the sense that the state has been the arena for group interaction, or the arbiter between competing groups. Although there is much debate about whether the power of states is in decline, there is much more agreement that that of groups is on the rise. The variety of groups who are now claiming prominence is so diverse that it is hard to say that pluralism has been invalidated; on the contrary, a new significance is clearly indicated. Indeed the emphasis on the political significance of groups such as ethnic groups, local and multinational companies, guerrilla and terrorist groups, and social movements has been one of the most persuasive arguments of globalisation (Scholte 1993; Shaw 1994a).

The most problematic aspect for pluralists will be redefining the arena where groups compete and the implications for understanding the institutional setting or rules of the game. In some cases it is relatively straightforward, such as in the European Union, where there is a defined arena, organised interest groups and recognised policy communities (see Ch. 6). In other cases, however, where the arena is less clear, there is not such a neat translation, but many of the concepts are still useful, for example the idea of insider and outsider groups in examining the politics of environmental agreements (Willetts 1996). Other useful adaptations have emerged in international relations in the form of regime theory (Krasner 1983; Young 1989). These examples suggest that there are uses within the globalisation context for pluralism and its variants, though as Lukes (1974) would argue, only to explain observable decision-making. As globalisation suggests a deep and complex set of events, pluralism may be insufficient to gain a full understanding of the process.

A traditional alternative to pluralism is *elite theory*. The core assumptions of elite theory are possibly the most universal of all theories of the state. As set out by Gaetano Mosca:

> In all societies – from societies that are very meagrely developed and have barely attained the dawning of civilisation, down to the most advanced and powerful societies – two classes of people appear; a class that rules and a class that is ruled (Mosca 1939: 50).

It is important to note that the potential for translating elite theory into the global context is enhanced by the reference to societies rather than states, which stems from the theory's sociological roots.

The other universal aspect of elite theory is its assumption that the basis for elites' authority is superiority. Different variations of elite theory emphasise different sources for this: classic elitism emphasises aristocracy; democratic elite theory emphasises administrative ability; and radical elitism emphasises business management. These competing and conflicting variations illustrate the lack of consensus on the elite process or outcomes. Globalisation may introduce new societal boundaries and new bases for superiority, and therefore complicate the argument, but the basic assumption of the inevitability of elites may remain intact. For example, while the role of the state may be called into question as the appropriate referent for security, the importance of elites in determining types, levels and challenges to security remains strong (Fordham 1998). In this way, C. Wright Mills' (1956) concept of the power elite (military, economic and political) might be developed to analyse security issues in a global context.

Elite theory also provides the useful insight of the 'two faces of power', decision-making and non-decision-making (Bachrach and Baratz 1970). The importance of agenda setting seems to only be increasing in importance with fast-moving communication and large-scale decisions being considered. The concept of elites has been employed at the international level – although in a broadly Marxist framework – through the work on transnational elites and classes (van der Pijl 1984; Gill 1990). This work makes the point that the lack of state constraints makes elites even more powerful. It therefore becomes more important to understand and analyse their role in policy-making.

While some might argue that *new institutionalism* is not a fully developed body of theory, its prominence comes from the backlash against behaviouralism and the recognition that many of the existing theories of political science are ignoring institutions as a major source of power (March and Olsen 1984, 1989). While its political-science advocates do not argue for examining institutions on a global scale, they make the point that institutions impact almost all political decisions. This point has been widely acknowledged in international relations, and with globalisation, this strand of investigation is crucial. Some traditional international relations scholars have focused on formal international institutions such as the United Nations and the International Monetary Fund, but most have assumed that the state is the primary international institution. As Ferguson and Mansback (1989: 2) observe, 'Without the concept [of the state] to fall back on, scholars would have to abandon the claim that there is something unique about the "international" or "interstate" realm'. More recent work though has emphasised the importance of less formal institutions, such as rules, norms and conventions at the international level (Krasner 1983; Keohane 1989).

Ultimately, both domestic and international institutions, formal and informal, will be affected by and affect globalisation. In light of globalisation, work is already being done on re-engineering existing institutions in order to better institutional outcomes (Jessop 1993; Albo, Langille and Panitch 1993; Bakker and Miller 1996). Though this work in political science focuses on the structure of the state, it has a parallel in much work on international institutions in the 1990s.

Another beneficiary from the backlash against behaviouralism has been *public choice theory*, also known as rational, formal, positive or collective theory. The basic premise of this body of theory is that individuals act to maximise their own utility. While there is some element of this assumption in all theories (no theory assumes that individuals act in random ways), public choice theory contains the most explicit formulations of this premise. There is also the underlying belief that a unified, cumulative political science theory, built from universal axioms and assumptions, is possible (Almond 1996: 86).

While public choice theory posits the individual as the basic unit of analysis, there is no limit to its level of aggregation (for instance Realist international relations theory also incorporates rational choice assumptions). The most obvious application of public choice theory to the international level is in game theory, such as the use of the 'prisoners' dilemma' to explain the classic international security problem (Axelrod 1970; Snyder and Deising 1977). More recently two-level game theory has been used to explain how actors incorporate international and domestic factors when negotiating (Evans, Jacobson and Putnam 1993). Two-level games have proved especially useful for examining many international political economy issues such as agriculture, trade, finance and regulation (Milner 1988; Frieden 1991; Paarlberg 1997). Though useful for understanding international level action, much more work needs to be done before such models could, if at all, be applied to the more complex set of interactions involved in globalisation.

The notion of a universal theory, stemming from basic individual attributes, is very attractive in the face of the confusion and uncertainty brought about by globalisation. However, strong allegiance to formal models and mathematics may render public choice theory obsolete if the basic assumptions and tests are not grounded in strong empirical evidence. Some argue even further that scholars who use public choice theory methods only as tools and also incorporate culture, social structures and institutions, will be able to make a contribution to the understanding of fast political change occurring under globalisation (Bates 1990; Fiorina 1995).

Some problems identified by public choice theorists, such as the collective action problem, persist unaffected by globalisation, because the need for collective action and the scarcity of resources continues or is even exacerbated. Solutions to the collective action problem, however, will need to consider the impact of globalisation if they are to be effective. For example, Ostrom (1990) demonstrates that there are many different ways to solve the problem of the overuse of common assets. The insight that neither total regulation by the state nor the free-market are possible solutions may prove important, as scholars and practitioners alike seek solutions to the collective action problem in light of continuing globalisation.

Other developments in the diversification following the backlash against behavioralism were *structuralist theories*, such as post-Fordism and neo-Marxism, which re-emerged in the 1970s and 1980s. Though these theories seem closest to what might be considered a global theory, it is questionable how far these approaches have addressed globalisation in the contemporary sense. These sets of theories represent one of the greatest areas of inter-disciplinarity in political science, since they clearly overlap with sociology, economics and history. As structural theories can come from the left (e.g. Marxism) or the right (e.g. Darwinism) they cover an enormous range of material and are often at odds with each other.

For structuralist theorists, globalisation may raise the questions of whether political science has been using the correct paradigm (Janos 1997). Rather than arguing that the world has changed, it might be that the world is evolving in the same way as before, but that we have not been focusing on the important structural elements. In this book, Neil Stammers makes an ambitious attempt to rework structural theories to understand the role of social movements in an emancipatory and democratising global society. While this is not a direction that all or even many political scientists would take, it provides a useful example of work that expands political science to global events and uses existing tools in an original way. This work, like other studies mentioned in this section, shows that traditional explanatory theories in political science are already being used to analyse different aspects of a globalised world and others offer the potential to be adapted. The biggest problem may be that these theories are seen as 'theories of the state' rather than the general explanatory theories of political science which in fact they are.

Traditional methodology

Closely linked to the dominant theories of political science has been a positivist methodology. From this perspective, the methodology of political science is based on rules of evidence and inference (Almond 1996). Thus, the discipline is defined by a transferable range of methodologies based on the use of hypotheses, theories, models and empirical evidence. The range of evidence which can be encompassed is, however, diverse, incorporating behavioural, philosophy and empirical case studies, systematic comparative studies, statistical studies, and formal mathematical modelling and experiments. This wide array of approaches facilitates the matching of appropriate research techniques with many aspects of policy and politics.

While the theoretical value of methodological rigour is essential, it is not easy to attain, so that the pursuit of tight methodology and greater rigour has often led to only a narrow range of questions for study. For example, the most substantial data sets in the UK focus on voting in national elections (the British Election Surveys). While such studies can be useful, research needs to be more broadly conceived if it is to be useful in answering the larger questions raised by issues such as globalisation.

This 'scientific' approach to political science is not, moreover, without question within and beyond the discipline. There are those who question the ability of academics to separate fact from value (Strauss 1963), as well as those who argue that positivism is only one of many valid approaches to political science (Dryzek and Leonard 1988; Farr and Seidelman 1993). Ultimately, critics argue that such an approach limits the nature and content of political agency and process (see Chapter 12). As such, the limits of what positivist methodologies can achieve must be kept in mind. While alternative approaches should be explored to gain greater insights into the areas where traditional methodologies fall short, the latter should not be discarded until their usefulness has been fully achieved.

Political science has developed, borrowed and adapted useful methods for understanding politics at the local, regional and state levels. Because the global includes these as well as another overarching layer, the methods developed by political scientists cannot be dismissed as outdated and remain of value. The theoretical and empirical methods of political science will be useful not only for addressing issues on the global agenda, but also determining whether and to what extent globalisation has changed the political world. Establishing what has changed, especially as it may still be changing, may be the most difficult aspect to determine of all globalisation issues, as Nicholson discusses in Chapter 2.

Conclusion

In this last section, I propose two future research agendas: how political science might contribute towards an eventual explanation of globalisation; and how globalisation might contribute to the advancement of political science.

The globalisation agenda

It is important to put globalisation into context. Globalisation is a broad development encompassing economics, sociology and history as well as politics. While politics has long needed to be in dialogue with these other disciplines, it has not always been successful in doing so. Today, political science has come to embrace all areas of social life such as gender, race and class (Gamble 1990), as well as the economic environment (Dearlove and Saunders 1984). Ironically these key issues have been problems throughout modern history. Issues such as welfare, poverty, the environment, security, legitimacy, authority, human rights, class divisions and social conflict, equality, war and violence remain at the forefront of the politics as well as the globalisation agenda.

These continuities suggest that globalisation is only one of many forces affecting political outcomes. So that while incorporating globalisation is crucial to understanding current political outcomes, it is also important to recognise that pre-existing political structures, actors and ideologies have a major impact. Some argue that the future must necessarily be global, either in the sense of homogenisation (Waters 1995) or of a movement towards cosmopolitan global governance (Held 1991a). The view of political science presented here, however, suggests that the future of globalisation is not predetermined, and to a large extent will depend on the institutions, ideologies and actors with which it interacts.

The problem remains of how to conceptualise policy-making when the boundaries between the local, regional, national and international are becoming more fluid. While it is a difficult and necessary test for political science theories to look beyond the state level, it is not sufficient. Globalisation does not necessarily mean internationalisation; in fact, according to most authors on the subject, it is just as likely to mean localisation. Therefore, the ability to examine units smaller than the state remains essential – a task for which political science is well suited (Stoker 1991; John 1994). Thus political science can contribute to the globalisation agenda by examining questions such as: In what areas is state power waning? To whose benefit and to whose detriment? In what areas is state power growing? What does Ruggie's (1996) 'leaner, meaner' state look like? In addition, political science can contribute by re-working theory and methodology to encompass the full range of variables from local to state to regional to global which are important to political outcomes.

Furthermore, while political science provides a means to describe and understand this wide array of political factors, as well as to predict and recommend policy change, a fully satisfying approach must be broader. Only an interdisciplinary approach to globalisation can comprehensively address these key problems. Political science can also contribute by becoming involved in interdisciplinary projects and addressing questions such as: How do groups form? How do institutions impact an individual's preference formation? What resources are most effective for political action by groups? How can societies reduce social problems such as poverty, environmental pollution and inequality?

A future agenda for political science

The debate surrounding globalisation highlights some of the problems in the discipline, primarily defining the state, combining multiple layers, creating consistent definitions and categories, and incorporating comparisons (international and over time) and uneasy relations between sub-disciplines.

In order to study globalisation, let alone explain or affect its progress, political science must move beyond its insularity and progressive specialisation. The debate about globalisation may also awaken political scientists to the fact that the broader world context is not stable and that, as Jan Aart Scholte and Martin Shaw have suggested in Chapters 1 and 11, large-scale historical change continues. Much of the work being done in political science focuses on small-scale change with little acknowledgement of its broader implications. Too much political science has also focused on traditional political players – elected officials and elites, civil servants, well-organised pressure groups, and voters. Globalisation adds to the pressure on political science to improve its work in fields like social movements, institutions and processes.

The issues raised by globalisation debates highlight the lack of communication between international relations and other political science fields. As indicated above, there are several areas of overlap – pluralism, elites, game theory, institutional and structural theories – and yet there were surprisingly few cross-references between the sources I examined. Globalisation can also contribute to political science – as arguably it has done to international relations – by stimulating interdisciplinary scholarship. Specialisation is only beneficial if it is placed in a broad context which links it to other specialisations, so that advances can be shared and employed broadly within and beyond academia.

While explanation and understanding are crucial, there is also an important role for normative discussions as to the fairness, justness, appropriateness, or even usefulness of a particular policy or set of processes. Political scientists can go further, proposing new policies, strategies, processes and institutions. While academics who take this step are often re-named practitioners, there is no reason for them to be ostracised from the discipline. As Hirschman (1970) has advocated, there is room for theorising based both on what is probable and also on what is possible. He also sets forth an ideal rule: any one who discovered an obstacle to a current policy is obliged to look for ways in which this obstacle can also be overcome (1970: 340).

Globalisation can contribute to the political science agenda by examining questions such as: Which political actors are creating and distributing economic growth? In which policy areas are states losing control? Are there new policies, strategies or institutions which can enhance political actors' power in the face of globalisation? To what extent do states have a choice in changing? These questions suggest not only new avenues for the discipline to explore, including a range of political actors and institutions as well as factors beyond state boundaries, but also a reassessment of traditional methodologies, particularly positivism. Yet these questions also build on traditional strengths of political science.

Part IV

ETHICS AND POLITICS

8

ANTI-POLITICS AND CIVIL SOCIETY IN CENTRAL EUROPE

Zdenek Kavan

It is often stated that the 1989 revolutions contained no new ideas (Ash 1990: 154; Dahrendorf 1991: 28–9). The stated general aims of most of the post-Communist regimes that emerged in 1989 in Central and Eastern Europe were the free-market economy, democracy and a return to Europe. This tended to be interpreted in the West as indicating that these countries had embarked on the path of transforming themselves into Western-type countries – a process that would require these countries to learn from the West and to adopt Western institutions and practices. Most Western assistance was geared towards this outcome and the enlargement of Western organisations to accommodate new members from the Eastern part of Europe was perceived largely as a process of change in the East and not as requiring any fundamental reconsideration of Western institutions and practices.

This chapter starts with a different assumption: that the ideas of civil society and anti-politics that emerged from the Central European dissident movements in the 1970s and 1980s had a significant impact not just on the post-Communist transformation in these countries but also on thinking among social movements and non-governmental organisations elsewhere. This chapter will analyse the ideas of civil society and anti-politics in their contexts and consider the practices they gave rise to and then consider what has happened to them in the strongly neo-liberal mood that followed the 1989 revolutions. Transnational factors affecting the development and impact of these ideas and practices will be analysed and finally the relevance of these ideas and practices for global politics will be assessed. This chapter will concentrate on Czechoslovakia and her two successor states but, where relevant, references will be made to the developments in some of the other Central European countries, particularly Poland and Hungary.

Civil society, anti-politics and dissent in Central Europe

The central ideas associated with these concepts emerged in the work of dissenting intellectuals such as Adam Michnik in Poland, Gyorgy Konrad in Hungary and Vaclav Havel in Czechoslovakia. They found their main expression in the activities of varieties of dissident movements and organisations such as KOR (*Komitet Oborony Robotnikov* – Workers' Defence Committee) in Poland and Charta 77 in Czechoslovakia. To understand them and the differences between them it is important to analyse the historical contexts. In Czechoslovakia the role of dissent and the ideas it generated must be understood in the context of the failure of the attempts to reform the failing Communist system in the 1960s. The origins of the reform movement in that period lay in the failure of the centralised system to modernise the economy and to deal with the effects of the scientific and technological revolution (particularly with the fast-developing information technology: Richta *et al.* 1969). However, a number of critiques of the regime went beyond this: these addressed the problem of state power and individual responsibility, identifying moral corruption of society as the central issue. Given Czech traditions it is not surprising that some of the most radical critiques came from the artistic intelligentsia and particularly from writers such as Milan Kundera, Ludvik Vaculik and Havel.

At the crucial Writers' Congress in 1967 Vaculik raised an issue that was to become one of the central themes of anti-politics – that of citizenship in the Communist state. For Vaculik, power was a human problem affecting both the government and the governed, which is universal in nature and survives successful social revolutions. Its rules are neutral – independent of personality and class – and involve homogenisation of power, growth of its independence, efforts to stay in power and the forming of dynasties. The advantage of democracies over totalitarian systems is that in the former governments fall and are replaced but the citizen is renewed, whereas in the systems where the government does not change the citizen falls and the system will breed fear, political apathy and dependence on the ever more corrupt rulers. Such power prefers people whose character is similar to that of its organisation, i.e. power seekers, servile people, people with bad consciences and those whose desire for happiness and profit is not constrained by any moral considerations. Those who care more for their conscience will not enter the realm of state power. It is, therefore, vital that real citizenship be reconstituted and power of the state limited (IV Sjezd 1967: 141–51). Vaculik's speech and those of some of the other writers provoked a severe reprisal from the government and the resulting repression proved one of the last straws that brought down the Novotny regime, ushering in the Prague Spring of 1968.

Developments during the Prague Spring brought further support for the centrality of the ideas of citizenship and civic activity. The Communist Party's Action Programme which sought 'to reestablish democracy not by the introduction of political pluralism but by the revitalisation of the elective organs of the state, guaranteeing a full range of human rights while restructuring the leading role of the party' (Wheaton and Kavan 1992: 4) was soon overcome by more radical demands for change coming from various civic initiatives and groupings.

The Soviet military intervention terminated the reforms and ushered in a period of 'normalisation'. It is this which is central to the understanding of the peculiarities of the Czech conceptualisation of anti-politics or parallel polis. The government that took over during this period lacked any real legitimacy, as its hold on power originated in the intervention and was maintained on the basis of Soviet support. Normalisation involved the purge of the party, the state and all major social institutions – including those concerned with the construction and dissemination of knowledge – of all reformist elements to ensure that new reformism would not emerge in the future. Economic reforms were reversed, centralisation reimposed and a tendency quickly evolved to tend 'to ignore major structural economic weaknesses in favour of dealing with short term economic problems' (Wheaton and Kavan 1992: 7).

After the initial period of harsh repression, the regime embarked on a dual policy designed to ensure obedience to the government. The purged reformers and 'enemies' apart, society was offered a kind of social contract whereby in exchange for its political apathy and obedience – symbolised by ritualistic affirmation of faith in the system and its works – the people were promised work, security, a reasonable standard of living and relative non-interference in their domestic sphere. For the majority of the population that led to a kind of inner emigration characterised symbolically by the preoccupation with country cottages. Those who refused this contract were subjected to punishment – much less severe than the Stalinist terror of the early 1950s, but quite pervasive in that it attempted to isolate and marginalise such people and their families (Simecka 1979). The dissent that emerged in these conditions was multifarious ranging from purged reform Communists – by far the largest group – who hoped that sooner or later the regime would reopen a dialogue with them, to liberals, Christian democrats and ideological anti-Communists who had abandoned any serious thought concerning the reformability of the Communist system.

It was international developments in the mid-1970s and specifically the Helsinki Accords that provided the spur for cooperation between them and the creation of Charta 77. The human rights basket of these accords provided an opportunity to utilise the formal international obligations to implement the rights specified against the Communist governments and combine internal pressure on the government with appeals to both domestic public opinion and the outside world. The basket provided the glue for common action and a form of organisation for another reason – the divergent groups of dissenters (cutting across the Left versus Right divide) could all agree on the vital importance of human rights. Charta 77 provided a basis for common action and continuing dialogue between the different factions. The debate on anti-politics or the parallel polis was one of the first fruits of this commitment to dialogic democracy.

The original Charta documents contain some of the common ground shared by the signatories which provided a basis for the debate on Chartism and the parallel polis. First is the conviction that politics and ethics are not separate and that the latter provides the framework within which the former operates. The first spokesperson of the Charta, the philosopher Jan Patocka put it as follows: 'the concept of human rights is nothing else than a conviction that even states and whole societies recognise the supremacy of moral sensibility and the sovereignty of something unconditional and sacred. ... The purpose of Charta 77 is a spontaneous solidarity of all who have understood the significance of ethics for society and its normal functioning' (in Znoj 1995: 16–17). The reestablishment of the ethical foundation of society and politics was the starting point and allied to that is the recognition of the central importance of the individual and his conscience. There is also an important distinction drawn between different types of politics – politics in a narrow sense, meaning technology of and contest for power, and politics in a broad sense of acting publicly on matters of common concern. The intention of the Chartists was to be apolitical in the former sense – 'Charta 77 is not about any act political in a narrow sense of the word or about competing for power and intervening in the functions of state power' (Patocka, in Znoj 1995: 16).

Havel's conceptualisation of anti-politics, formulated in this debate, involved an acute analysis of power in late Communist or post-totalitarian society and the recognition that power is not monopolised by the government entirely, nor are the governed powerless. In such societies everybody tends to be implicated in the reproduction of power relations. By participating in ritualised acts of obeisance, people enforce the rules of the game and create pressure on everybody to do so as well. This pressure is, of course, reinforced by threats of punishment, though these tend to be relatively low-level ones (loss of a good job, etc.). In Havel's view the main function of Charta 77 was thus to break the game by showing that compliance in it is not necessary and that one does not have to live a lie, i.e. participate in something one does not believe in. Living in truth in this sense is not an epistemological position but a refusal to participate in the game that is designed to reinforce the regime. Chartists thus serve as moral examples to the rest of society – they not only reveal to them that alternatives are possible but in fact generate some sense of obligation for the rest to accept the responsibility for their actions and their consequences (Havel *et al.* 1985).

It is noteworthy that this proposition of moral leadership divided the Chartists and that a number of participants, particularly from the Left, adopted a somewhat critical view of this position. Indeed Patocka himself argued against Charta setting itself up as the moral authority or conscience of society. Kusy in his contribution goes further and argues that Charta is likely to generate hostility not just from the regime but also from ordinary people who have gained something from their bargain with the regime – security – and have more to lose from radical change and from living in truth – more work, less security (Kusy in Havel *et al.* 1985). For the critics Charta's role in formulating proposals for political change is more central.

The other aspects of Havel's position generated greater agreement. Though he formulated a critique of politics in general, he was fundamentally concerned with post-totalitarian society. The aim of pushing back the state into much narrower spheres than those occupied by the Communist state was shared by all. This required the establishment of a proper public sphere in which individuals acted as citizens rather than as servants of the regime. Civil society based on a variety of civic initiatives and actions is such a public sphere in which solidarity is created and a sense of community arises. The parallel polis is the emergent civil society in the post-totalitarian states. This civil society is non-political only in the narrow sense referred to earlier, i.e. not involving competition for power.

The development of these ideas among dissidents in Poland and Hungary was influenced by the different experiences in these countries. In Hungary, where reformism from above flourished right up to 1989, Konrad developed a concept of anti-politics that was less concerned with a parallel polis and more with exercising control over politicians and the state. Thus he considered anti-politics to be the 'rejection of the power monopoly of the political class and if the political opposition comes to power, anti-politics keeps at the same distance from, and shows the same independence of, the new government' (Konrad 1984: 231). Some tension between the state – which tends to be expansionist in its activities – and society is presupposed and the task of anti-political politics is to keep the state to what it should do.

For Michnik, the Polish experience of 1956 and the Czechoslovak experience of 1968 indicated that change (reform) was possible but that it is fragile and has its limits – the ruthlessness of the repression suggests that revolutionary change is not possible. Thus 'an unceasing struggle for reform and evolution that seeks an expansion of civil liberties and human rights is the only course East European dissidents can take. The Polish example demonstrated that real concessions can be won by applying steady public pressure on the government' (Michnik 1985: 142). Politics from below supplements reformism from above.

The encouragement of civic initiatives, activities and solidarity had an international dimension too. The Chartists had recognised that as the repression had an international aspect, based on frequent consultations and common action of European Communist governments to suppress particularly unwanted developments in any one Bloc country, 'the best defence for those (civic and human rights) movements must be to organise cooperation across frontiers . . . to exchange experiences, visits, books, samizdat publications and hold joint seminars, etc. . . . in short to establish international solidarity, such as Charta 77 has done with the Polish KOR' (Ruml, in Havel *et al.* 1985: 186).

Similar cooperation was extended to Western peace movements. The dialogue between the Western peace movement and the dissidents was initiated by groups such as European Nuclear Disarmament (END) at least partly in order to demonstrate that they were not manipulated by the Soviet government (Kaldor 1999). The participants needed to confront a degree of mutual suspicion and the recognition of lack of symmetry in their respective positions. As Havel (1985) pointed out, whereas for the Western peace activists their activities could be considered to be normal expressions of their civic responsibility and commitment, there were no such public spaces available for ordinary non-dissidents in the East. Civic *rapprochement* across the East–West divide required a common struggle for the development of such public spaces in the East.

Therefore human rights had to be placed at the centre of the agenda, with a recognition on the part of the Western movements that a struggle for peace in Europe required a struggle for democracy throughout the whole of Europe. For the dissidents, on the other hand, this required the recognition that their allies in the West were not just governments, and that the struggle for democracy contained a commitment to the struggle for peace. The extent of the resulting cooperation should not be overstated – not all Western peace campaigners came to support this position and a number of Eastern dissidents remained suspicious of the peace movement as being insufficiently anti-Soviet. However, it can nevertheless be argued that this collaboration in the second half of the 1980s generated the beginnings of a more genuinely pan-European transnational civil society.

A further international aspect was the growth of interest in the concept of civil society in the Western academia. This interest was clearly multicausal: it could be linked to the triumph of neo-liberalism in the 1980s, the failure of traditional Left-oriented approaches to generate effective responses, the relative decline of party politics and the growth of social movements. However, the impact of the East European developments and of dissident thought was undeniable and was acknowledged (Keane 1988; Cohen and Arato 1992; Touraine 1997).

Civil society, anti-politics and post-Communist transformation

The role of anti-politics and civil society in the post-Communist transition needs to be set within the context of multiple radical economic, political, social and international changes. The collapse of Communism in Czechoslovakia came quickly and bloodlessly. Paralysed by protracted economic crisis and deprived of Soviet support, the regime lost its will to power when faced with mass public demonstrations in Prague and other major cities in November 1989. The role of the general public in the collapse of the old regime was crucial but it cannot be taken as proof of developed civic society and citizenship. That the regime was ready to give way was amply demonstrated by the fact that it negotiated its way out of power and handed it over to the leadership of the quickly organised Civic Forum.

The Forum was formed during the November upheaval as an umbrella organisation of disparate groups, devoted to uniting all members of society as a prelude to a dialogue and negotiation with the government. Its centre consisted mainly of the dissidents from Charta 77 though a number of experts, mainly economists, were drafted in. Inevitably, as Civic Forum took over the government, ambitious individuals joined in and gradually the dissident core came to be outnumbered by the *arrivistes*. For some dissidents, the Forum was civil society in practice – the Foreign Minister, Jiri Dienstbier, proclaimed after the June 1990 elections overwhelmingly won by the Civic Forum that 'civil society was now in power'. This formulation indicates some weakness of conceptualisation as it neglects the issues of the rootedness of civil society and how it coped with the pluralism of interests that existed in post-Communist society. Indeed, this approach contrasts sharply with the more pessimistic view of Dahrendorf who estimated that the process of developing a democratic civil society would take sixty years (Dahrendorf 1991).

The consensus politics represented by Civic Forum soon came under strain when disagreements over economic reforms began to emerge. It became evident that the alliance between the dissidents and the neo-liberal economists was based on rather limited shared ground. The dissidents' defeat in the debates over economic policy began to spell the end of their central role in post-Communist politics. It also resulted in a serious decline in the importance of civil society and anti-politics approaches. Disagreements over economic policy concerned the speed of the proposed changes and the extent to which social and ethical issues should play a role in the formation of this policy. The neo-liberals led by the Finance Minister, Vaclav Klaus, advocated rapid change that would usher in a free market economy unencumbered by any other than economic considerations. The search for some 'third way', a synthesis of socialist and capitalist principles, or a gradualist approach that would express the demands of social justice, was dismissed as ignorant and intellectually arrogant.

Klaus argued that 'we show insufficient humility before the accumulated intellectual heritage ... I agree with one of the greatest Western experts on Eastern Europe, T. G. Ash, that "East European revolutions in the late 1980s did not offer any fundamentally new ideas regarding the key questions of politics and economics." ... We should realise this and humbly accept tested solutions and old truths' (Klaus 1991b: 20–1). What these tested truths in economics were was revealed by the author of the privatisation programme, Tomas Jezek: 'Today we have an iron-cast certainty that economic theory has built over the last two hundred years a body of knowledge which is beyond dispute. ... This core knowledge is accepted by all significant economists and thus the other approaches can be ignored' (Husak 1997: 49). The impact of Western economic theory throughout the period of the normalised regime, he claimed, was based on 'the reading of classical works, particularly those of the Vienna school such as von Mises and Hayek, that is to say that branch of the Western economic thought that we were increasingly convinced was correct and should form the basis upon which we ought to build our own ideas' (1997: 43).

The few economists among the dissidents were dismissed as being professionally out of date, ironically due to having been punished for their dissent by being deprived of their professional jobs! The authority of the International Monetary Fund was frequently invoked to strengthen the case for a speedy and radical reform. Klaus was careful to avoid the impression that the Fund dictated economic policy to the Czechoslovak government, claiming that it becomes involved in policy creation only in countries which are incapable of formulating their own rational programme – and this was not the case in Czechoslovakia. International Monetary Fund approval was thus invoked as the authority for the government's policy (Klaus 1991b: 79–80).

The authority of prominent Western economists was also solicited. For example, Milton Friedman visited Prague in September 1990: he 'publicly dismissed the arguments in favour of the social market economy and expressed support for the position represented by Klaus at a time coinciding with the parliamentary debates on the government economic plan' (Wheaton and Kavan 1992: 155–6). Economic developments in the West were also referred to to strengthen the neo-liberal argument for the rapid liberalisation of the economy – Klaus again: 'at a time when the whole of Europe is changing over to a market economy and to payment in hard currency we cannot lag behind. There is no time for us to demonopolise the economy first' (Wheaton and Kavan 1992: 155).

The neo-liberal economic policy ironically required, because of the speed of the reforms, a strong state to ensure their implementation. It had no truck with the politics of consensus-building, large-scale civic engagement or public dialogue. The prioritisation of economic reform required politics based virtually entirely on political parties acting as instruments for the conquest of power. The minister for the economy, Vladimir Dlouhy put it succinctly:

> In the world, an economic programme is usually associated with the election cycle, that is, with a political party or coalition. These parties do not usually submit such programmes to the people for widespread discussion. Their programmes tend to be formulated by experts, and the elected government then simply implements them. The democratic control of its implementation is then guaranteed by Parliament and the plurality of political parties (cited in Wheaton and Kavan 1992: 163).

Civic Forum had to be transformed, therefore, into a standard political party with one main task – to ensure that the right experts at the head of such a party were elected into office. And as the greatest threat to democracy during the transition period was perceived to be weak government, this position identified all sorts of civic activities from below and all forms of politics based on civil society as dangerous and destabilising (Kavan and Palous 1999). The neo-liberals quite soon prevailed within Civic Forum and by spring of 1991 it was in effect replaced by two political parties – the neo-liberal Civic Democratic Party led by Klaus took the majority of Civic Forum's members and the Civic Movement led by Dienstbier tried for a while to maintain a Forum position before transforming itself into a centrist liberal party – too late, however, to succeed in the 1992 elections. The era of the civic movement's dominance was at an end.

Why did the neo-liberals succeed so quickly given that Havel – who as President of the Republic still retained a position of great influence – was opposed to the transformation of politics to a party-political system? As mentioned above, the dissidents were a rather small group who were relatively isolated from the rest of society during the era of late Communism. After the revolution they were admired for a time but their prescriptions did not appeal to the population, whose main interests were in the economic sphere where the neo-liberals had distinct advantages with their presumed expertise and promise of quick results. Anti-politics addressed the issue of citizenship and state power in the political and social spheres but not really the issue of citizenship and economic power. For the *arrivistes*, the old dissidents were an obstacle to their ambitions and not surprisingly most of them went along with the neo-liberals. The crude forms of *Realpolitik* practised found expression in simplistic forms of anti-Communism, spawning purges (the lustration law) and a reduction of public dialogue by various forms of delegitimation of stances other than the dominant one. Contest replaced solidarity.

A Czech liberal theorist explained the change as follows:

> At the core of the new approach to human and civil rights was the conception of antipolitical politics .... This concept of human rights oriented towards the idea of authentic freedom and moral good could not prevail over the actual pluralisation of values in society .... It appeared that civil society is not just a community of people sharing a moral conviction but also a community of people who pursue their own interests .... The moderates attempted to supplement anti-political politics with the liberal concept of the rule of law, emphasizing the equality of rights of citizens. This concept was not accepted by the people (Znoj 1995: 114).

Nationalism and the dissolution of Czechoslovakia

A broad consensus existed among the post-Communist elites in Czechoslovakia that the civic principle had priority over nationalism. However, in practice nationalism played a crucial role in the dissolution of the country and the process itself showed the severe limitations on the strength of ideas of citizenship in the country. Even though in Slovakia, Public Against Violence – the Slovak equivalent of the Civic Forum – won the elections in 1990 and the nationalist Slovak National Party did relatively badly, nonetheless most of the new Slovak political parties adopted positions sympathetic to nationalism. The reasons why nationalism was a relatively potent force in Slovakia had to do with the asymmetry in the relationship between the Czechs and the Slovaks, and the Slovak perceptions that the common state was really the state belonging to the Czechs and that the Czechs had little understanding or sympathy for the Slovak cause. The Slovak economy, having been only recently industrialised under the central planning system, was much more vulnerable to the negative consequences of the type of economic liberalisation that the federal government pursued. As very much higher rates of unemployment were being experienced in Slovakia, it is not surprising that many Slovaks felt that the uneven impact of the economic policy was another example of the lack of consideration for Slovakia displayed traditionally by the government in Prague.

Demands for increasing autonomy, leading up to a form of confederal arrangement, gained significant currency right across the political spectrum. For the neo-liberals in Prague any form of compromise that would slow down the process of economic reform was unacceptable. The resulting impasse, which threatened to paralyse the government under the terms of the federal constitution, was broken (after the elections of 1992 which were won by the neo-liberals in Prague and by populist moderate nationalists in Slovakia) by an agreed dissolution of the country. For the neo-liberals in Prague the dissolution was preferable to a compromise based on increased Slovak autonomy, for several reasons. Without the Slovaks the economy could be reformed more quickly and successfully and the country would be in a position to join the European Union sooner. Without the more populist and left-leaning Slovaks the political Right would be in a much stronger position to retain effective power in the Czech republic.

The process of dissolution showed the constraints on the power of citizens to affect even such a fundamental policy development. In the 1992 elections none of the parties in either part of the republic advocated the dissolution of the state – with the exception of the Slovak National Party, which polled less than ten per cent of the vote in Slovakia. Dissolution was agreed by the respective governments who resolutely refused to test the legitimacy of their decision by calling a referendum. In circumstances where according to opinion polls only a relatively small minority in both parts supported dissolution this is not surprising.

Dissolution has strengthened nationalism, particularly in Slovakia where state-building strengthened the tendency to view the new state as belonging to Slovaks rather than the citizens of Slovakia. The exacerbation of tensions between the Slovaks and the Hungarian minority has plagued Slovakia ever since. Even in the Czech Republic nationalism was strengthened by the dissolution. For the first time in history the Czechs had a largely monoethnic state. The new constitution and particularly the legislation on citizenship implied an overt nationalist agenda in the way it discriminated against the Roma minority.

Civil society in the Czech Republic

The first few years of the independent Czech state were characterised by relative economic success and political stability. Until 1997 the neo-liberals remained in power and so were able to push through economic reforms based on liberalisation and privatisation. The political system stabilised round a gradual development of something akin to a two-party, Left-Right divide. The formal processes of democracy were successfully introduced, albeit with some deficiencies in the area of citizenship, the rule of law and human rights (see Kavan and Palous 1999). The government retained its hostile view of civil society, or rather of the anti-political view of civil society.

In May 1994 a televised debate on the subject of civil society took place between President Havel and Prime Minister Klaus which well demonstrated the gulf between the two positions. Whereas Havel identified the creation of civil society as one of the main tasks of our time, arguing that civil society constituted 'an important intervening layer between the citizen's private microcosm and top state agencies', for Klaus no such intervening layers were desirable. Both Havel and Klaus put emphasis on the citizen, but that had a different meaning for each of them. For Klaus the citizen is a free individual who enjoys certain rights; for Havel the citizen should also be actively involved in communal life (Pehe 1994: 13–14).

The differences between Klaus and Havel showed in their disagreements over regional government, over the need for a law on non-profit organisations and on the desirability of various forms of direct, non-representative democracy, particularly the use of referenda. Klaus opposed the creation of regional governments as a form of decentralisation of power perceiving it as a threat to the government's ability to control the reform process. He also saw it as an attempt 'by the proponents of civil society to give more power to the people at the local level' (Pehe 1994: 15). Klaus was also opposed to the legislation on non-profit organisations arguing that 'the defenders of non-profit organisations think they know best what is good for public welfare and they want to impose their views on us' (Pehe 1994: 16). Havel took the opposite view claiming that both are vital steps towards the creation of social and legal conditions for the growth of civil society. Havel also retained his aversion to the dominance of party politics, arguing that the increased partisanship and lack of civility in Czech politics was caused by the absence of a developed civil society. Institutional development was not enough and democracy not upheld by civil society would degenerate.

There has been, in fact a steady growth of the number of non-profit and non-governmental organisations in the Czech Republic and this process has been supported by external bodies such as major Western foundations and the

European Union. It is somewhat paradoxical that the European Union has been much more keen on the development of civil society and the various non-governmental organisations contained in it. The Union's PHARE Democracy Programme and Programme for the Development of Civil Society provided financial support for the development of civic organisations and activities, as did major private bodies such as the Soros Foundation. Several observations could be made in this context. Anti-politics and civil society ideas had influenced Western thought and institutional practice – and now they in turn were influencing developments in Central Europe. Clearly thought and practice had not remained unmodified. Indeed, Western financial support was offered within a strict framework of rules, which tended to push non-governmental organisations towards professionalisation and was thus somewhat removed from the original conception of spontaneous civic activity. The emphasis was also placed on non-governmental organisations rather than social movements. At the same time, however, the development of trans-national links and cooperation between non-governmental organisations, both East–East and East–West, have been encouraged by such programmes.

Civil society in Slovakia

Slovakia after independence developed differently from the Czech Republic. The government of Vladimir Meciar which assumed power and remained in office until 1998 (with one brief interruption), was a populist one with increasing disregard for some of the basic rules of democracy. The party political system has remained underdeveloped, with this ruling party sharing more of the characteristics of a social movement than of an established party. The opposition parties remained ineffective and were not particularly popular, although in 1998 a coalition of them finally managed to dislodge Meciar from power. Until then, the government was able to hold on to power through a successful combination of clientelism, populist appeals and the use of nationalist rhetoric. The increased authoritarianism and intolerance of any real plurality of views was identified in the West as constituting a real threat to democracy and it removed Slovakia from the list of countries deemed eligible for membership of Western institutions such as the North Atlantic Treaty Organisation and the European Union.

The major check on this growing authoritarianism in Slovakia has been provided by its well organised and highly active civil-society sector. The growth in the number of non-governmental organisations has been highly impressive as has been the institutional cooperation between them. Part of the explanation lies in the way that numbers of former dissidents found their niche in the non-governmental-organisation sector and that this sector is able to recruit from disaffected sectors of society, particularly the urban intelligentsia which has been on the receiving end of government hostility. It is noteworthy that the Meciar government came to identify the independent non-governmental sector as a greater threat to its power than that posed by the opposition parties and embarked on a set of legal, political and financial measures designed to bring this whole sector under governmental control. Withdrawal of financial support from independent organisations, the creation of parallel organisations sponsored by the government, and legal measures designed to place government appointees on the board of directors of non-governmental organisations are examples of this policy.

In the circumstances Western support is crucial for the maintenance of this sector in Slovakia. Financial support is important, because such organisations not only lack government support, but also there is a great dearth of available domestic private sponsors. Political support has also been significant, because Western pressures – particularly from Brussels – slowed down the Meciar government's attack. As in the Czech Republic, the non-governmental organisations have been developing partnerships with similar organisations both in the other post-Communist countries and in the West, partly spontaneously and partly because they have been encouraged to do so by the assistance programmes. Thus they have contributed to the process of the development of a transnational civil society in Europe.

Conclusion

Anti-political civil society ideas and practice developed in Central European dissident circles as a response to the aridity, ineffectiveness and oppression in late Communist societies. They were conceived as an ethical project designed to limit the power of the state through the development of a proper public sphere based on active citizenship and communal solidarity. This project had little to say about the economy, or the relationship between civil society and the economy, and had in some versions an elitist aspect that helped to isolate its protagonists in idealised moral communities. Given the realities of the Communist regime it is not surprising that its approach to civil society was further delimited by its concentration on the role of individuals as citizens and thus relatively little attention was paid to issues of institutional autonomy – including that of the Churches, the trade unions, universities or the media. The project had an impact on the parallel developments in the West. The outcome was a cross-fertilisation of ideas and forms of transnational civic cooperation that provided the basis for a transnational civil society.

After the revolutions, the anti-political civil society approach briefly held sway but soon was replaced as the dominant force by neo-liberalism, due at least partly to its neglect of the economy and of a clear conceptualisation of the place of self-interest. Civic organisations nevertheless appeared in significant numbers, though their political impact and significance varied greatly, being more significant in the less stable and only formally democratic Slovakia than in the Czech Republic. Anti-political civil society ideas have changed considerably as a result of the post-Communist experience and became much less anti-statist. Not only was the provision of a supportive state framework perceived as important for the development of civil society but as Mary Kaldor (1999) has noted, the experience of the former Yugoslavia shows that civil society alone cannot guarantee sufficient minimal security to its citizens and thus civil society itself may disintegrate under the impact of civil conflict. In Central Europe, civil society was unable to prevent the disintegration of the Czechoslovak state and society despite the wishes of the majority of the citizens.

Havel himself has argued that not only is state support important for the development of democratic civil society but that 'active social engagement improved the citizen's attitude towards the state because it generated a bridge between his private life and the state' (Pehe 1994: 13). The emphasis now is on civil society acting as an intermediary between the state and the citizens, facilitating a dialogue between them and encouraging the development of civility in public affairs (see Kavan and Palous 1999). Civil society thus requires not just active citizens, with the ability to organise themselves spontaneously into a variety of independent civic organisations, but also the autonomy of other institutions such as the media and the trade unions and a legal-constitutional framework guaranteeing this autonomy. The Central European experience also shows that the process of establishing a well functioning democratic civil society in a rooted way is a long-term project, though perhaps not as long as anticipated by Dahrendorf.

The transnational elements affecting the development of civil society theory and practice were varied – ranging from the way globalisation of knowledge affected policy creation to the growth of transnational civic cooperation. Western democratic assistance shows the process of dialectical interconnectedness of civil society theory and practice across the East–West European divide. The ideas and practice of civil society have become in some ways more modest than those expressed in the 'parallel polis' concept but in other ways they raise more complex issues. The growing transnational civil society is confronted with the question of whether it requires some form of institutionalised government at regional and global levels, to create and maintain frameworks within which civil society can flourish.

9

GLOBAL ETHICS AND THE IMPLICATIONS OF GLOBALISATION

Christien van den Anker

Globalisation has been welcomed by some as a possible way out of poverty for poor countries, while others predict that globalisation will increase global inequality. Whether or not one views globalisation as a positive development, if one accepts that it is a new phenomenon, it raises moral issues. In this chapter I look at the moral implications of the process of globalisation. The main question with which I am concerned is whether the process enhances moral obligations across the borders of nation-states. If globalisation implies a growing interdependence between actors in the world economy, moral duties across borders may play a larger role than they did in a world consisting mainly of sovereign nation-states governed by the principle of non-intervention. And if it is the case that a global culture is developing, and we are moving in the direction of 'one world', the cosmopolitans may be right that moral duties are owed to people independent of where they live.

The ethical theories arguing for fair global arrangements in the late 1970s and early 1980s relied on the growing interdependence and globalisation in the world to justify a major redistribution from rich to poor. An example is Beitz (1979) whose theory is broadly Kantian and continues the line of argument introduced by Rawls (1971). More recent contributors to the debate on globalisation often assume that there is a link between globalisation and increasing obligations across borders (Luard 1990; Horsman and Marshall 1994; Waters 1995).

This position raises important problems. If it is global interdependence that justifies redistribution, does that imply that in a less interdependent world the plight of poor people across borders could legitimately be ignored? In a strictly Kantian approach to global justice, the empirical fact of globalisation can never be the justification for global redistribution since an empirical fact, according to Kant, is irrelevant to our moral obligations. In his argument global justice is required on the basis of a universal moral theory, which cannot but include every rational human being on the planet. This point was later conceded by Beitz (1983) but that still leaves the question of the importance of globalisation as an empirical fact. Moreover, recent authors on globalisation still rely on global interdependence as a basis for more extensive global duties.

This chapter argues that although globalisation makes it impossible to deny any human being moral standing, the existence of moral duties beyond boundaries is independent of whether or not human relations are globalised. I agree with Kant that moral duties cannot simply rely on an empirical phenomenon. However, I am aware that a strictly Kantian, universalist approach brings problems of its own. Particularists have shown the difficulties in justifying such an approach, and the debate in ethics between particularism and universalism has presently reached a virtual impasse. I suggest that O'Neill's practical approach to the problem of moral obligations across borders can help us to begin to solve this stand-off. In my conclusion I explore some extensions to her argument.

The order in which I address these issues is as follows. In the first section I discuss the concepts of globalisation and interdependence and I consider whether these are new phenomena or accelerations of trends which are much older. In the second I assess the argument for obligations to global redistribution based on interdependence. In the third I formulate the Kantian critique of empirical justifications for moral duties and explore some universal theories of moral obligation. In the fourth section, I suggest a theory of universal global justice that recognises moral standing as undeniable in an era of globalisation. This theory is, however, not directly dependent upon globalisation in its argument for global obligations of justice and does not exclude the possibility that there may be global duties when a process of globalisation is not taking place. The final section contains the conclusion.

Globalisation and interdependence

So far I have defined neither globalisation nor interdependence. Although for the purposes of this chapter it is possible to remain relatively agnostic about the details of the process of globalisation, it is important to be clear about the general character of the process. The developments that are commonly believed to be constituent of globalisation are economic expansion and increased flexibility in the choice of locations for production; reduced influence of the governments of nation-states on their economies; and an intensification of the social and cultural connections between people in different parts of the world. The main cause is identified as the development of technology which speeds up communication, the transport of goods and the travel of people. These are sometimes complemented by factors such as the growth of global networks of social movements and non-governmental organisations, the growing awareness of environmental problems which need to be addressed globally and security issues in a nuclear age, all of which can be seen as important elements of globalisation. In short, globalisation is often defined as the process by which the world seems to shrink and actions in one place have major long-distance effects. This process is sometimes linked to the end of the Cold War and the global rise of liberal capitalism (Giddens 1990; Luard 1990, 1992; Held 1991a, b; McGrew *et al.* 1992; Scholte 1993, 1996b; Waters 1995; Robinson 1996).

In evaluating whether globalisation creates new types of duties across borders, it is also important to establish whether globalisation itself is new. If it is merely a continuation of the initial expansion of the world economy and the rise of modern states from the late sixteenth century onwards, then there would be no special occasion to re-evaluate our moral duties. This chapter therefore suggests that there are reasons to believe that globalisation in its present form is qualitatively different from earlier forms and requires a critical evaluation of its ethical implications. According to O'Neill, the time in which strangers were temporary visitors who had a right to hospitality for the length of their visit is now far away. Our relations to people across our national borders are very different. 'We live in a world where action and interaction at a distance are possible. [. . .] Distant strangers may be benefited or harmed, at the limit sustained or destroyed, by our action or inaction as we may be by theirs' (O'Neill 1995).

An objection to this type of view claims that there is nothing new about global interconnections. According to this view, a dense pattern of worldwide linkages began to emerge with the initial expansion of the world economy and the rise of the modern state from the late sixteenth century. Held admits that the complex interplay between state and non-state actors is hardly new. But claiming an element of continuity in the formation of the states system is quite different from claiming that there is nothing new about the present global system. The first new feature of our time is that political, economic and social activity is becoming worldwide in scope and the second new feature is the intensification of levels of interaction and interconnectedness within and between states (Held 1991a, b). If globalisation is both an expansion of the scope of activities and an intensification, it is clear that this is a relatively new trend even though expansion of networks of trade across the globe has been going on for centuries. It is the intensification and the acceleration that make a qualitative difference. Scholte holds that only in recent history something approximating 'planetary' social relations has emerged (Scholte 1993).

These developments are going on mainly in the economic, the political and the cultural sphere. There is some debate as to which sphere is most important and whether or not some drive others towards globalisation. For the purposes of this chapter that discussion is less relevant. We can conclude that globalisation has its origins in much earlier developments but has accelerated since the end of the Second World War. Luard refers to 'the breathtaking shrinkage of the world, which has taken place over the last fifty years or so' (Luard 1990: vi). Waters agrees that some measure of globalisation has always occurred but until the middle of the millennium it was non-linear in its development. The linear period of globalisation that we are now experiencing began, according to Waters, in the fifteenth and sixteenth centuries. Globalisation could not really begin until then since it was only the Copernican revolution that convinced humanity that it inhabited a globe (Waters 1995: 4).

An important element in the debate on globalisation is the connection between the two sides of a paradoxical relationship. On the one hand globalisation can be defined as the intensification of worldwide social relations which link distant localities in such a way that local happenings are shaped by events occurring many miles away and vice versa (Giddens 1990: 64). On the other hand local transformation also forms an intrinsic part of globalisation. While the nation-state becomes less influential and cross-border influences become stronger, the connection between local communities and their national state may become weaker and the identity of the smaller unit more pronounced. In Scholte's view the process of globalisation is characterised by 'an intertwining of processes of globalisation and the promotion of subnational, substate territorial identities' (Scholte 1996b). This has important implications for the way duties are perceived and for debates on who is included in the scope of distributive justice. Universalists and particularists make references in support of their argument to these different sides of the process of globalisation. (This point will be taken up further below.)

There is also a reflexive element in globalisation which may be very important for its moral implications. The growing interconnectedness and expansion of contacts across borders as well as their intensification and the speeding up of communication, transport and travel have made many people aware of the fact that they live in a more globalised world. This element of realisation and self-reflection is sometimes connected by observers to a larger awareness of others in distant locations as fellow human beings. According to cosmopolitans the awareness of sharing one world may make it easier to see that we have moral obligations towards others even if they live outside our borders. I suggest, however, that this is a matter of motivating people to act on principles of justice rather than a justification for a particular scope of principles of justice. Globalisation may make it easier for people to act on universal cosmopolitan principles of justice but it does not make those principles right or wrong.

The sometimes implicit cosmopolitan stance of authors on globalisation contributes to the common assumption that the causal link between globalisation and global moral duties no longer needs explicit justification. For example Luard views the centre of decision making as moving away from nation-states and towards collective institutions: 'The welfare of ordinary men and women no longer depends primarily on the actions of their own governments. It depends, far more, on actions and decisions reached, far beyond the frontiers of their own state, by other governments, or by international bodies taking decisions collectively' (1990: vi). It remains to be seen to what extent the space created by the diminishing powers of the nation-state will be occupied by transnational or global institutions. It may well be that regional institutions are going to play a more important role than global ones in the near future. Waters sketches a picture of what he calls 'a fully globalised world' as far from a cosmopolitan Utopia of one world community. He foresees that in a globalised world there will be a single society and culture occupying the planet but neither will social relations be harmoniously integrated nor will there be a central government. Territoriality will disappear as an organising principle for social and cultural life and we will be unable to predict social practices and preferences on the basis of geographical location. We can expect relationships between people in disparate locations to be formed as easily as relationships between people in proximate ones (Waters 1995: 3). The picture of a global village (McLuhan 1964: 93) can obviously no longer be taken for granted.

A further point worth making when assessing cosmopolitan claims about the ethical impact of globalisation is that globalisation and interdependence do not automatically imply equality. Inequality between and within nation-states is frequently increased by integration in the global economy. The Newly Industrialised Countries are often mentioned as an example of how beneficial the integration into the world economy is for countries in the South. Although there may be some success stories, there is a wide divergence between countries in the South in how well their integration in the global economy has paid off and who has benefited from it. In the heyday of Structural Adjustment Programmes, for example, many countries were advised to focus on the production of primary goods for the world market. As a consequence of the additional supply, the price for those goods declined and the results are well known.

Even for countries which successfully integrated into the world economy, the results were not beneficial for everyone. In Brazil, for example, economic growth over the past twenty years has been remarkable. Yet the internal distribution of income has not advanced. Instead of becoming more equal, the situation has deteriorated. Globalisation and integration in the world economy have not had positive effects for Brazil's poor. Furthermore, the use of the term interdependence in the world economy conceals that the poorer countries in the world are part of this integrated economy on the basis of dependence rather than genuine interdependence. Even if one does not hold that dependence causes underdevelopment, the fact of dependence cannot be denied. While everyone may take part in the process of globalisation, not everyone takes part to the same extent. Therefore it must be noted that interdependence does not coincide with equality (Gilpin 1987).

So far, globalisation has been widely held to mean the increased freedom of market forces and the diminishing roles of political actors, mainly nation-states, in softening the impact of market outcomes. In the context of national societies it is now common practice to smooth out the worst implications of market capitalism. With the decreasing influence over economics of national governments, the sombre situation of the world's poor has sometimes been seen as capable of generating social change in the direction of some form of power to contain global capitalism. In reality this can only be a coordinated power between nation-states and other global actors since single nation-states have no longer so many instruments to control the major players in the global economy. 'The strongest impetus towards the re-imagining of our communities', Horsman and Marshall (1994) argue, 'will come from the realisation that without political opposition capitalism will not on its own accord provide the conditions for narrowing the gap between the rich and the poor, a redistribution of wealth globally nor even much more than a basic level of security and stability. Without the articulation of a political balance to the international economy, the likely result will be a perpetuation of the system's inequalities'. Luard (1990) argues that the vacuum left by national governments in the provision of welfare will make welfare a global issue like the environment: 'If national politicians are not always capable of making decisions to protect the well-being of their citizens, there is a vacuum in which human welfare must be considered. If we use the analogy of the environment human welfare becomes a global problem which requires an open debate about the extent of duties across boundaries.'

Political philosophers can be of great help in opening up the debate by providing relevant concepts and arguments. Seeing a role for political philosophers in the debate on the impact of globalisation is, however, not the same as viewing globalisation as the basis for duties across borders. The direct route of arguing that global interdependence creates duties to fellow human beings across boundaries raises philosophical problems. The issue here is whether or not globalisation changes the moral obligations people have towards others in the world.

The main element in globalisation that causes the need to look freshly at moral obligations is sometimes seen as the growing knowledge about others in the world. Luard, for example, maintains that people are more prepared to take human rights issues seriously across the globe 'because the world is so much smaller that we are all today more conscious of the human rights violations that occur in other parts of the world and more determined to do something about them' (1992: 296). Robinson (1996: 1) suggests that '[i]n an interdependent world, questions of justice and fairness, duty and obligation, rights and responsibilities, and trust and care are more pressing than ever'. However, it is clear from the argument in this section that globalisation and interdependence do not lead automatically to the cosmopolitan ideal. For a further critical evaluation the next section looks in more detail at the cosmopolitan political theory of duties based on global interdependence developed by Charles Beitz.

Moral duties based on global interdependence

The main proponent of a moral theory based on growing interdependence is Beitz (1979). Although he altered his argument (Beitz 1983) the original theory is worth looking at in more detail since many people share his intuition that globalisation causes a shift in the moral duties towards people across boundaries. In some ways interaction is the obvious condition for moral duties. Even though morality may come into play in situations where there is no interaction, such as the balance between present and future generations, it cannot be plausibly excluded from situations in which there is human interaction. We could argue that in the period before communities knew about the existence of other communities in the world, the members of those communities did not have moral duties towards one another. However, in a historical period where we know of the existence of others and have intensive interaction with them, morality and obligations are denied only by outright moral sceptics. The form global interaction has taken, according to Beitz (1979), leads to a strong argument for global duties of redistribution. Since nation-states are no longer self-contained justice becomes a global matter and cannot be coherently theorised within models of one society.

Beitz's original argument follows in the Rawlsian tradition. He uses the persuasive force of a hypothetical contract agreed on by all those involved. As long as the situation in which the choice of the principles is made satisfies the criteria of justice, the principles that result from the deliberations are also just. Rawls himself argued that two principles of justice would follow from an imaginary original position. People who did not know their future position in society would opt for the greatest equal liberty for all and a second principle, specifying equality of opportunity by guaranteeing offices open to all. The second principle would also include, according to Rawls, the Difference Principle, which holds that benefits and burdens of social cooperation should be divided equally unless the worst off in society benefit from any inequalities. Rawls believes in the trickle-down process of wealth and he assumes that incentives for the rich are needed to get them to invest their money and talents in the society. This is why inequality may benefit the least advantaged up to a certain point (Rawls 1971).

Rawls argued, however, that in the question of international justice, the second principle would not be opted for. The theory of international justice would justify the non-intervention principle that presently rules the international order albeit combined with a basic set of human rights, including the right to life and security, the right to personal property, and the elements of the rule of law, as well as the right to a certain liberty of conscience and freedom of association, and the right to emigration (Rawls 1993b: 68). The Difference Principle was not applicable to international justice, according to Rawls, for the following reason: 'persons' adverse fate is more often to be born into a distorted and corrupt political culture than into a country lacking resources. The only principle that does away with that misfortune is to make the political traditions and culture of all peoples reasonable and able to sustain just political and social institutions that secure human rights. [...] We do not need a liberal principle of distributive justice for this purpose' (Rawls 1993b: n. 52).

Beitz criticised Rawls and argued that the Difference Principle should also hold internationally. He makes two basic points. Firstly, even if we accept that states are separate self-contained societies, their representatives would insist on a more wide-ranging contract than Rawls envisages. Secondly, since states are not self-contained there is no reason to look for a second contract between them; instead Rawls's full account of justice should be applied worldwide, including the Difference Principle. Beitz's first point concerns the distribution of natural resources. He argues that the initial distribution of resources is morally arbitrary and therefore subject to procedures of distributive justice. His argument is roughly that if representatives in an international original position do not know how rich their country is in resources, their aversion of risk will make them opt for an equivalent of an international Difference Principle (Beitz 1985).

The main concern here is the second argument. Beitz's position that the world is now in practice a single society as a result of interdependence and that therefore Rawls's principles should be applied without exception brings up some interesting problems (Beitz 1979: 129 and onwards and Beitz 1985: 295 and onwards). The argument runs as follows: 'if evidence of global economic and political interdependence shows the existence of a global scheme of social cooperation, we should not view national boundaries as having fundamental moral significance. Since boundaries are not coextensive with the scope of social cooperation, they do not make the limits of social obligations. Thus, the parties to the original position cannot be assumed to know that they are members of a particular national society, choosing principles of justice for that society. The veil of ignorance must extend to all matters of national citizenship' (Beitz 1985: 298). In conclusion, Beitz argues that there is no reason why the content of the chosen principles of justice would change when the original position is thus transformed.

A first difficulty is that the present interdependent world system cannot plausibly be defined as a cooperative venture for mutual advantage, which is the definition of society Rawls presents in his original theory of justice. 'Possibly parts of the industrial world could be seen in this way – the European Union, for example – but it would be difficult to see relations between rich and poor countries in this light' (Brown 1997: 290). One way out of this dilemma is to adopt a position which is no longer dependent on a society as a scheme of cooperation for mutual advantage, as has been done by Brian Barry. He argues against Rawls that impartiality is the crucial principle of international justice. His theory is universalist and includes all human beings. A reasonable agreement on the principles of international justice can be reached on the basis of their motivation to justify behaviour to others (Barry 1995).

Further critics have attacked the causal link Beitz presupposes between the currently growing interdependence and moral duties of redistribution across borders. Brown (1995: 94), for example, writes that a sense of obligation towards people across national boundaries is not 'something that can be expected to emerge simply as a result of individuals and peoples coming to have more contact with one another, because such contact need not generate the essentially moral consciousness of common identity that is required'. And, similarly, Robinson, F. (1996: 17) rejects the 'dubious causality whereby the increasing scope and range of influence and contact among individuals, institutions and states is thought to bring about the creation of a set of universal norms, universalised moral commitments and a global shared identity'.

The critics expect that there may be certain trends, commonly associated with globalisation, which hinder rather than assist the creation of positive moral relations across borders. They do not see why, for example, the expansion of the global market economy would contribute to an extension of moral concern to other communities when the global capitalist system is characterised not only by interdependence, but often by dependence and increasing inequalities between (and within) North and South. Moreover, these critics argue, certain trends associated with the spread of what might be called a 'global consumer culture' – the fact that young people everywhere desire the same jeans, trainers and electronic games (Brown 1995: 93) – do not suggest any movement towards new understandings between cultures or heightened moral awareness of the well-being of distant others. Scholte also warns for over-enthusiasm on the side of cosmopolitan arguments: '[...] [W]orld interdependence is not by definition a good thing. World social relations do not guarantee us equality or community, although these eventualities are not logical impossibilities, either' (Scholte 1993: 39).

The points made by these critics are essentially about the fact that increasing contact between people across the globe does not necessarily lead to moral concerns between them. I would add that some parts of the globalisation process may seem to include more contact with people in other parts of the world, but in fact they add to the increasing isolation in which people (especially in the North) sometimes live. For example, the contacts made through the internet talk-rooms are often based on complete fantasy stories about one's life and the home-shopping trend means that people can withdraw even more behind the walls of their flats. In some instances the point is even further developed, arguing that even if some moral obligations are the result of these contacts, they may never add up to the same kind of obligations people have towards their fellow nationals. Brown, for example, concludes that '[I]n practice, and quite sensibly, we recognise degrees of obligations towards family, friends, acquaintances, fellow citizens, and so on, and as long as this recognition does not lead us to disregard the interests of those in the outer circles of our concern, there is no reason to see this as immoral' (Brown 1995: 96). The discussion of priorities in moral obligations is beyond the scope of this chapter.

A point in favour of Beitz's argument is that in his original version, he does not argue that globalisation leads to moral concern and to equality among nations. Beitz clearly suggests that the benefits of globalisation are distributed unequally and that therefore principles of global distributive justice are required: 'Economic interdependence, then, involves a pattern of relationships which are largely non-voluntary from the point of view of the worst-off participants, and which produces benefits for some while imposing burdens on others. These facts, by now part of the conventional wisdom of international relations, describe a world in which national boundaries can no longer be regarded as the outer limits of social cooperation' (1985: 296). In this way Beitz rejects the criterion of cooperation for mutual advantage which Rawls developed for principles of justice.

The final and most important criticism posed the hardest problem for Beitz's initial position. It can be argued that not only his prediction of the effect of globalisation is at least uncertain and at worst wrong, but the use of an empirical fact to justify moral duties as in the sense described above is methodologically unsound. In Beitz's original theory his account of the international Difference Principle relies on the empirical fact of interdependence. Inclusion of all human beings alive on earth now in a universal theory of international or global justice may be morally obligatory even when the states system has not evolved into anything like a global society. Exactly how relevant the present circumstances of globalisation and mutual dependence are is questioned by the more strictly Kantian approaches.

Beitz himself has answered this objection, which was first formulated by Barry (1982), by stating that his argument that the members of the Original Position should be global rather than national because national societies are not self-sufficient misses the point although he still agrees with its conclusion (Beitz 1983: 595). The basis from which Beitz (1983 and 1991) now includes all human beings in the theory of justice is the two basic powers which we all possess: a capacity for an effective sense of justice and a capacity to form, revise and pursue a conception of the good. This formulation is found in Rawls's (1980) article on Kantian constructivism. Beitz (1983: 595) concludes: 'Since human beings possess these essential powers regardless of whether, at present, they belong to a common co-operative scheme, the argument for construing the original position globally need not depend on my claim about the existence of international social co-operation.'

It may well be that Beitz has revised his theory arguing for global redistribution but many continue to link globalisation with worldwide duties. If it is put forward in the form Beitz chose in 1985, namely, using the increasing global inequalities as a result of the unfair global economic and political institutions as an illustration of why a theory of global justice is needed, then this seems a plausible argument. The crux of this version of his argument is the denial of any moral relevance to national boundaries. This would be in line with a Kantian moral theory. The problematic version of the argument is the one that relies on global interdependence *per se* to invoke duties of redistribution. In the next section I look at the Kantian objection to this type of argument, which holds that empirical phenomena cannot influence moral universal principles.

Kant and universal moral obligations

Since the Enlightenment moral and political philosophy has seen morality as independent from the actually existing world. This is evidence of a Kantian influence. Kant himself said: '[w]hen we have the course of nature alone in view, "ought" has no meaning whatsoever. It is just as absurd to ask what ought to happen in the natural world as to ask what properties a circle ought to have' (Kant 1787 (1929): 473). Kantian moral theory is based on universal principles and the conviction that principles have precedence over consequential or collective considerations. Kantian universality means that principles stand independently from place or time. The analysis of the world as it is cannot alter those principles. The widespread opinion that globalisation in itself raises questions of a moral nature in determining the obligations we have towards people who live outside our nation-state would be denied by strict Kantians. This is not to say that in a Kantian perspective duties across borders cannot be justified. On the contrary, duties across borders are part of the underlying universality of the Kantian morality. Both Kant and modern-day cosmopolitans argue that national boundaries are arbitrary and do not plausibly limit the duties we have to other people.

In Kant's view, existing or potential cooperation is largely irrelevant when framing the responsibility of global actors. Just as for domestic morality, the basis for international morality is the moral demand of reason (Donaldson 1992). The main source for Kant's cosmopolitanism is his Categorical Imperative: 'act only in such a way that I can also will that my maxim should become a universal law' (Kant 1991: 67). The Categorical Imperative is valid independently of any desires or inclinations towards alternative actions; it is also valid for all rational human beings. O'Neill has illustrated the importance of universality by considering some non-universalisable principles. There are, according to O'Neill, certain principles of action which can be held coherently by one agent but which cannot be coherently proposed as principles for all. For example, if coercion and deception were universalised, then all projects of individual coercion or deception would be made incoherent: '[s]ince nobody who hopes to deceive can coherently will that a principle of deception be fundamental to the practice of any plurality, justice requires that it be rejected' (O'Neill 1992: 64). The Categorical Imperative leads to a universal theory of ethics.

Many of the contemporary cosmopolitan liberal theories rely to some extent on Kantian universalism. Their focus on theories of justice rather than virtue and their prioritising of just principles over the consequences of actions are examples of this Kantian heritage. Kantian ethics is sometimes criticised for its reliance on a metaphysical conception of the person. Any strong metaphysical position is claimed to be avoided in a contractual scenario, along the lines of Rawls's original position or Scanlon's more inclusive notions of reasonable agreement as used by Barry (Scanlon 1982; Barry 1995).

If we were to take Kant's work seriously, whether in its original form or in the revised form of the contemporary cosmopolitans, the question of the ethical implications of globalisation would have to be answered in a balanced way. It is not due to globalisation that duties beyond borders are owed but to the principle of universalisability or the Categorical Imperative. In the contractarian theories duties are owed according to the principles of justice. In these theories, Kant's universality of principle was taken seriously from the start but the universality of scope was at first not accepted. The cosmopolitan versions of contractarian theories, developed by Beitz (1979), Barry (1995), and Pogge (1987) used globalisation to show why theories of justice should no longer be confined to models of one society. Strictly speaking, however, it is not globalisation in itself that creates moral duties. Humanity should have accepted universal moral obligations before globalisation became as influential as it is. People knew of the existence of others in the world and contact was possible.

If globalisation was the necessary condition for a global theory of justice then it is implied that practices like the slave trade and imperialism were morally acceptable. Barry (1973) had already pointed out this problem in Rawls's work. However, globalisation is empirically no longer disputed and therefore it is even less plausible to deny duties across borders. It might make sense to hold that globalisation, strictly speaking, cannot alter our duties across borders, since we were already in a position to influence others' lives for a long time. The process of globalisation only makes it extra clear that the effects of interaction demand moral responsibility. In the next section I sketch a view which includes globalisation in this careful way, without denying that in a less globalised world duties could have been due to the same extent.

Universal moral standing and global justice

After discussing the problems with a cosmopolitan position which relies on globalisation, and mentioning the Kantian problem of relying on metaphysical notions of the person and human rationality, I now turn to a recently suggested alternative which takes globalisation seriously as an element in moral reasoning while not relying on it. As I pointed out earlier, the two main positions in ethics, universalism and particularism, each deal well with one aspect of the globalisation process but not with both at the same time.

Universalism, broadly speaking, holds that judgements in ethics should be made according to universal principles which hold for all lives and in all situations. The scope of universal principles is mostly seen as cosmopolitan. Universalism uses as evidence for its position the aspects of globalisation such as the process of growing worldwide interdependence, the expansion of supranational institutions and the development of a cosmopolitan frame of mind. Particularism, in contrast, appeals to the actual practices or traditions of particular communities, which rule out the cosmopolitan scope of the universalists. Particularists emphasise the aspect of globalisation which causes the reassertion of subnational local communities and of groups coming together on the basis of particular identities.

If it is true that these two aspects of globalisation are causally linked, it may be best to reach for an approach in ethics which could include both universal principles and an account of existing local practices. O'Neill's version of practical ethics aims to arrive at universal principles without having to rely on a metaphysical account of the person. O'Neill avoids the question 'what are the obligations from one person to others in the world?' and asks instead 'what are our obligations in the present time?' (O'Neill 1996). In her search for an answer to the questions of global or transnational justice she acknowledges that in today's world, theories of justice with a wider scope than national societies are unavoidable: 'today questions of global distributive justice will arise whether or not we can find the theoretical possibilities to handle them. Modern technical and institutional possibilities make far wider intervention not only possible but unavoidable' (O'Neill 1991: 277). In order to solve those questions, according to O'Neill, we need to look at who is obliged to take which sorts of actions for whom. In her later work she therefore focuses on the question of moral standing.

O'Neill takes a practical approach rather than a theoretical one because cosmopolitan, universal principles have not convincingly overcome the objections from the communitarians and liberal nationalists. One way forward could be to focus on the practical approach to moral standing. This approach holds that assumptions of moral standing we show when acting cannot be denied in the realm of moral obligations. In summary, when we interact with others across borders we make quite complicated assumptions about the agents and subjects we deal with. It would be incoherent to deny those agents or subjects moral standing while clearly assuming their complexities when we interact.

A possible objection would be to argue that people were treated immorally, for example, by the Nazis in Germany in the 1930s and 1940s and the victims were denied moral standing by the perpetrators. But even in that case the moral standing of the people mistreated was not in question. Despite what the Nazis claimed in their rhetoric their actions showed what they believed to be true about their victims. According to O'Neill their actions reveal that the Nazis held their victims to be 'intelligent, foresighted, literate and capable of complex mental suffering' (O'Neill 1995). The organisation of deportation and of the camps makes no sense except against those background assumptions. 'In short, the claim that these others were "Untermenschen" was simply a lie. It was inconsistent with other assumptions' (O'Neill 1995).

Clearly, O'Neill has a point when she argues that it is not possible to have complex relations with others without conceding that they are indeed agents or subjects. In her view agents must accord moral standing to neighbours and strangers, near and far, but her theory does not need any account of essential features of beings deserving moral standing. In this way she avoids the trap that universalists are often accused of falling into. The result is a less universalistic approach which still defends the principles that the universalists hold so dearly. O'Neill's practical approach will yield results which are different for different people at different times. A theoretical universalist approach would not. The approach does not say anything about agents on whom we cannot act (like inhabitants of distant planets) and whether or not they have moral standing.

What, then, is the importance of empirical facts for moral obligations in the practical approach to ethics? O'Neill makes three assumptions relevant to fixing ethical standing. From an agent perspective, the first assumption is that there are others who are separate from the agent. Secondly, the agent assumes that those others are somehow connected to him or her. Thirdly, the assumption is made by an agent that the others have limited but determinate powers. These three assumptions are respectively called plurality, connection and finitude. 'Where assumptions under all three headings are made, there will be a basis for agents to determine which others they are committed to according ethical standing and consideration' (O'Neill 1996: 101). In O'Neill's theory of moral standing, connection means that agents can be or are acted on by others. For this it is necessary that the agents believe they are connected to others by some causal link. This causal pathway may be a very indirect route as is the case in many instances in the modern, globalising world. This is a much more modest claim than what is sometimes thought to be a necessary condition of moral standing, namely that agents share a language, normative ties and so on. (For a discussion see Brown 1995.)

O'Neill presents some examples to show that moral standing is not due if communities are not aware of each other's existence. One such example are the inhabitants of Anglo-Saxon England and their T'ang Chinese contemporaries (O'Neill 1996: 105) and another the Vikings living in Dublin and their Peruvian contemporaries (O'Neill 1995). These communities lived beyond the pales of each other's known world. They did not and could not premise actions on assumptions on one another's capacities to act or to suffer. It would be absurd to accuse them of acting either justly or unjustly to the members of the other group.

Since in our world action which is globally institutionalised is a reality, O'Neill's approach shows that a more or less cosmopolitan view of moral standing is contingently appropriate. Due to the assumptions we make about others as soon as we take part in practices in which they play a part moral standing cannot be denied. Examples of such assumptions are that others can trade and negotiate, translate and settle payments, pollute the environment and contribute to its renewal and so on. O'Neill concludes therefore that '[i]f we owe justice to those whose moral standing we acknowledge [by our actions] we will owe it to strangers as well as to neighbours and to distant strangers as well as to those who are relatively near at hand' (O'Neill 1995).

Further considerations

There are two main aproaches to the question of what the moral implications are of the current process of globalisation. Firstly, the theoretical, universal approach which abstracts away from empirical details and seeks to resolve moral questions by strictly moral reasoning. A problem with the universal or strictly cosmopolitan Kantian approach is that it relies on a conception of the person as a moral agent and is in need of an account of the central characteristics of beings which are accorded moral standing. The second, practical, approach avoids that trap and argues instead that since we interact in many ways with people all over the world, it would be incoherent not to accord all human beings in the world moral standing. This means that globalisation and global interdependence are relevant to the claim that the scope of justice is universal in the present world. However, it is not coherent to argue, as Charles Beitz did in 1979 and many others have done more or less implicitly since then, that global interdependence in itself means that we now have global obligations. As Brown and Robinson have objected, interdependence can add to global inequality and does not necessarily bring about a broadening of moral scope in common sense morality. Although this observation may be right there is a possibility that globalisation and global interdependence generate moral obligations to others outside national boundaries even if common-sense morality is not that way inclined. Moral reasoning needs a critical edge and the reliance on common-sense morality leads to inherently conservative outcomes. However, in order to show the existence of moral obligations beyond those recognised in common-sense morality, a separate argument is required since global interdependence cannot provide the grounds for global obligations.

Such an argument is provided by the practical approach to moral standing as proposed by O'Neill. The main advantage of her approach is that cosmopolitan universal principles are defended without having to rely on metaphysical assumptions. This strengthens the argument for a universal scope of justice I make elsewhere (van den Anker, forthcoming) and weakens grounds for arguments that duties across borders are based on humanitarian considerations rather than principles of justice.

However, O'Neill is vulnerable to two reactions. Firstly, the practical approach to global ethics cannot answer the question of what duties we owe based on our common humanity. This is because moral standing relies on people already being recognised as human beings in shared practices (communication, trade, etc.). O'Neill's theory explicitly starts from the question of what we owe others in the present world, rather than the question of what human beings as such owe to each other. O'Neill's more modest approach may help us to move ahead and establish obligations here and now which is helpful in a world where action to reduce poverty and other injustices is urgently needed. Moreover, I do not believe that the contingency O'Neill brings into the debate is a threat to the universality of justice in her theory, since her notion of complex moral assumptions does not require one-to-one contact between all people in the world but a network of intricate causal links which can only exist if we assume moral standing of others involved in this network of interactions. From the perspective of ethical debate, however, it is still interesting to discuss the question of what human beings owe to each other.

Secondly, O'Neill's approach can be questioned on the grounds of whether it provides a model of which duties follow from the recognition of moral standing. An important part of the ethical debate on duties across borders is focused on the strength of those duties. Although it is important that O'Neill argues for duties based on justice rather than on common humanity, a theory of the hierarchy of duties and the relevance of the borders of nation-states needs to be developed. I have suggested elsewhere (van den Anker 1993, 1995) that a valid principle of global justice is impartiality as applied to institutions and not to personal morality. In the same way as individuals can give away (part of) their resources to 'significant others', groups (whether nation-states or not) can institutionalise care and obligations to others over and above the requirements of global principles of justice. However, these arrangements may not interfere with the duties owed to others across borders and those duties must be part of a theory of justice rather than of charity.

Finally, it is important to note that this chapter has dealt with the moral implications of globalisation in a rather abstract and theoretical way. This does not mean to say that specific effects of globalisation, such as increased poverty and the exclusion of certain social groups within Northern and Southern societies, do not affect the understanding of global duties. This chapter aimed to show, however, that these effects need to be theorised in the context of a distinct theory of global justice rather than as part of an argument for duties across borders based on global interdependence.

10

GLOBALISING LIBERALISM?

Morality and legitimacy in a liberal global order

Fiona Robinson

> It seems to me that liberalism imposes extraordinary ethical difficulties on us: to live with contradictions, unresolvable conflicts, and a balancing between public and private imperatives which are neither opposed to nor at one with each other. (Shklar 1984: 249)

It is widely accepted that, in international relations, liberalism has always played second fiddle to realism. While liberal values and practices may flourish within societies, it is argued that structural obstacles to progress, justice and freedom ensure that the international system remains the realm of anarchy. Until very recently, the consensus in international theory seems to have been that 'whereas liberals can claim impressive victories in the realm of domestic politics, the relations among states have proven to be remarkably resistant to liberal reform', and that in contrast to the domestic political realm in many states, 'the international realm in the era of the modern states system has been characterised by a precarious order and the absence of justice' (Smith, R.M. 1996: 201; Dunne 1997: 147).

Recently, however, there appears to have been somewhat of a change. It is argued that the end of the Cold War has brought with it an explicit and renewed commitment to liberalism on a global scale, along with a strengthened belief in the possibilities for achieving reform in the direction of global liberalism. Fukuyama (1992) has proclaimed the 'end of history', based on the argument that the collapse of the Soviet Union demonstrates the demise of any serious ideological challenge to liberalism. Moreover, it has been suggested that liberalism, within the international realm, although limited by the states-system, is of growing importance because of its dominance as a value system against which state forms are legitimised. In addition, the growth, over the last four or five decades, of an increasingly global capitalist economy is currently recognised as a powerful force in international relations, penetrating states, cultures and communities and acting as a 'transmission belt for the normative ideas about the states-system and the nature of statehood' (Williams 1996: 52, 56). Human rights, global democracy and global responsibility are once again on the agendas of Western governments and liberal academics, as the cosmopolitan ideal finds new credibility in a post-Cold War, globalising world.

In response to these developments, moreover, liberalism appears to have gained a new lease of life in international relations theory. From the explicitly normative to the solidly positivist, liberals of very different persuasions are claiming to present a challenge to neo-realist orthodoxy. Fukuyama's triumphant Hegelian liberalism, for example, expresses an explicitly normative, distinctly global liberalism. From a very different yet no less influential perspective, neo-liberal institutionalism, as represented by authors such as Robert Keohane (1984, 1989) and Robert Axelrod (Axelrod and Keohane 1993), has been described as 'the new orthodoxy in a number of key North American schools of international relations' (Dunne 1997: 158). Dominated by US scholars, the 'neo-liberal challenge' is said to respond to the question of whether realism can account meaningfully for the new issues and cleavages that define today's global agenda (Kegley 1995: 6). Neo-liberal institutionalists argue that realism is wrong to discount the possibilities for international cooperation and the capacities of international institutions. They claim that institutions can help states work together and that the prospects for international cooperation are better than realism allows (Keohane, quoted in Grieco 1995: 156). Finally, in addition to these theoretical developments, there is currently a proliferation of 'policy-relevant' research exploring the Clinton administration's foreign policy priority of the 'enlargement' of the democratic community. Charles Kegley and Margaret Hermann, for example, have undertaken research funded by the US Institute of Peace, exploring the question of whether military intervention is an effective instrument for pursuing and achieving pro-liberalisation policies throughout the world (Kegley and Hermann 1998). Similarly, Sean Lynn-Jones, of the Kennedy School at Harvard, has presented an argument explaining why the United States should spread liberal democracy; notably, he argues in favour of the promotion not just of 'electoral democracy', but also of 'liberal values' (Lynn-Jones 1998).

This chapter begins by questioning whether contemporary liberal international theory can provide a satisfactory account of not just if and how liberalism should be 'exported' and ultimately globalised, but on what grounds this 'globalisation' of liberalism can be justified. If, in the post-Cold War era, liberalism is claiming 'global reach' – if liberals are asserting that liberal principles do or ought to inhere not just in already liberal societies, but in non-liberal regions of the world – then the question of what makes a liberal way of life better than a non-liberal one is an important question for liberal theorists in international relations. Attention to this question would involve a recognition that – despite the fact that both the political practice and the theoretical analysis of liberalism have generally been restricted within national borders – liberalism is, and has always been, a political philosophy with universal aspirations.

In an era of globalisation, this fact cannot be ignored. If liberals are seeking to claim that liberal values set standards for the international community, and if liberal states are engaged in promoting liberal values such as human rights throughout the world, then it becomes the task of international theory to explore, and question, the moral basis of these liberal claims. Can liberalism be vindicated simply because of its historical dominance and its current, apparently global, reach? What foundations – transcendental or immanent, metaphysical or political – can be supplied to support the claim that liberal values must apply not only in Western already-liberal societies like 'ours', but indeed throughout the world, for all of humanity?

This project of the search for 'objective' foundations is nothing new to moral and political philosophy; indeed, this quest has preoccupied political theorists for decades. Over the past thirty years – more precisely, since the publication of Rawls's *A Theory of Justice* in 1971 – political theorists have engaged in an assiduous debate regarding the nature of liberal philosophy. Moral and political philosophers have reacted in opposing directions to both the early and the later work of Rawls, to deontological liberalism more generally, and indeed, to the entire tradition of thought which is commonly referred to as the Enlightenment project. In international relations, moreover, questions of the scope of moral inclusion and the source of moral value have recently begun to preoccupy the new 'normative' theorists. While cosmopolitans follow Kantian and rights-based liberal political theories to argue in favour of a universal human community, communitarians reject universalism, maintaining that the source of moral value lies within constitutive communities – normally nation-states – and that, hence, the scope of moral inclusion is limited. But this 'normative theory' appears to have a monopoly on such lines of inquiry. Orthodox neo-liberals, foreign policy experts and even theorists of 'globalisation' – from both international political economy and historical sociological perspectives – still regard this territory as at best marginal; at worst, irrelevant.

The first section of this chapter, therefore, will briefly examine traditional liberal international theory, as well as the current context of the neo-liberal resurgence in international relations theory. The second will explore the contradictions and conflicts that are inherent in the idea of globalising liberalism and, specifically, those which arise from moral and political philosophy. It will be argued that liberal international theorists must be aware that amidst what may seem to be the overwhelming evidence that liberalism has 'won the day' – proving that it is, finally, *the* global ideology with universal relevance – there are deep contradictions within liberalism. The final part of the chapter will argue that in order to explore the morality and legitimacy of liberalism on a global scale, the real focus ought not to be the search for 'foundations', but rather the nature of the social relations of a world increasingly governed by liberal values and institutions. Ultimately, then, this chapter will argue that attempts to 'ground', or to provide some sort of 'objective foundation' for liberalism are flawed. These preoccupations have served to limit and channel the moral debate over liberalism into questions regarding epistemological certainty, and thus to obfuscate the more important questions regarding the ability of liberal societies and, indeed, a liberal world order to prevent harm, reduce suffering and provide the basis for a just and humane world.

I will argue that, if we question the morality and legitimacy of liberalism on a global scale, another option is to eschew the debate over universality in liberal political theory and much normative international theory. We could explore, instead, the historical development of the globalisation of liberalism, and the causes, manifestations and potential solutions to patterns of domination and exclusion in a world dominated by a particular brand of liberal values and institutions. This will involve examining both different aspects and types of liberalism, and the relationship between liberal ideas such as freedom and rights, to the increasingly global dynamics of democratisation and the liberalisation of the world economy. I will argue that liberal international theory must rid itself of complacency and triumphalism and occupy itself instead with an evaluation of the ability of a global liberal order to contribute towards the mitigation of exclusion and suffering in the world today.

Liberal international relations theory

Liberal political thought has clearly played a crucial role in the development of international relations theory. Although liberal thinking on international relations is said to have originated with the various plans for peace articulated by philosophers and theologians from the early sixteenth century onwards (Dunne 1997: 149), the most authoritative statements of early liberal internationalism are usually thought to be found in the work of the Enlightenment philosophers – primarily in the philosophical rationalism of Kant and the moral utilitarianism of Jeremy Bentham. Earlier in the twentieth century, liberal thinking in international relations found a voice in the idealism of the post-war period. Personified in Woodrow Wilson, idealism argued that although war was irrational, peace was not necessarily a natural condition. Rather, it had to be constructed through the creation of international institutions to regulate international anarchy. Later, realists used the failure to sustain such an institution – the League of Nations – as a way of discrediting idealism, and of affirming their own view.

Liberals in international relations – from Kant to Wilson – are thus generally thought to contribute to a view of international relations which emphasises (to a greater or lesser degree) the inherent and essential goodness of human nature and the possibility of progress, embraces the spirit of unfettered commerce and rejects the realist assumption of the inevitability of war. Liberals in international relations argue that the possibilities for peace lie in the restructuring of international society and that collective or multilateral action – especially in the form of international organisation and institutions – is not only possible but desirable. Liberal internationalists, taking their arguments from Kant, believe that the spread of legitimate political orders will eventually bring an end to international conflict. Wars, then, are created by undemocratic governments for their own vested interests. Through their faith in the power of human reason, liberals believe in progress and the perfectibility of the human condition; thus, they are confident that war is a scourge that can be removed utterly from the human experience (Burchill 1996: 29, 31).

Moreover, liberalism has traditionally been seen, in contrast to realism, as the 'moral' approach to international relations. Indeed, it is argued that the liberal tradition in international relations takes 'ethical values and their consequences as the bedrock of its perspective for analyzing how states should and do act'. 'In this vision', it is argued, 'international relations is inherently a domain of moral choice'. As Kegley claims, 'liberalism holds that the choices international actors make should be judged against a moral code, a conception of right and wrong' (Kegley 1995: 296).

> Liberals are moved by deontological imperatives – the requirements of moral duty. They insist on the universalizability of moral principles and the notion that they are accessible through reason. Liberals reject any calculation that resembles 'the end justifies the means'. All moral action must be rooted in calculation that is true to a universalizable moral principle (Rosenthal 1995: 321).

This widespread but misleading assumption begins to highlight the insolubility of the quest for foundations, as well as the Janus-faced nature of liberalism. The emphasis on deontology and universality – both in terms of scope and in terms of the universalisability of moral principles – serves to reinforce the often overstated dichotomy between realism and liberalism, but ignores the fact that there are forms of liberalism which reject universalism on the grounds of either ontology or value advocacy, or both (see Taylor 1995: 181–2).

Liberalism is equated with a strong, universalist, deontological tradition, and liberal international relations theory is taken as 'moral' by definition, standing in opposition to the amoral, or sometimes immoral, claims of realism. But this suggestion that deontological, cosmopolitan liberalism is the only 'moral' position in international relations belies the fact that so-called 'universal' moral principles can often be used to support very particular ends. It also obfuscates the contradictory norms and values that exist within liberalism itself. The conflict between 'self-determination' and 'human rights' is perhaps the most notorious of them all; both notions are supported by distinctly and intrinsically liberal values, and yet in policy as well as philosophical terms they create a seemingly intractable dilemma. Liberalism seems to underwrite both universal and particular moral claims; as Dunne asks, 'how can liberalism be our guide when, from different perspectives, it can support intervention and non-intervention?' (Dunne 1997: 160).

Of course, it could be argued that any version which does not insist on the universalisability of its principles will always be a diluted liberalism. Liberalism as a political philosophy has always claimed universal applicability; it claims universal scope and proposes an account of progress and justice that does not stop at national or other boundaries. Its central normative aspiration – freedom – has always been thought of as a human and not merely a national goal (O'Neill 1988: 705). Thus, while it has been argued that 'historically, international politics has not been hospitable to liberal ideas' (Dunne 1997: 148), it could reasonably be claimed that in fact all liberal ideas are ultimately expressions of an international theory.

This, however, is one of the paradoxes of liberalism, since it is widely accepted that liberalism as a political practice has been limited by the boundaries of sovereign states, and that it is realism not liberalism which has provided the most convincing explanatory theory of international relations. The received view is that Stanley Hoffmann's claim – 'international affairs have been the nemesis of liberalism' (Hoffmann 1981: 400) – is an accurate assessment of the relationship between liberal values and the real world of international relations. It is because this view is widely accepted, moreover, that so-called 'neo-liberal challenge' to realism is perceived as such – a resurgence of liberal theorising given new credibility by the circumstances of globalisation.

Neo-liberalism in an era of globalisation

It is evident that the end of the Cold War and the intensification of processes of globalisation have prompted a proliferation of liberal theorising in international relations. Perhaps the best known of the post-Cold War neo-liberal arguments is Fukuyama's *The End of History and the Last Man* (1992). Fukuyama makes the bold and provocative claim that while there still may be many parts of the world that remain untouched by the liberal 'revolution', it is the liberal idea, more than liberal practice, which is currently emerging victorious. For a very large part of the world, he argues, there is now no ideology with pretensions to universality that is in a position to challenge liberal democracy, and no universal principle of legitimacy other than the sovereignty of the people (Fukuyama 1992: 45). Indeed, he makes the quite remarkable claim that, today, we have trouble imagining a world that is radically better than our own, or a future that is not essentially democratic and capitalist (1992: 46). For Fukuyama, of course, what this demonstrates is the unfolding of the Universal History of mankind in the direction of liberal democracy (1992: 48). He points to the success of democracy in a wide variety of places and among many different peoples to support his claim that

> the principles of liberty and equality on which they are based are not accidents or the results of ethnocentric prejudice, but are in fact *discoveries about the nature of man as man*, whose truth does not diminish but grows more evident as one's point of view becomes more cosmopolitan (1992: 51, emphasis added).

Fukuyama's liberalism is explicitly linked to the globlisation of the capitalist economy and a commitment to a *laissez-faire*, rights-based individualism. It is also expressly tied to the collapse of Communism in Eastern Europe, asserting the lack of any viable alternative to liberal democracy in the global system today: '[t]he countries of Eastern Europe all opted for a return to market economic systems after their democratic revolutions in 1989, even though they differed amongst themselves on the timing and pace of marketisation' (1992: 96). As he argues,

> ... the unfolding of technologically driven economic modernisation creates strong incentives for developed countries to accept the basic terms of the universal capitalist economic culture, by permitting a substantial degree of economic competition and letting prices be determined by market mechanisms. No other path toward full economic modernity has been proven to be viable (1992: 96–7).

Also emerging from the United States is a vast array of literature which argues that promoting liberal democracy in other countries should be a key element of America's global strategy. Although this work tends to refer more to 'democracy' than to liberalism, it is evident that what is being promoted is a particular brand of democracy characterised by liberal conceptions of 'political' and 'economic' freedom. Thus Lynn-Jones (1998: 7–9) explicitly states that '"liberal" and "democracy" often go hand in hand', and that the United States can and should attempt to 'build support for' and 'promote' liberalism. Among the reasons he gives for justifying this promotion are the bonds of common humanity, the universalisability of American values and United States national interest. Lynn-Jones suggests that 'as human beings, Americans should and do feel some obligation to improve the well-being of other human beings. The bonds of common humanity do not stop at the borders of the United States' (1998: 10). Moreover, quoting the Deputy Secretary of State, Lynn-Jones also asserts that '[t]he United States is uniquely and self-consciously a country founded on a set of ideas, and ideals, applicable to people everywhere' (1998: 11). Finally, he concedes that given the 'growing interconnectedness of international relations', the spread of democracy 'will directly advance the national interests of the United States' (Lynn-Jones 1998: 12). Later in the paper, the argument turns to the links between liberal democracies and free markets:

> Democracies are more likely to adopt market economies, so democracies will tend to have more prosperous and open economies. The United States generally will be able to establish mutually beneficial trading relationships with democracies. And democracies provide better climates for American overseas investment, by virtue of their political stability and market economies (Lynn-Jones 1998: 33).

This analysis, like Fukuyama's, portrays liberalism as mutually beneficial for the newly liberalising state that adopts its values and institutions and for those already liberal states with which it interacts. Thus these liberal advocates find themselves in the most agreeable position of being able to advocate measures which are in line with their own interests while at the same time claiming the moral high ground, by asserting that the spread of liberal democracy is about recognising the obligations that Americans have to other human beings beyond their borders. Moreover, by basing their argument loosely around the changes emerging out of 'globalisation', the argument is then portrayed not as normative, and thus value-laden, but simply as a response to empirical conditions, and thus objective and legitimate. This complacency is not only arrogant, but naive. It is a long-standing argument (it lies, for example, behind the rhetoric of international human rights) which has fuelled its own fire with the collapse of the Soviet Union and the accelerated globalisation of the world economy. That the primacy, legitimacy and universality of liberal values should simply be asserted and the moral basis of liberalism should be left unexplored is, I have suggested, unacceptable. The section which follows explores the ways in which we may interrogate the norms and values that lie beneath this globalisation of liberalism.

Triumph or crisis? The debate over foundations and universality

In spite of the confidence of the liberal international relations scholars described above, most political philosophers would accept that today the ideology of liberalism finds itself in a most uncomfortable position, being hailed by some as triumphant and by others as decidedly dead. As Rogers Smith (1996: 241) has argued, assessments regarding the prospects for the future of liberalism in recent years have been 'wildly different'. Far from experiencing a global triumph, it has been argued that liberalism is in fact in the midst of a crisis, due to its close relationship with an increasingly discredited Enlightenment view of the world. 'Contrary to the hopes of liberal internationalists', Dunne (1997: 160) argues, 'the application of reason and science to politics has not brought communities together'.

Nowhere is this crisis more evident than in the work of political philosophers who are engaged in exploring the moral principles, values and foundations of liberalism. While Kantian liberals maintain that liberalism is an inherently universalist political philosophy, that must, by definition, be able to 'travel' beyond the domestic context, and, specifically, beyond the borders of already liberal societies, sceptics – from 'communitarians' to anti-foundationalists – have argued that liberal values emerge out of and thus are embedded in only certain political cultures, and that there can be no moral or political basis for seeking to export them beyond these borders. Onora O'Neill neatly summarises the debate: '[t]he very universality which has traditionally been part of the appeal of liberal thinking is now often cited as evidence of its inadequate and abstract conception of morality and its reliance on conceptions of the human subject that abstract from social and historical context'. Specifically, she cites Rawls's 'political' reading of *A Theory of Justice* which emerged at least partially in response to the book's critics. The implications of this 'modest liberalism', O'Neill (1988: 706–8) argues, is that 'its internationalist commitments (if any) can be defended only to those who are *already liberals* of a certain sort' (italics added).

O'Neill's central point is that the internationalist commitments and implications of liberalism are damaged if they are vindicated by reference to an aspect of the *Sittlichkeit* – or particular, situated morality – of a specific tradition. If liberal principles of justice, she claims, are simply 'our' principles which reflect 'our' traditions and 'our' institutions, any universalist aspirations they might have will be uncomfortably based on intellectual imperialism (O'Neill 1988: 709). What is required (and what O'Neill and other deontological liberals attempt to provide) is a foundation – based on the demands of rationality or some other 'essential' feature of humanity – which can transcend cultural differences.

Rogers Smith also argues that the difficulties that centre on the demands that liberalism cannot meet include, perhaps most famously, problems of justification for liberal principles. Early liberals like Locke, he argues, blended appeals to divine will, rationalistic natural law and human consent in politically palatable but philosophically unstable combinations, leaving the true intellectual and moral foundations of liberalism unclear. Contemporary liberals, following Rawls, have tried to reduce their justificatory burdens by not trying to offer any robust theory of the human good. Rather they defend only minimal conceptions of the good that are sufficient to justify allegiance to liberal theories of justice or right. Thus traditional liberal theorists answer the challenge that liberalism is self-destructive by explaining that liberal principles are deontic principles – principles of right which do not depend on any particular theory of value or any specific conception of the good. They designate regulative principles which specify the terms and constraints under which substantive goods may be promoted and pursued (Gray 1998: 71). In a liberal society, any regulative principles of justice should not themselves presuppose any particular conception of the good but should guarantee an equal freedom to individuals (Seidler 1986: 123). Because of the separation of the right and the good, and the priority of the right over the good, liberalism remains intact in spite of value pluralism. Values reflect substantive understandings of the good and thus not only are but should be plural. Principles of right, however, are universal and foundational; it is only these principles which can mandate or vindicate liberalism and its internationalist commitments.

It is this sleight of hand which has, for centuries, masked the contradictions in liberalism. This is the illusion which allows philosophers and statespersons to defend the universal moral rectitude of the liberal position, while at the same time achieving the goals that are often egoistic and particular. As Rogers Smith explains:

> That move (the separation of the right and the good) has rightly prompted a thundering chorus of criticism that liberal 'neutrality' is misleading. Liberalism narrows the range of permissible conceptions of the good in ways that must be defended not merely as just but also as good (1996: 254).

Thus it would appear that the project of justifying or 'grounding' the universality of liberalism is unsustainable and even fruitless; even these so-called 'deontic', regulative principles of 'right' are heavily laden with thick notions of the good and thus fail the 'test' of generalisability. In response to this apparent problem, anti-foundationalists such as Richard Rorty have, paradoxically, based their liberal theories on the impossibility of finding a universal justification. Rorty is relentless in his attack on deontology and foundationalist reasoning while remaining committed to the importance of spreading 'our' liberal values; he readily admits to a kind of ethnocentrism in which a specific group – 'we twentieth-century liberals' – is dedicated to enlarging itself, to creating an ever larger and more variegated *ethnos* (Rorty 1989: 196–8). This liberal ironist stance allows Rorty to advocate the most traditional of liberal values – such as individual human rights, for example – while rejecting the claim that we must search for well-grounded theoretical answers to questions regarding 'essence', 'nature' and 'foundation'.

Rorty's postmodern liberal ironist, then, would argue that any universalist convictions that were ever held by liberals must now be abandoned. Instead of pressing theorists to justify their global liberalism with foundational principles which can guarantee the epistemological status of liberalism's claims to truth and justice, these arguments deny that any such foundations exist, and thus bring the entire project of the 'liberalisation' of the global order into question. But these arguments, like their universalist counterparts, are themselves preoccupied with the question of foundations, and hence are guilty of ignoring the more vital moral questions surrounding inequality and exclusion in a liberal world order.

Thus, while the search for foundations could certainly propel much liberal international relations theory beyond its narrow methodological and epistemological frontiers, there are, as has been suggested above, some dangers associated with the philosophical debate over foundations. The controversy over whether liberalism's claim to universal validity can be justified is one which centres on epistemological certainty – on whether liberal values have, over any other values, particular claims to the status of truth. Thus the focus in not on the values themselves but on whether or not and to whom they may be justified. The result is, ironically, a debate in political philosophy which exists at a metatheoretical level and which, to put it bluntly, refuses to get its hands dirty. Ultimately, these debates are immersed in an insoluble theoretical dilemma surrounding the existence of value pluralism and the quest for universalisable values. What they ignore are the more fundamental questions surrounding the circumstances of liberalism's rise to its position of hegemony, and the contradictions which threaten to unseat liberalism's claims to provide and preserve freedom, equality and justice.

Interrogating global liberalism

So far I have argued that much recent liberal international relations theory takes for granted not only that liberalism is the only viable basis for political and economic organisation today, but also that its values are increasingly being spread across the global system and that this process is a good thing. In orthodox liberal international relations theory, the 'morality' of liberalism is assumed and questions surrounding the normative basis of liberalism are rarely explored. By contrast, within the traditions of analytical political philosophy and (increasingly) in the new normative theory in international relations, there is a deep concern to provide (or, indeed, to deny the possibility of) objective foundations which can vindicate the neutrality and universality of liberal principles, thus proving their applicability beyond the borders of already liberal societies.

I have argued that, although the unquestioning acceptance of liberalism's global relevance by much contemporary international relations theory must be challenged, the search for foundations is unlikely to be a fruitful way of confronting this complacency. What must be questioned, instead, is liberalism itself, and its ability to achieve basic levels of well-being for the world and its inhabitants. How is it that liberalism comes to claim, at the end of the twentieth century, global reach? What is the relationship between political liberalism and democracy, including the liberal conceptions of freedom and justice, and the workings of the global capitalist economy? What substantive moral goods are being advocated by liberals, and what kind of social relations – personal, political and economic – can we expect, and should we seek to achieve, in a liberal global order?

We might begin such an analysis from the rather gloomy yet uncontestable observation that many contemporary manifestations of liberal values leave much to be desired for *most* of the world's peoples. Although we may inhabit a world with fewer dictators, it remains plagued by gender inequality, racism and the oppression of cultural minorities, as well as 'vicious environmental abuse' caused by market systems impelled by productivity (Rogers Smith 1996: 244). Perhaps most prodigious, however – insofar as it can only be said to be increasing – is the gap between rich and poor. As Wallerstein (1995: 161) has recently argued: 'The self-contradiction of liberal ideology is total. If all humans have equal rights, and all peoples have equal rights, we cannot maintain the kind of inegalitarian system that the capitalist world-economy has always been and always will be.' However, it is precisely this system – the capitalist world economy – that many liberal international relations theorists regard as the context in which freedom, equality and individual rights can be guaranteed. How is it, then, that a system that perpetuates such vast inequalities can be almost universally upheld for its moral rectitude?

As I have already argued, liberalism's pretence of neutrality allows it both to transcend the variability of time and place, and to stand apart from, and above, any particular conception of the good. This appearance of universality masks the extent to which liberal values can be used to support and underwrite the interests of those in power. Moreover, through its focus on individual rights and formal equality, liberalism claims a privileged moral position, again masking the extent to which those same 'rights' can lead to inequality and social exclusion. Liberals must recognise, and confront, the serious potential for illiberality that is inherent in liberalism. As Walzer (1996: 24) explains:

> I think that libertarianism is the name we use for a liberalism set loose from its own negativity. In this version of liberal politics and society, individual autonomy, unlimited in its scope, gives rise to a pattern of domination: the strong over the weak, the rich over the poor. Since such a pattern, once established, opens the way for cruelty and oppression, it is certain to produce, as a characteristic recoil, the liberalism of fear.

Seen from this perspective, there is considerably less room from which to claim the moral high ground. Far from proclaiming that liberalism has all the answers to how to achieve global peace and prosperity, this analysis demonstrates that liberalism can undermine itself and give rise to cruelty and fear. This suggests that liberals must not be complacent but critical of their own values. Indeed, the contradiction set out by Wallerstein – between 'individual rights' and the inequalities of global capitalism – might provide a good starting point for international theorists to begin an interrogation of the legitimacy, and the moral basis, of global liberalism.

A similar enquiry can be conducted into the relationship between liberalism and democracy in the modern era. Benjamin Barber (1989: 57) has argued that the doctrine of consent, the historical basis for the legitimacy of Western liberal-democratic political forms, has permitted liberal ideas to take precedence over democratic ideas. Through the idea of consent – as in social contract theory, for example – politics becomes purely defensive; the model political act, he argues, is resistance to encroachment on a private sphere defined by the autonomous and solitary person (Barber 1989: 59). On this view, liberalism is not regarded as fundamentally linked to democracy; on the contrary, the values of liberalism may be seen as oppressors of the true spirit of democracy and, ironically, of liberty as well:

> Indeed, it is arguable that the forces that created the greatest pressures on the liberty of individuals in the twentieth century are, at least in part, the consequences of deracination, social anarchy, and rampant individualism – the consequence not of too much democracy and too little liberalism but of too little democracy and too much liberalism (Barber 1989: 55).

Without participation, public-mindedness, public discourse and action, the primary substantive moral value of liberalism – liberty – is rendered impotent:

> Liberty rings hollow to women and men whose lives lack purpose and meaning: it is then only the right to do everything in a world where one has no idea of what to do. In emancipating us from authority, liberalism separated us from one another (Barber 1989: 66).

Here we have a powerful rebuttal of the claim that liberalism and democracy 'go hand in hand'. Although, as Barber argues (1989: 62), liberalism established an alliance with democracy through the idea of consent, the result of this alliance is the dogmatic justification of the priority of liberty, and of the liberty of the abstract individual over the needs of community-created citizens. Such historical analyses should impel advocates of global liberalism to rethink their claim that the 'first way in which the spread of democracy enhances the lives of those who live in democracies is by promoting individual liberty ... including freedom to own private property' (Lynn-Jones 1998: 12). This derivative view of the importance of democracy – i.e., reducing its importance to the individual liberty, and the right to private property it allows – belittles the significance of participation and belonging in the lives of peoples. Moreover, when it is asserted that there 'appears to be a universal demand for liberty among human beings', it is important that we question the root of those demands, and the extent to which protests against dictatorial rule are motivated not just by the 'demand for liberty' but also by the desperate rejection of the material inequality resulting from the tyranny of oppressive regimes; most importantly, however, we should eschew the assumption that once liberty – of a peculiarly liberal kind – is achieved, well-being will follow.

Conclusion

In this chapter, I have argued that the complacent, triumphalist liberalism which has emerged since the end of the Cold War must be confronted. Liberal international theory must engage with questions more challenging than those which require us to count up numbers of 'elected' governments and to construct 'league tables' of human rights performance. However, I have also argued that a concern to interrogate the moral basis of liberalism on a global scale should not be preoccupied with the insoluble theoretical problem of 'foundations'. Rather a liberal theory of international relations must confront the moral contradictions inherent in much liberal theory. It must explore the relationship between liberal values, such as human rights, and the practices and relations of global capitalism, as well as the links between liberalism and democracy. While interrogating liberalism may indeed involve asking to what extent its values and institutions can be universally applied, we must pose this question, not through attention to abstract principles and justifications, but through an historical and situated analysis of the political, economic, social and personal relations which inhere in an increasingly liberal world order.

Part V

AGENCY AND GLOBALITY

11

GLOBALITY AS A REVOLUTIONARY TRANSFORMATION

Martin Shaw

This chapter argues that we must see global change as constituted by deep transformations of state relations and forms, and that we therefore must be concerned first with its political *meaning* rather than with the political *consequences* of technological, economic or cultural processes. I argue further that the global transformation can be seen as revolutionary in a serious political sense. In order to develop these arguments, I first examine the meaning of 'global' change and the adequacy of the concepts and explanations current in the debate, and second ask what happens to our understanding of 'global' processes if we try to bring an historical understanding of war and revolution systematically into the argument.

The meaning of global change

Many contributors to this book follow the broad consensus that globalisation concerns, as Anthony Giddens (1990) puts it, 'the intensification of worldwide social relations which link distant localities in such a way that local happenings are shaped by events occurring many miles away and vice versa'. However, if globalisation is identified as such an intensification of the long-established tendencies towards worldwide linkages in social relations, it is not implausible to argue (as Nicholson does in Chapter 2) that although important, it does not involve a fundamental change.

According to other contributors, however, notably Jan Aart Scholte, the consequences of globalisation are far more substantial shifts in world realities. In this chapter I agree with him that 'global' changes are fundamental, but I analyse them in terms which make 'globalisation' rather more problematic. If it involves wide-ranging and deep-seated changes, then it is important to ask what 'global' means. It is surprising how little attention is given to the concept. Even in academic circles, the term is often used loosely, as interchangeable not only with 'world' but even with 'international' – hence the often unremarked slippage between 'international' and 'global' political economy.

In this book, as in most globalisation literature, the word global has been used more precisely, in clear distinction to international, with the complexity of relations between global and international recognised as a central issue. But even here the meaning of global is confined, including by some contributors, to something like 'worldwide'. Global has therefore a primarily spatial reference, to the world as a whole and social processes which intensify worldwide linkages.

Although the term globalisation has been used only for about three decades, the word global has a long usage in this kind of sense. It is of course an extension of the oldest reference, which lies at the root of the word, meaning connected to the physical sphere of the Earth. This has gained enhanced meaning and currency in environmental discourse, in which global means belonging to the world as a whole in the sense of its common natural environment. Global in this sense is sometimes equivalent to 'planetary': global concern, for example, may aim to 'protect' nature even in opposition to social needs.

The planetary, like the worldwide and supraterritorial aspects, is clearly an intrinsic part of the meaning of global at the beginning of the twenty-first century. However, its meaning is being – and should be – extended still further in contemporary discourse. What these extant meanings indicate are the worldwide spatial dimensions and physical context of contemporary human society. The spatial meaning of global was refined in Chapter 1 to refer to 'supraterritorial' as opposed to territorially based spatial relations; thus globality refers to a transformation of the spatial content of social relations. I contend, however, that the emergent meaning of the global goes beyond this, to concern the social meaning of these spatially transformed relations. Global now refers, maximally, to the self-consciously common framework of human society worldwide. In this sense, global has a fully social as well as spatial and environmental meaning.

This idea of global as referring to the commonality of worldwide human society is not entirely new. It has long been anticipated by the universalist claims of both religious and secular world-views. It is also implicit, to some degree, in both the planetary concept of the global as the common natural environment of humankind, and in the idea of intensified relations through worldwide spatial connectedness. In my 1994 book I argued that the latter was creating the factual basis or 'system integration' of a 'global society'. I now put this more strongly: there is, in addition to such integration, a strongly emerging practical consciousness of worldwide human commonality. Within the proliferating particularist ideologies of our time there is also a powerful recognition of a common framework of values and the need for institutions which embody this.

How far this actually creates the possibility of worldwide 'social integration' (for the distinction of system and social integration, see Shaw 1994a, Chapter 1) is another question. Societies are not the harmonious, value-unified 'social systems' dreamed up by functionalist sociologists. The emergent global society is highly segmented, stratified and conflict-ridden, its cohesion manifestly weak – in a different order from tensions in the vastly more restricted national and other 'societies' which it contains. Extending global social cohesion depends on the practical relations between global values and institutions and the interests and organisation of particular social groups. But despite the very powerful limitations on global cohesion, the growing consciousness of worldwide human commonality relativises all particularist nationalisms and other ideologies. Even Islam, often seen as the ultimate obstacle to Western-centred globality, exists in tension with this framework.

In this sense, we can understand that the global involves far more than most analyses of globalisation suggest. Indeed the discussion of global change in terms of globalisation can itself be regarded as too restrictive. The term globalisation carries with it the connotations of the inexorable, mechanical spread of market relations. What it does not convey is the role of conscious global-oriented action, even in the very spread of the market, let alone in all the other manifestations of global change.

Because of these limitations of the idea of globalisation, there has been discussion instead of 'globality' (Albrow 1996). While this could be taken as implying that there is a 'finished' global world, it is more helpfully understood as referring to the emergent and contradictory condition of global-ness. The point is not the degree of completeness but the distinct quality of a global world. Globality depends on the more mechanical interconnectedness indicated by globalisation analysis, but is far more than this. The relation between the two can be specified thus: globalisation is a necessary but not a sufficient condition for globality.

The fuller meaning of global and globality suggests that we understand the process of global change as involving more than globalisation, as this is generally understood. We need to ask whether there is indeed a deep change, of major historic significance, in our time? Is the current transition no more than the rapid extension of the process of commodification, as some Marxist and radical critics of globalisation contend? If there is something more, in what does that consist? Of what is the emergence of globality the development? To what kinds of historical processes does it respond?

The answer proposed here (developed more fully in Shaw, forthcoming), is that the historical process which globality represents is centred not in economic or cultural but in political changes. It follows that we should be concerned not so much with the political consequences as with the core political meaning of global change. In the remainder of this chapter I attempt to put some historical flesh on my argument.

Globality in the perspective of a century of war and revolution

To the historically minded scholar it must seem curious that global change should be seen as primarily economic and cultural, with the political and military as reactive or epiphenomenal. We might find a precedent for globalisation in the industrial revolution – a change of technical, economic and social organisation so fundamental as to be called 'revolutionary'. But while technical and economic change in the modern era involves, just as Marx and Engels (1998) argued in a much earlier period, the constant 'revolutionisation' of the means and social relations of production, the idea of revolution has retained its most precise meaning in the idea of social and political upheaval.

Indeed, fundamental economic and social change has always had its concomitant in social and political revolution. The period of industrial 'revolution' in the West was framed by the French revolution of 1789 and the Russian of 1917, with the 'age of revolution' (Hobsbawm 1968) intervening. If globalisation is a fundamental change, then it seems plausible that there will be correspondingly important political events to which it is related – as both cause and effect. A major part of our problems in grasping globality are to do with the shallowness of the historical understanding employed.

This lack of historical depth is evident in many of the concepts of contemporary change which have dominated the social sciences in recent decades. The idea of postmodernity crystallised a diffuse sense of movement beyond the classic categories of modern social life. This idea was influential first in literary and cultural fields: it was generally unrooted in a coherent, broad-based historical conception. Indeed a central point of postmodern writing was often the very impossibility of such a conception. (Although Anderson (1998) argues that the idea of postmodernity was most coherently elaborated by Frederic Jameson in work which was situated in the Marxist tradition, this has not been the context of most self-consciously postmodernist writing.) These ideas became most influential in the 1980s, the decade during which a decisive world political change was maturing but had not yet taken shape. Postmodernism can thus be seen as a broad cultural intimation of historic change, rather than an understanding of it.

When the moment of decisive political change arrived, in the crisis and dissolution of the Soviet bloc in 1989–91 and its many ramifications, a new discourse of a 'post-Cold War' world emerged. Widely developed in the early 1990s, this concept identified a little more precisely what was being transcended – the Cold War involved quite a tangible set of relations – but the 'post-' tag gave away its relative incoherence. Although there was agreement about some of the specific trends involved (e.g., growing international cooperation on the one hand, state-fragmentation on the other), there was little consensus on the overall meaning of what was replacing the Cold War world order. The idea of a simple triumph of Western liberalism was widely contested.

Globalisation discourse, which probably attained its maximum influence in the mid-1990s, appeared – unlike these various 'post-' ideas – to have positive content, and to indicate a definite change of direction. It had a seemingly more coherent centre, the 'global' – but as we have seen there was no clear content to this notion. Globalisation ideas came into their own in the middle of the decade, as the dust appeared to be settling from the upheavals of 1989–91. In proclaiming increasingly supraterritorial, technologically led worldwide economic and cultural integration, globalisation discourse often nodded in passing to the end of the Cold War. It did not come, however, with a coherent historical understanding of the links between the economic and cultural changes which it highlighted and the military and political upheavals of our times.

At the end of the 1990s, as the linked financial and political crises of Asia and Russia have been followed by a major war (Kosova), the limits of all three narratives of the contemporary historical transition have become increasingly clear. The transition involved major political and military changes – to which the idea of the end of the Cold War hardly did justice – which were closely bound up with economic and cultural change. An overall historical perspective which linked these changes and explained the development of globality in the broader sense was badly needed.

Inevitably, achieving such a perspective involves tying the changes of the final quarter of the twentieth century back into an understanding of the century, and modern history, as a whole. We need to do this, however, not in the spirit of global-sceptics, trying to show how much old categories still apply, but in order to define precisely which important features of the modern world have been changing, how far and why. In an essay of this kind, it is possible to do no more than indicate the broad thrust of an alternative account of global transformation. However I propose that globality is, in a serious sense, a revolutionary change, centred on fundamental political transformations.

Few really doubt that the defining moments of change in modern history have been wars and revolutions. Although the narratives of contemporary change which I have discussed have begun to suggest more recent turning points, 1945 remains the benchmark of what is still called the 'post-war' era. As a glance at popular culture as much as political debate will tell us, we are still settling the accounts of the war of 1939–45 – not to mention the Great War and the Revolution of 1917. It seems curious *not* to ask how contemporary global change relates to these kinds of upheaval.

The argument here is that war has been the fulcrum of the emerging global consciousness (in the sense of commonality which I have defined) of the twentieth century. It is often suggested, of course, that nations have a special hold on collective versions of memory, which larger communities lack; certainly wars have been profoundly national experiences. But it is also clear that the world wars of the twentieth century have been common experiences – however much their effects have differed among nations and groups – and the naming of them as 'world' wars recognises their fundamental role in human history as well as their geographically worldwide scope.

The recognition of worldwide human commonality is rooted in the disastrous effects of human division in the world wars. While the most profoundly shocking of these effects belong partly to particular communities – so that the Holocaust can be seen as a Jewish experience and even be appropriated by Israeli nationalism – they are also widely recognised as symbols of our common experience of human cruelty, and the hope that survival and resistance generate are common inspirations for humankind.

So in fundamental cultural senses, a common experience of war is a foundation of globality. This is arguably a far more powerful and durable foundation than those lowest common denominators of globalisation – the dross of worldwide commerce such as Coca Cola and McDonald's – which have been emphasised by too many commentators. But the growing commonality of human history, in which the world wars are key events, is not simply a cultural acquisition. World wars have been levers for powerful changes in the social relations surrounding state power, leading to immense political upheavals. Globality is more than a matter of culture in general or even political culture; it is a matter of practice, institutions and changing structures of social power.

Global change was not a mechanical result of war, but the outcome of changed consciousness and practice at many levels in the changed relations of power which war produced. Among political elites, a key foundation for contemporary globality was the recognition across Western Europe and Japan, especially in defeated states but also among semi-bankrupt victors, that autonomous nationalism of the kind which had brought states to total war was no longer viable. 'National' states and identities were revived after 1945, but no longer based in really independent centres of power with the potential for war against each other. They were no longer classic monopolists of violence in Max Weber's sense, but junior partners of an emerging American hegemony. In the foundation of the United Nations, there was an aspiration among elites – reflecting a powerful sense among the people – for the worldwide peaceful cooperation of states.

The road to global consciousness among state elites, opened in 1945, has hardly been an easy one. The Cold War quickly subsumed old national rivalries into a new worldwide ideological contest, in which larger hopes for the United Nations were stillborn. An overarching military rivalry threatened not only the populations of the rival alliances but the survival of humanity, maybe even of the planet. The threat of nuclear war was, however, another major stimulus to emerging global consciousness and the containment of military rivalries between major powers. As it became virtually inconceivable that a nuclear war could be fought successfully, superpower rivalry also spawned latent cooperation. Eventually, in the dissolution of the Cold War, the elites of the two former blocs recognised that their states would no longer fight each other.

From 1945 onwards, moreover, the growing infrastructure of globality was not simply an elite matter, but a result of popular movements and struggles. The most manifestly 'revolutionary' movements of the world war and post-war period were the militarised Communist-led national movements in China, Vietnam, Korea, Yugoslavia and elsewhere. Although these movements were all successful in gaining power, in the longer term the state institutions they established – most of which became opposed not only to the dominant West but also to the Soviet bloc – were failures. The most nationalist of all routes from 1945 was an historic dead-end.

More important transformative movements, with more lasting legacies, were actually the democratic reform trends within the West itself, the anti-colonial movements in what became known as the Third World and, of course, the democratic revolutions against the Soviet bloc. The convergence of these worldwide popular trends – contradicting the ideological construction of First, Second and Third worlds – was manifest in the student-coordinated movements of 1968 which, although now mostly neglected, were actually the harbinger of many democratic, anti-Cold War impulses in the period leading to 1989.

All these broad kinds of movement were more congruent with the dominant Western state-bloc than its Soviet rival, but they also came up against its limitations: the limited, formal character of democracy even in the most parliamentary states; the West's readiness to sacrifice democracy to anti-Communism, notably in its support for authoritarian regimes worldwide; and its inability to offer real support to democratic movements within the Soviet bloc. Popular movements were of crucial importance in consolidating democracy as the most legitimate political model not only throughout the West – where it was far from universal – but in some at least of the post-colonial world, and among large sections of the population in the Soviet bloc itself. The alternatives – the one-party regimes which flourished in many African states as well as in the Soviet-controlled region, the authoritarianism and military dictatorship which the West widely supported – all lost legitimacy because of courageous democratic movements.

Taken together, these elite and popular movements contributed to a fundamental transition in political power which can be seen in retrospect as pre-global, laying some of the foundations for contemporary globality. A fundamental structural transformation was accomplished in the changes of the 1940s. The abolition of war between the major centres of the expanded West – it was quite a new conception of the West which included Japan as well as Western Europe and North America – went a long way towards removing the core function of the nation-state. Long before globalisation was thought of, Western states were no longer nation-states in the classic sense. Interdependence was the result first of war, not commerce, although the latter reinforced it.

Within the West, therefore, national units were subsumed in an increasingly integrated Western conglomerate of state power. The paradox of this conglomerate was that while core state functions – war-making, law, economic management – were effectively shared in various but generally increasing degrees, political authority remained organised primarily in national, and only secondarily in international terms. National forms remained dominant even while the content of autonomous national power drained away. The consolidation of democracy as the common political form of the West was the consolidation of national democracies. American hegemony raised, moreover, a single nation-state to a unique position within the international framework of Western power.

The global significance of these changes was limited, of course, by more than national and international forms within which they were cast. Indeed the 1940s transition remained decidedly pre-global because it resulted in the state-bloc as the new form of state and the bloc-system as the dominant set of power relations, not merely between states but also between state and society. The bloc system was doubly asymmetric, in the balance of power between blocs (the West was always much stronger in most senses than the Soviet bloc) and also in their internal structures (in the West, unlike the East, these involved genuinely cooperative elements of both inter-state and state-society relations). For both these reasons, the Western bloc proved the foundation for the new global order, while the Soviet bloc disintegrated both internationally and socially in its terminal crisis of the late 1980s.

This conception of global transition is therefore the opposite of the conventional view that economic, technological and cultural changes undermined the nation-state. On the contrary, state relations and forms had already moved beyond the classic national framework after the Second World War. The world order based on competing blocs, centred on a dominant Western bloc, was the political structure which made possible all the economic, technological and cultural changes which are now held to constitute globalisation. Of course these other changes also contributed in many ways to the global transition of our times (and none of this polemic should be read as denying their significance). But the key to the end-of-the-twentieth-century global change is precisely a new set of political changes which have moved us on still further. These, I contend, are both sufficiently radical in structural terms and consciously based in large-scale social upheavals as to constitute a global revolution.

Character and elements of the unfinished global revolution

The global revolution, in the sense used here, is not therefore a fundamental transformation of socio-economic relations – the overwhelmingly capitalist character of which has been confirmed and even in some ways intensified by it. It is not a social revolution as such, although like any deep political change it has manifold social causes, effects and significance (and these are not as simply or uniformly negative as many radical critics believe). The global revolution is above all, however, a fundamental transformation of political relations and forms, which extends and in some ways completes the 'pre-global' revolution of the 1940s. The new upheaval is itself profoundly incomplete, however, at the turn of the twenty-first century and for this reason I prefer to describe it as the *unfinished* global revolution.

Since this concept of global change is radically different from most others, including those of other writers in this book, I will list the most important components of the revolutionary global change of our times.

1. *The abolition of war between the major centres of state power.* The end of the Cold War between the Western and Soviet blocs has extended the process begun in the results of the Second World War. Where that war abolished war among the major North American and West European states and Japan, the outcome of the Cold War has largely removed any possibility of war between the West and the Russian Federation, the main successor state of the Soviet bloc.

   Certainly, this abolition of war between major states remains fundamentally incomplete. This is not only because political instability in Russia makes it impossible to exclude the emergence of an aggressive nationalist regime there. More broadly it is because even more than Russia, other major states (China, India and Pakistan) as well as smaller ones (Iran and Iraq) remain weakly integrated with the dominant Western system of power. However the potential for war is probably less between these states and the West than among themselves, and very considerably less than the potential for war between smaller non-Western states and between such states and groups within society.

   All this suggests a process in which war is squeezed out of central inter-state relations, although it remains a fundamental problem of state and society in many non-Western zones, and (as the Gulf and Kosova suggest) in relations of Western and non-Western states.
2. *The emergence of a single, more or less legitimate world centre of state power, the basis for a 'global state'.* With the end of the Soviet bloc, the Western state conglomerate has become the undisputed, although not unchallenged, centre of power, which it increasingly exercises worldwide. This broadly legitimate conglomerate of state power with worldwide ramifications has come to function as what I have called a 'global state' (Shaw 1997). This Western, increasingly global state represents far more than United States power, even if it remains strongly centred on it.

   The dominant conglomerate exercises power within a global framework of legitimate international state institutions, centred on the United Nations and the other global organisations linked to it, but also including a wide range of less inclusive institutions developed from those of the Cold War West. Some, like the International Monetary Fund and World Trade Organisation, have worldwide remits; others including the still-crucial military alliance, the North Atlantic Treaty Organisation, have regional scope (although this is sometimes called pan-regional because of a mistaken essentialism in which regions are assumed to be based on 'natural' geographical continents). However, the legitimacy of many international institutions remains weak even among state elites, let alone in society at large, and they are notoriously ineffective.

This 'global' state depends very much on the inherited infrastructure of national-and-international forms (so that, as Scholte argues, global supra-territoriality coexists with transformations of territorial relations). However, one particular development, that of the European Community – now Union – clearly involves a deep as well as extensive modification of traditional political forms, to produce what is juridically as well as in practice a novel composite form of national-cum-regional polity in western, central and southern Europe. The European Union is a special case, but a case nonetheless of the growing integration of state forms as well as of power relations within the West and worldwide. There are many less clear-cut ways in which this integration is developing across a wider range of states, including the growing harmonisation of law in all sorts of areas from commerce, transportation and communications to medicine (Wiener 1999), and the developing structures of cooperation between courts and police forces. In these ways, the key law and law-enforcement functions of states are being globalised.

Central to the integration of state power worldwide is the regulation of what is increasingly recognised as a global economy. At the same time as individual nation-states become consciously 'competition' states (Cerny 1990), promoting national economies within world markets, they are also forced to develop new ways of collectively managing these markets, and the world economy, so as to avoid worldwide recession and slump. Institutions like the Group of 7 major Western states, developed during the Cold War, are increasingly pressured to adapt not only their membership (now G8, including Russia), but their role, to respond to worldwide threats of economic instability, although it remains very unclear how effectively they will be able to achieve this.

3. *The worldwide extension of democracy as a normal model of political development, together with a fundamental deepening and broadening of democratic concepts.* The earlier period saw the spread of democracy within or on the immediate margins of the West (e.g. southern Europe), as well as in parts of the post-colonial world (e.g. India). Democratisation in the current transition has by no means been confined to the former Soviet bloc. On the contrary, the new trend was widely evident in Latin America in the 1980s and spread in the 1990s to large parts of Asia and Africa, as well as east-central Europe, Russia and other Soviet successor states. Democratisation has hardly been unproblematic or unchallenged, but even ex-Communist and other authoritarian-inclined elites increasingly find it

necessary to clothe themselves in democratic forms. The scope of many freedoms has been substantially extended even if they are still heavily restricted by would-be democratic as well as openly authoritarian states.

The limitations of formal democracy (confined to electoral processes and representative institutions) and the importance of embedding democracy in a wide range of practices (international law, human rights) are increasingly widely understood, together with a recognition of the importance of non-state institutions (increasingly understood as involving a distinct sphere of civil society which also needs to be developed worldwide).

4. *The increasing consolidation of a more or less universally accepted framework of global norms and institutions.* The United Nations has become much more than it could ever be during the Cold War, a globally accepted framework of authority. The values on which the United Nations system is based, although sometimes derided as purely 'Western' values, in fact have a deep resonance in society across the world, and are appealed to by individuals and social groups of many kinds. Both the values themselves and the idea of global institutions have become increasingly embedded in social consciousness and practice, even if the actual institutions are often seen as highly compromised and ineffective.

Thus the dominant Western states, despite continuing opposition in powerful quarters in the United States, generally accept the need for United Nations legitimation for their actions. Their reluctant partners among the other major states (Russia, China, etc.) may see international organisation as a framework for constraining Western power, but they also pay at least lip service to the global democratic norms which it increasingly represents. Even oppositional, 'rogue' states like Iraq accept United Nations authority in principle, as much as they may try to subvert it. Non-governmental organisations, social movements, oppressed minorities and victims of injustice worldwide, all look to the United Nations framework of legitimate institutions for support and action. Of course, the United Nations remains weakly funded and supported by states, often denied the necessary means to function effectively, and internally often semi-paralysed. It often fails to deliver, and year-on-year its failures often seem more substantial than its successes.

The significance of global norms and institutions since 1989 has also been reflected in the growing importance of international law. Symbolically important developments include the creation of war crimes tribunals for Yugoslavia and Rwanda, which have extended the principle (established at the Nuremberg trials) that state leaders can be held liable in international law for genocide, war crimes and crimes against humanity. The creation of a permanent International Criminal Court, although weakened by American opposition to its having real powers, will consolidate this development. International agreements between states mean that national law, too, may be used to apprehend those who have committed crimes against humanity across the world – the 1998 arrest of the former Chilean dictator, Augusto Pinochet, in London at the behest of a Spanish court, provided a glimpse of what may develop.

Taking these four sets of developments together, I believe that we are in the middle of a major transformation of political order on a world scale. In conventional terms, this includes transformations both of international order and relations between states and societies. In reality it is even more than this: it is a recasting of the very categories of 'international system', 'state' and 'society'. An international system in the core of which war has been more or less abolished is hardly an international system in the sense that this has been known and understood for the last three hundred years. National states which are parts of a Western conglomerate and global order are hardly classic nation-states. Societies are hardly national in the classically discrete sense when not only are they as integrated and cross-cutting in all sorts of ways (as Scholte shows), but they are also defined within global norms and structures of authority. Some still dispute the significance of the changes: for realists, state-blocs are still comprised of states; for Marxists, super-imperialism is still imperialism. For fundamentalists in both schools, if the American nation-state is still 'hegemonic' among other such entities, then *plus ça change c'est la même chose*. Others might acknowledge some of the changes but dispute the idea that overall they can be considered 'revolutionary'.

Revolutionary agency in global transformation

Certainly the idea of revolution is problematic. Classically, revolutions were social and political upheavals which took place, even if in international waves of revolution (1789, 1848, 1917–19, 1944–5, 1968), within nation-states. Even those who have stressed the international context (e.g. Skocpol 1979) have accepted the framework of international system, nation-state and social forces. However, the concept of revolution in this classic context is no longer viable, just as these categories themselves have been transformed. And yet the changes which are overthrowing these very categories are surely quite as, indeed more, profound than any changes within them. The four major changes which we have defined, if they overcome the nation-state and international system as we have known them, are surely *prima facie* revolutionary.

However, revolution has classically meant not just deep structural transformation, but popular self-activity as the agent of change. Some sceptics, while accepting that important changes in states and international systems are taking place, deny a major popular role – let alone a progressive one – in these changes. For Halliday (1999), for example, the 'revolutions' of 1989 were not revolutions, since they moved state and society from socialist forms, however deformed, back into the dominant world order of liberal-democratic capitalism. For Robinson (1996), democratisation is not so much a popular movement as the outcome of the 'promotion of polyarchy' from above, especially in United States foreign policy.

There are, of course, important elements of truth in these positions. The global revolution, as I argued above, far from overcoming capitalism, partially reinforces it. But there are gains as well as losses for society in the transition from the Soviet system – not only in political freedom, or in consumer choice (so far mainly for some elites, and in some countries much more than others), but also in the possibilities of self-organisation by workers and other subordinate social groups which democratisation opens up. Similarly, it is clearly correct to emphasise how Western elites – especially the United States – have shifted from backing authoritarian anti-Communist regimes in the non-Western world, to supporting formally democratic regimes which produce pro-Western leaders. According to the concept of American manipulation of democratisation – ironically popular among those influenced by Marxism – the changes of our time are the product of elite policy adjustments.

But this argument begs the question of what has caused Western policies to change – are Western policy shifts really the principal, independent cause of democratisation? This view ignores the long and often heroic history of democratic revolution since 1945. Communism and the Soviet bloc did not collapse simply because of their economic failures, their defeat by Reagan in the Second Cold War or Gorbachev's reform movement. After the Red Army brought Soviet rule to eastern and central Europe after 1945, popular uprisings challenged it continuously, from East Germany in 1953 to Hungary and Poland in 1956, the Czechoslovak reform movement of 1968 and the Solidarity movement in Poland in 1989–91, not to mention many lesser or more localised events. The constant pressure and threat of such movements denied the Soviet-bloc order legitimacy and put elites permanently on the defensive against their citizens.

The democratic transitions of 1989–91 in the Communist states were centred on popular uprisings. The 1989 revolutions in East Germany, Czechoslovakia and Romania were not simply street theatre accompanying inevitable elite changes. Without these movements, and less dramatic but still important popular pressure elsewhere, the Soviet bloc might have been reformed rather than overthrown. Democratic change might have been far less complete, as indeed it has been in Russia itself where the popular democratic movement was weaker and more sidelined by conflicts between various elements of the old elites. The defeat of democratic movements might have consolidated, like the Tiananmen Square events in China, a market-oriented continuation of Communist authoritarianism, rather than its removal.

The dialectics between popular movements and local elites can be seen in a variety of forms in worldwide democratisation. Clearly in some cases elites have managed change so as largely to exclude popular action. But in many of the more radical local transformations, from South Africa to South Korea as well as in central Europe, mass democratic movements played key roles. And where such movements have been defeated in struggle, in Serbia and Burma for example, market-oriented reform – if it has occurred at all – has taken profoundly undemocratic forms. Western policy elites have been significant actors in all these conflicts, but they have hardly been decisive in whether, how or by whom fundamental local reforms have been achieved.

The condescension of some Western social scientists as well as policy elites, who dismiss popular democratic movements and downplay their successes, thus also ignores these very real costs where movements are defeated. The global counter-revolution – of authoritarian nationalist regimes and movements opposed to democratic change – has involved the appalling violence of 'new wars' (Kaldor and Vashee 1997) directed against civilian populations. The gains in the development of international law enforcement, referred to above, have been responses to some of the worst, genocidal episodes among many crimes against humanity, in which millions have suffered. A global human-rights-based democratic order is not something simply, or mainly, promoted by Western elites and imposed on the non-Western world. On the contrary, it is a response to the demands of movements of the oppressed, from Kurdistan to Bosnia to Rwanda, however little or indirectly their voices are allowed to be expressed in global media (Shaw 1996).

It is not unrealistic therefore to see the global transition as one of an unfinished global revolution. It is a movement away from a fragmented state system based on war, and towards a common, worldwide democratic order with flourishing global institutions. It encounters fierce resistance from local elites and other social groups whose power and/or identity is threatened. There is thus a worldwide power struggle between global-democratic revolution and nationalist-authoritarian counter-revolution, which in many regions outside the West often erupts in war and genocide. Increasingly, globalised Western state power plays a balancing role in these struggles; sharing some core assumptions with the democratic forces, it nevertheless fails to advance both decisive victories for local democratic forces or principled extensions of global order.

The argument of this chapter is, therefore, that the dynamics of world political change do not originate simply with Western policy-makers, but with the actions of millions in many different kinds of collective action worldwide. Western elites find themselves in the midst of conflicting processes which they can hardly control in many specific locations, let alone in their entirety, because of the hugely varied sources of political power and mobilisation – both elite and popular – and to which they have only moderate interest in giving clear or distinctive direction.

Varied pressures push Western policy-makers towards some forms of global integration, but they have also to be seen in the context of the continuing primacy of national sources of political legitimation. Here is a major paradox of the global transition, which argues against any simple equation of globality with supra-terrritoriality. While states – especially in the West – are increasingly integrated, pooling monopolies of violence, harmonising law and extending cooperation, direct sovereignty remains largely (with the major partial exception of the European Union) national in form, and direct political authority derives almost exclusively (with the so far relatively minor exception of the European Parliament) from national electorates. Global institutions remain international in form, deriving legitimacy indirectly from national states with their parliamentary and democratic bases. The end of the Cold War leaves Western elites fumbling towards global rhetoric, but dependent on mainly national constituencies. This is one source of their contradictory and often uncertain roles.

Indeed, the global revolution itself has been made up of national revolutionary or democratic movements, in the various states of the former Communist and Third worlds. In virtually every case the manifest demands of the movements have concerned national-democratic goals, but they have had equally conscious connections with regional and worldwide international changes. Thus the movements in east-central Europe depended on Gorbachev's reform movement and the new East–West *détente* of the late 1980s. Their success manifestly derived from, but also deepened, the end of the Cold War. Similarly, the worldwide democratic movements of the 1990s, such as the Indonesian upheaval of 1998, have depended as much as the Latin American democratisations of the 1980s on the knowledge of the shift in American and Western policies which is pulling the rug from under old authoritarian regimes.

Although in some cases the consolidation of national democracy has led to the rise of new national-authoritarianisms which have come into conflict with global change, in general national democracy and internationalism have been complementary to, and necessary ingredients of, global political change. Globality is not the simple negation of nationality and internationality; although it transcends their classical conflictual forms, it relies on producing new forms of both. Democratic nationality and cooperative internationality become parts of the infrastructure of a global world.

12

TOWARDS A POLITICAL ECONOMY OF AGENCY IN CONTEMPORARY INTERNATIONAL RELATIONS

John MacLean

The aim of this chapter is to analyse the nature of 'agency' in the late-modern world. Its core question is: what kinds of agency, particularly political and economic agency, are capable of being realised in contemporary international relations? The question's apparently simple form belies its deep complexity. At first sight, it appears as empirical – resolvable through careful observation. But social life is not wholly constituted through those elements capable of being captured (and rendered intelligible) by observation statements. Besides, what 'agency' consists in, and whether it is important to understanding international relations, is neither clear nor settled. Already implicated in the question are second-order questions, both conceptual and substantive, some of which must be addressed.

In addition, the question of what kinds of political and economic agency can be realised is simultaneously a question about what kinds are marginalised, enclosed, made invisible, removed or not thought of. Answers to the first question hinge upon answers to the second, since certain historically specific forms of agency are continuously privileged over other possible forms. Furthermore, developing a concrete historical analysis cannot be simply a matter of 'agency' constructed as an external substantive item. Instead, analysis must include meta-theoretical considerations; part of what agency is or might be in the world is constituted in and mediated by theoretical orthodoxies within the discipline of international relations. International theory is not external to political and economic agency, but part of what needs to be explained within the latter.

In the first section I offer a critical account of concern with agency and how this has been articulated within the discipline. In the second section, I develop a concrete analysis of political and economic agency in international relations, using globalisation as an analytical framework. Finally, I will say a little about the role of formal regional and global international organisations in relation to agency, and offer some thoughts about what possible forms of emancipatory, or counter-agency, might be developed out of this critique.

Two caveats must be noted. First, I am not defining agency at the outset in wholly abstract and ahistorical terms; rather, the meaning and possibilities of agency will be established through the analysis. However, I assume that agency is a generic term. It is as important to the establishment and realisation of systematic poverty and inequality, as it is to the possibility of emancipatory practices, so that successfully establishing the latter (which I am most interested to develop) hinges upon critical interrogation and disclosure of the former. Second, my focus within this generic domain of agency upon political and economic agency in particular is not an entailment of adopting a 'political economy' approach. I do not use the term as an empirical referent. It includes the political and economic elements of social life, but is not restricted to them. Political economy here is a general meta-methodology for social analysis, based in but not identical to that of Marx's *Grundrisse* (1973: 100–8; MacLean 1988a: 300–7). In this approach, cultural, legal or other dimensions could also be starting-points for analysis; I have selected political and economic agency for reasons which will become clear later.

International relations and the invisibility of agency

Agency has not been a problematic issue within international relations until recently. Its entry into the array of disciplinary concerns has been somewhat forced; it is not yet seen as central. This intervention – posing agency as central to emancipatory practices – emerged from conceptualisations developed initially outside the discipline, in philosophy, sociology, etc. The intellectual movements involved were linked to substantive developments in the world which were viewed as only marginally, if at all, important within the mainstream of international relations.

These developments included: the break-up of the Soviet Union and Yugoslavia with their consequent conflicts; the demise of centrally planned political-economies across the world; the development of apparently competitive non-Atlantic political-economies in Asia, the assumed success of which is presently in doubt; the growth of institutionalised regional economic organisation; the emergence of global firms, markets, production, distribution and consumption systems; and the development of new information and communications systems, apparently compressing time and space and rendering territorial borders partially redundant.

These developments partially engaged the discipline's realist and neo-realist orthodoxy and its economistic wing, international political economy. Attention was facilitated by neo-realist refinements to realism – the focus on transnational relations and complex interdependence (Keohane and Nye 1972, 1977), so-called structural realism (Waltz 1979), regime theory (Krasner 1983) and international society (Bull 1977). These developments could be included in the scope of the discipline because they had deep resonances with state-centric phenomena, long-established as central objects of enquiry. Traditional concerns with states as unitary political actors meant that these developments were recognisable, with only minor refinements of core motifs in the disciplinary orthodoxy. However, the focus on the state as the only (or major) actor and unit of analysis has played a central role in the capacity of the discipline to render the more inclusive concept of agency invisible.

Other developments in the world, which did not have these metaphorical links with the disciplinary tradition, in principle presented the possibility of disturbing and disrupting it in a variety of ways, conceptual and substantive. I have in mind transnational social movements; feminist projects; human rights; animal rights; labour and trades union rights; ethnicity and nationalism; problems of refugee formation and migration; health and safety; poverty; ethical trading; consumer rights and intellectual property. As Shaw (1994a) and Stammers (1996 and this volume) have pointed out, not all these movements can be declared progressive. However, they are intimately linked to – but not synonymous with – recent ideas about civil society, local and global (Shaw 1994a: 68–70; Giddens 1994: 2–4, 250–2; Albrow 1996: 164–8).

Because the international relations tradition has maintained a distinction between 'high' and 'low' politics, it was primed to resist the implications of such developments by placing them outside the discipline, or at its farthest margins. However, these issues generate questions of agency in varying degrees, because they are all concerned with change – either moving to new or returning to old forms of political economy. The major vehicles of – limited and controlled – entry into the discipline have been *critical neo-Marxist theory*, based in either the Frankfurt School or Gramsci's projects, and occasionally in both (Cox 1981, 1983, 1987; MacLean 1981a, 1981b, 1988a, 1996); *historical sociology*, with its more sophisticated theorising of state and society and focus upon civil society (Skocpol 1979; Mann 1993; Giddens 1985, 1990; Held 1995; Scholte 1993; Shaw 1994a, 1997); *postmodernism*, with its denial of foundationalism, and methodologies of genealogy, deconstruction and double-reading (Ashley 1988, 1996; Der Derian 1987, 1990, 1992; Klein 1988; Dalby 1990, 1996; Campbell 1993; Walker 1993; Weber 1995; Sylvester 1993; *International Studies Quarterly* 1990); and *feminist theory*, with diverse accounts, liberal, radical, Marxist/socialist and postmodern (Grant and Newland 1991; Krause 1995; Peterson 1992; Peterson and Runyan 1993; Hoskyns 1994; Enloe 1989; Sylvester 1993; Brown 1988; Weber 1995; Steans 1998).

Within this range of projects, constructions of agency are diverse and developed more or less explicitly. Many are inadequate for locating agency within contemporary international relations; I develop this claim below. The prior task is to explain how the issue of agency has been simultaneously resolved and yet made invisible. Although the 'high–low politics' dichotomy has played a large part, this alone has not accomplished this complex task.

Indeed, it is of less importance than the transformation of the concept of agency (which always carried with it the possibility of critical interrogation and radical alternatives) into the categorical concept of agent or actor.

The problem of agency in general is close to Abrams' description: 'the problem of finding a way of accounting for human experience which recognizes simultaneously and in equal measure that history and society are made by constant and more or less purposeful individual action, and that individual action, however purposeful, is made by history and society' (1982: xiii). Here the possibility of a reflexive, critical theorisation of international relations – in the sense of Cox's distinction between problem-solving and critical theory (1981), stated earlier and more powerfully by Horkheimer (1972) – is heavily implicated.

There are two distinct, related dimensions to the removal of agency in international relations; one inchoate, pursing a nomadic, fragmented existence, sometimes implicit sometimes explicit, the other historically specific, explicit, sharply defined, disciplined and focused. The first I shall call the dominant taxonomic lineage. In international relations, the problem of abstraction, and within this, agency, has been continuously resolved through classification, categorisation, separation and difference. From the start of the discipline, the dominant mode of abstraction has been methodological individualism (MacLean 1981a).

International relations were rendered intelligible through the identification and separation of core agents or actors. The primary dichotomy has been that of state and non-state actors (as with all dichotomies, one side is always privileged over the other) constructed mistakenly as a pre-theoretical task of ordering data, and reinforced by a set of secondary dichotomies; discrete territorial spaces (wherein territory was assumed to be 'at rest') against discrete levels of analysis, politics against economics, and non-normative against normative analysis. Together these dichotomies have invested the centrality of actors/agents in international relations with a quality of physicality or three-dimensionality, in which they necessarily occupy space and are therefore capable of being observed. In turn, the quality of observability became a necessary feature for anything to qualify as an actor/agent. Consequently even though the state has mainly been defined ahistorically, as a legal abstraction, the nature of the state form was held unproblematic. The abstraction was brought to life with observation statements, assumed to refer to discrete named units – the United States, France, Tunisia. These actors are assumed to be capable of being known through metricity along a range of indices: size, population, gross domestic product, etc.

The consequences of 'fixing' actors in ahistorical time and territorial space have been enormous. First, the issue of agency has been transformed into one of actors or agents. The question of emancipatory potential – what kinds of agency are capable of being realised within the discourse of international relations, and which are simultaneously marginalised or removed – is replaced by the behavioural question of actors; who gets what, where, when and how. The taxonomic device of non-normative against normative incises the intimate causal links between actors and agency. Actors became located in the non-normative sphere and rendered apparently real because empirical; agency is located in the normative sphere and rendered unreal, or idealistic, because not-empirical – illegitimate. Agency is classified as a non-observable item and divested of any causal status. So-called 'new' normative theory has done nothing to resolve this enclosure, even though it purports to deal directly with agency, because it assumes the non-normative/normative dichotomy and reproduces its disciplining authority – assigning itself to the assumed separate world of normative as distinct from non-normative concerns (Brown 1992: 1–4; Robinson and van den Anker in this volume).

Secondly, by disciplining attention upon actors as the normal gaze of international relations, the mobilisation of bias is towards policy-making analysis and problem-solving theory – inherently static because it takes the world as presented as the only secure basis for validating propositions (Cox 1981, 1983; MacLean 1981b, 1988a, 1988b; Sayer 1992). It privileges the views of participants. However, the reasons that statespersons – or members of social movements – give for what they do, do not necessarily constitute an explanation. Rather, what they do and their reasons are parts of what needs explaining.

Thirdly, possibilities of structural analysis in the discipline were substituted by the 'level-of-analysis' problem. This intensely simplistic conception has shown remarkable endurance in the disciplinary arsenal; originally associated with J. D. Singer (1960), as Barry Buzan (1995: 200–2) points out in his reassertion of the motif, this resolution of the issue, linked closely as it was to the intervention of General Systems Theory into the discipline, was posed earlier by Kaplan (1957) and Waltz (1959).

Fourthly, the conception of power in the discipline was heavily encircled. It focused mainly upon observable outcomes and the capacity of actors to control the agenda. This limitation was central in privileging war and conflict as real over peace as a not-real (and thus only to be desired) future state-of-affairs. Ideas about structural or three-dimensional power (Lukes 1974: 21–5), or hegemony (except as reducible to aims, capabilities and intentions of particular actors) were rendered unintelligible or metaphysical, because incapable of being empirically operationalised.

Fifthly, the discipline privileged politics over economics. This was, of course, intimately connected with the state focus, but behind it was the philosophical context of classical political theory. This severely derivative relationship is still maintained by an influential few (Williams, H. 1992, 1996; Donelan 1990; Jackson 1990, 1996; for criticisms, MacLean 1981a, 1999; Walker 1993). In addition, the first chair in the discipline (Aberystwyth in 1919) was in International Politics, and many book titles continue this focus

(Waltz 1979; Baylis and Smith 1997) as indeed does the present volume. Notwithstanding neo-realist international political economy, the effect of privileging 'the political' has not only constrained what can be said to be significant actors, but has further limited the notion of agency to political agency. However, political and economic agency are separated only by social and theoretical constructions. At the level of explanation they are internally and necessarily related; to treat them as categorically separate leads to incoherence.

The second major dimension of the problem of agency in international relations is its more precise articulation as the 'agent-structure problem'. Interestingly, orthodoxy already had a hold upon the issue. Waltz's development of a more strictly scientific and so-called 'structural realism' (1979), seems to have focused the collective mind more abstractly, coherently and precisely than the previous reduction of agency to actors and agents only. This debate is well enough known as not to require restating; it can be tracked through Wendt (1987, 1992), Hollis and Smith (1991, 1994, 1996), Carlsnaes (1992), Scholte (1993), Jabri and Chan (1996) and Yurdesev (1993).

There were two fundamental flaws in the construction of the 'agent-structure problem'. First, placing the issue in the meta-theoretical domain was mistaken; it has philosophical content but is not wholly philosophical. What the debate (especially Waltz, Wendt and Hollis and Smith) assumed is that the agent-structure problem is centrally theoretical, capable of being resolved by abstracted meta-theoretical discussion alone. But this can be so only if we suppose that the theoretical domain is categorically separate from social practice. This dominant supposition of social science cannot be sustained (MacLean 1981a, 1988b, 1999; Mészaros 1986; Murphy and Tooze 1996; Bhaskar 1986, 1989, 1991; Sayer 1992). It begs the question of the nature of subject–object relations. Actually, the agent-structure problem is continuously and historically resolved – through the concrete establishment of what are taken to be the limits of social reality by social agents and academic practice. Secondly, the inchoate dichotomous element in the discipline (agency translated into actors) received an ironic boost from the very formulation of the 'agent-structure problem'.

It was difficult if not impossible to pose the problem of agency, in particular whether it is constrained by structures, clearly enough to generate concrete historical analysis of emancipatory forms. However, some contemporary developments in international relations and some conceptual interventions could not be rendered intelligible and disciplined into the orthodoxy. Although the potential of these contributions has been obscured by their rag-bag categorisation as a 'post-positivist, third Great Debate' (Lapid 1989; Smith, Booth and Zalewski 1996), they contain the promise of reasserting a disruptive and subversive project of agency within the discipline.

Agency reconceptualised

To answer my question – what kinds of agency are capable of being realised in contemporary international relations? – what remains is to establish a concrete historical analysis of agency, and the possibilities within it for emancipatory agency. This I will do first by drawing out some interim postulates, which taken together constitute a reconceptualisation of agency. In the final section, with this new analytical framework, I will develop a concrete analysis of the deep structure of agency.

First, 'agency' is a generic term: attention to its meaning is central to explaining international relations practices in general. The implicit interest of the discipline in maintaining agency's relative invisibility is because analysing it carries with it the possibility of specifying radical counter-hegemonic forms. This in turn carries the possibility of subverting the causal relationship between hegemony in theory and in international practice.

Secondly, agency has not been considered problematic in international relations until recently. Despite its entry into the discourse, textually at least, from other disciplines, it is mistaken to suppose that agency can be added as an already-coherent concept. There is really a double omission; just as international relations failed to theorise agency, so attempts outside the discipline, generally in work on social movements and civil society, have largely failed to theorise 'the international'. Consequently, it is mistaken to see sociological (Giddens 1990, 1994; Touraine 1981, 1998; Shaw 1994a, 1994b; Albrow 1996) or political (Habermas 1989; Scott 1992; Cohen and Arato 1992) approaches to agency as constituting comprehensive theoretical and substantive alternatives to international theory.

The theoretical and empirical conditions which temporarily allowed some coherence to the distinctiveness of sociology and politics as disciplines no longer hold. It is not that the substantive contents of these disciplines have disappeared or no longer require analysis, but political, social, cultural and economic practices have themselves become transformed, initially through internationalisation and now through globalisation. International relations is not the external environment of political and social activities; they are already causally embedded in international space, even though in observational terms they are enacted in specific geographical places. This means that understanding political and economic agency cannot be effected only by 'socialising' international concepts. Sociological and political concepts need to be simultaneously theorised in relation to globalisation.

Thirdly, agency is not reducible to (although it includes) the aims, interests, activities, capabilities and ideologies of individual or collective entities. Emancipatory forms of agency are not reducible to the characteristics of those groups – social movements and non-governmental organisations located in civil society – which actively seek to expand possibilities for agency. Agency cannot be attached only to actors or agents, for this is to construct agency as categorically separate from and necessarily external to social structures. Nor can agency be attached only to social structures for this is to categorically detach agency from agents; to render actors mere 'dupes', 'automata' or 'bearers of roles', unalterably 'programmed to reproduce' (Sayer 1992: 96).

Agency is a complex abstract concept (although nonetheless real) referring to what become socially established in any particular historical period as the natural limits of social reality and thence practice (Bourdieu 1977: 164, 168). Consequently, agency refers not only to practices which are capable of being realised, but also and simultaneously to those which are not. Agency is a shorthand term for the resolution of the agent-structure problem achieved in any historical period. Thus agency in general, and defensive or emancipatory agency in particular, cannot acquire meaning through abstract ahistorical definitions or closed sets of ideal-typical empirical characteristics. What agency is, or might be, in international relations can only be established as the conclusion of a historicised analysis, exposing the complex set of relations in and through which it is constituted – theoretically and substantively.

Fourthly, a corollary is that although agency generically may be seen as the site of emancipatory agency or counter-hegemonic struggle, it is predominantly the site of dominant agency or taken-for-granted ways of acting. Consequently, agency cannot be assumed to be emancipatory simply because it is intentionally oppositional to prevailing ways of doing things. For example, although constructions of emancipatory agency through individually selected alternative lifestyles may well offer apparently alternative ways of acting; they may also simultaneously reproduce, albeit unintentionally, some of the core conditions of the dominant form of agency in the world, for example possessive individualism. Emancipatory agency can only be established through analysis of those forms of agency which have become historically necessary to the reproduction of particular social structures – structures which are at the same time a necessary condition of those forms of agency (Bhaskar 1978). This means agency is not disinterested or impartial in relation to power – agency is itself unequally distributed. Consequently, possibilities for radical agency cannot be coherently articulated outside a concrete analysis of forms of agency already inscribed within the hegemonic core of international practices.

Fifthly, possibilities for agency cannot be exposed by maintaining a categorical distinction of political and economic agency – even though actual forms of agency regularly present themselves as one or the other and most academic analyses also use this dichotomy. In its meta-theoretical aspect, the separation of polity and economy reveals their mutually constitutive character. Throughout the period of modernity, the assumed separation of polity and economy has taken different forms, but some form of separation has been causally necessary to reproduce modernity, particularly the naturalness of capitalist social relations. Concrete analysis of the possibilities of agency requires, therefore, the conceptual reinstatement of polity and economy as an internally (necessarily) related structure. A methodology of political economy, recovered from classical political economy offers the optimum possibility of achieving this.

Sixthly, concrete analysis of agency and its emancipatory forms cannot be fully established if agency is assigned only to the sphere of civil society. Certainly social movements need to be contextualised in relation to civil society and civil society is a site of potential counter-hegemonic struggle. But the argument cannot be left there, because civil society cannot be defined as only a site of opposition to dominant forms of polity and economy in the world. It is simultaneously a site of reproduction of those dominant forms, necessarily implicated in the polity-economy structure.

Finally, what agency (generically and in its particular representations) means in the late-modern world is necessarily constituted in international relations activity. This is not a parochial claim, but an assertion that as a matter of historically produced reality, social relations have become causally embedded (for better or worse) in the process widely referred to as globalisation. The aspect of this process most relevant to analysing the contemporary possibilities of agency is what is often called hegemony, which has been transformed historically. The first historical form was national, the second international: the third and most complex, recently developed, is that of global hegemony. This is not an evolutionary or teleological view. However, non-territorial and placeless (although not spaceless) global hegemony is qualitatively different from earlier forms of hegemony. Hegemony now appears as a form of power independent of any particular actor or agent. Locating agency, and in particular emancipatory agency, has to take account of this.

Agency recognised

Agency is located simultaneously in three key sites – polity, economy and civil society – within international practices. These are internally (necessarily) related and occupy the same geographical-empirical place which is today in principle global. The key to exposing their composition and the conditions which sustain their relationships – which conditions they in turn reproduce – is to be found in the complex concept of hegemony which temporarily binds them together. In the contemporary stage of modernity, hegemony has become global. Here, global is no longer a reference to a geographical-empirical *place*, nor is it a claim about increasing homogeneity of social practices. Instead, global here refers to a *space* of causal power in the world, which is no longer linked directly to observation statements. The three sites are only capable of being distinguished analytically; together, they represent a complex set of determinations, a totality. None of them bears causal primacy for agency on *a priori* or categorical grounds. However, from time to time any one may be decisive, which we can establish only through concrete analysis.

Since explicit concern with questions of agency has been pushed into international relations, the activities of contemporary social movements and academic writing about them do present a limited challenge, but it does not yet press critically as far into the discipline or into international practices as its most enthusiastic proponents claim. This is because the social movements/civil society project has at best underestimated and at worst failed to acknowledge the challenge which the international relations discipline and practices present to it. Even the exceptions to this relative blindness (Shaw 1994a, b; Walker 1993; Rosenberg 1994; Gill 1994, 1995) – who are sensitive to the problematic of international relations as more than simply an expanded context of action – underestimate the extent to which globalisation presents a qualitatively different set of causal relations within which agency in general, and the possibilities of emancipatory agency, are embedded.

There are not two distinct kinds of agency, dominant and emancipatory, capable of being specified empirically. We cannot unravel what agency is or might be simply by comparing its forms of appearance. Instead, it is necessary to return these apparently separated forms to their heavily obscured initial location – agency in its generic form. There is more to agency in general than the sum of observable acts. What is relevant here is the set of possible acts *not* practised, because they are not thought possible in the context of what has become socially constructed as natural (Bourdieu 1977: 164–9). There is always a hidden side – what Lukes (1974: 24–5) might term latent agency – which is causally necessary to maintain the social reproduction of a boundary between the disputed and undisputed in international relations. Three important implications flow from this construction. First, 'hidden agency' is not a ready-made alternative mode of agency, sitting within observable forms and waiting to be discovered. Nor is it agency already in practice but hidden by means of their removal from 'public, or official, accounts or transcripts' and which 'identify active sites of resistance' (Saurin 1996: 674, 676) – this is better termed marginalised agency. 'Hidden agency' can be found only by disturbing the boundary between the disputed and what is undisputed – because it is taken as undeniably given by dominant as well as by subordinated agents. This also means that the task of uncovering agency in the world is initially a conceptual task.

Secondly, although the articulation of emancipatory agency hinges on the deconstruction of agency in general and is therefore a matter of huge complexity, this need not lead to either pessimistic or indeed over-optimistic conclusions. What it can lead to is the realisation that agency in the world really can be other than its apparent limits. For, no matter how given the givens of international relations seem to be, because they are partly located in and reproduced by social practices they are continuously precarious and capable of disruption (MacLean 1999).

Thirdly, agency and its possibilities are not reducible to the attributes of named actors. Agency is not simply a composite outcome (effect) of agents' activities (cause): agents' activities are simultaneously an outcome (effect) of the structure of agency (cause) and themselves require explanation. Consequently, the dominant linear form of causality – itself an important indirect component of power – needs to be transformed into a conception of reciprocal causality.

There is not the space here to develop a full account of the deep structure of agency. Nevertheless, I will aim to set out the major fixing points of agency in contemporary international relations, together with some indication of substantive conditions which mediate them. First, radical agency, understood as potentially non-arbitrary ways of acting, can only be conceptualised in relation to dominant agency – which represents ways of acting which are actually arbitrary but reproduced intersubjectively as taken for granted. The relation is therefore continuously, although not inevitably, asymmetric. Thus agency can be characterised as combined and uneven, and might be supposed to be causally but indirectly related to the combined and uneven development of localities within global capitalist social relations. However, this intricate causal link cannot be established simply by opposing two stories – the first concerned with the official, public audition of practices such as development, modernisation and democratisation; the second with the unofficial, obscured and unaccounted-for practices of poverty, displacement and ill-health which are nevertheless active sites of resistance (Saurin 1996: 674–80). Such exposure is a necessary but not sufficient basis for establishing the full story of agency.

The unequal distribution of agency itself needs explaining, and this implies a third, meta-theoretical story of generic agency. This is always 'hidden' in that it is never amenable to direct observation. There is no set of actions to which it is reducible, but this does not mean it cannot be described. Generic agency – which kinds of practices are capable of being realised and which are disabled – is embedded in the everyday practices that together establish what constitutes dominant and subordinated agency. Generic agency is a structural concept, and has a different causal status from its mediated observable forms, whereas at the behavioural level dominant and subordinated practices may both be conceptualised as effects of other social items. In its structural form, agency itself possesses causal powers.

I have argued that the agent–structure debate cannot be resolved at the level of abstracted meta-theoretical discussion alone. I cannot now consistently leave my own argument as only meta-theoretical; it needs to be reconciled with observable social practices. The two stories of agent and structure (Hollis and Smith 1994) must be reconciled so that the two stories of agency – dominant and subordinated – can also be. The agent–structure issue is really one story of two connected structures. Structure I is a collective reference to the observable institutions, rules, norms and conventions in and through which social practices, and agency in particular, are realised in any specific historical period. Structure II refers to the simultaneous meta-theoretical elements, embedded in the everyday social practices signified by Structure I, and which give them meaning precisely because they are taken for granted.

Within modernity, the major meta-theoretical elements are private property, gender, heterodoxy defined as difference, force, time-space and rationality (MacLean 1999). Today, the distinctiveness of the combination within Structure II is that it is placeless, appears timeless, but is not spaceless. This transformation in the political economy of modernity is at the centre of globalisation. It gives coherence to the assertion that globalisation as a causal concept is universal, not in the sense of being identifiable everywhere in the world as a geographical place, but as the dominant framework within which possibilities for agency are articulated and evaluated – and hence included or excluded.

The concept of power must therefore be expanded from purely behavioural content to that of hegemony, which is now global. Modernity has thus displaced 'the global' from its spatial history, rooted in territory, to a new non-territorial, placeless conjunction – through which specific forms of agency in local, national, regional, and international places are disciplined and realised. Here difference is reproduced continuously, but also coherently bounded so that it is taken as given. The maintenance of difference is a central requirement in sustaining and naturalising large-scale inequality. Consequently difference itself needs explaining (Brown 1988: 470–3).

Secondly, this takes us back to the trinity of polity, economy and civil society and partly substantiates the claim that agency cannot be assigned only or even mainly to any one of these sites on definitional grounds alone. At the same time, we cannot suppose either that agency is equally distributed amongst them. Consequently, the nature and possibilities of and for agency must also be rooted in the substantive conditions which give a historically specific content to the observable aims and practices of agents. These arise from the causal liabilities of the Structure II elements of relations between polity, economy and civil society.

Thirdly, exposing the substantive content of agency does require serious attention initially to civil society. International relations has consistently marginalised this sphere of social practice, even though within the long structural history of modernity (Rosenberg 1994) civil society has been necessarily (causally) related to the establishment and transformations of the modern state – which the discipline has hidden through reifying the concept of sovereignty. The globalisation of social relations disrupted sites of political and economic agency – national and local government, mass political parties, national mass media, military–industrial complexes and trade unions. It led to the formation of 'new' social movements with 'new' concerns – ecology, rights, feminism, ethnicity, religion, nationalism, charity, welfare and citizenship – and to new non-governmental organisations (Willetts 1996; Nelson 1996).

These developments have led to the apparent transformation of civil society as a separated and transnational sphere. However, both assumptions are mistaken; they deal only symptomatically with civil society. While a transformation has indeed taken place, it was historically necessary to the establishment of the new global form of hegemony. Consequently civil society remains intimately linked, causally, with polity and economy within this new hegemony and does not constitute a pure location of radical agency.

The central requirement for reformulating civil society within the structural conditions of globalisation has been an incisive break with Marx's and Gramsci's formulations. In these, civil society was simultaneously an analytic concept and a reference to a complex aspect of capitalist social relations which represented the possibility of 'a new kind of struggle which would take the battle against capitalism not only to its economic formations but to its structural and ideological roots in everyday life' (Meiksins Wood 1995: 241). Meiksins Wood (1995: 241, 238) reminds us also that 'Gramsci's conception of "civil society" was unambiguously intended as a weapon against capitalism, not an accommodation to it', but asserts that in its most recent formulations the concept 'no longer has this unequivocally anti-capitalist intent' and indeed that 'civil society is now in danger of becoming an alibi for capitalism'.

While civil society has been a site of contestation against state coercion, to theorise it as necessarily or only a sphere of freedom and new forms of choice (anti-politics, non-politics, sub-politics, life-style politics, identity politics) is to forget the range of oppressions that have been inscribed historically within civil society. These are not just pathologies of practice, but integral causal elements of the social reproduction of hegemony within capitalist social relations – which depends upon the continuous acceptance of difference as given in the world. Civil society is as much, if not more, a causal element in dominant agency as it is the potential ground of radical agency. Its appropriation into the formal-technical apparatus of authority and legitimacy, now concentrated within the deep structure of globalisation, is constantly its most likely transformation.

The establishment of global hegemony has required hegemony in theory alongside, although not coeval with, hegemony in material social relations. Political and economic agency today is theoretically and substantively global, in the sense that a global hegemony defines its possibilities. Global hegemony is non-territorial, placeless and mediated by – but not reducible to – the capabilities and actions of dominant agents. It is quite different from the concept of hegemonic stability (Keohane 1981), meaning dominance by one state. Hegemony refers to a structure of dominance which may include a dominant state or group of states, but signifies a larger combination of political, economic and private power which sustains it.

Global hegemony is a historically recent phenomenon, emerging from a specific set of historical transformations. This does not mean it has only a short history, but it does not have a discernible linear, chronological history as many have argued (Robertson 1992; Waters 1995; Albrow 1996; Scholte 1997). Rather than asking the unanswerable question of precisely when it began, we can ask what conditions were historically necessary for it to occur. Global hegemony has a longer structural history, disrupting chronological conceptions of time and space; its core structural conditions have not all emerged simultaneously. Social developments can be thought of as embodying differentiated velocities in time and space; specific social elements have different speeds, for example as between the mobility of capital and of labour. In this view, it is coherent to talk about limited local, national and regional histories alongside structural history. Indeed, these items are necessary if we are to understand globalisation, global hegemony and agency within it.

Five main conditions have been historically necessary to constitute globalisation as qualitatively different from internationalisation and interdependence. Although these conditions have developed with different historical velocities, they can only be distinguished analytically. In their structural relations, they represent a coherent centre of 'causal powers' in the world, which reproduce 'difference' as given or natural, so that inequality is seen as capable of alleviation or management – in short, technical-rational control – but not removal. Taking the first four core conditions of globalisation and global hegemony in turn, I will locate them in relation to the discipline and demonstrate that, theorised as separated areas of both academic and social practice (political, economic, socio-cultural and intellectual) they reproduce the apparent fragmentary and individuated character of social relations.

The first condition is a global proto-state form, capable of collapsing the distinction between the state and international organisation. This has been much written about within international relations in terms of global governance (Rosenau and Czempiel 1992; Murphy 1994; Carlsson *et al.* 1995; Scholte 1997). Related is a more focused body of work concerning the possible development of a global state form, over and above the sovereign territorial state, but linked to arguments about the latter's transformation (Ohmae 1993; Shaw 1994a, b; Gill 1995; Saurin 1995; Taylor 1996b; Strange 1996; Scholte 1997). Central to both is a realisation that what is political and authoritative in international relations can no longer be comprehended through the traditional idea of the sovereign territorial state as the basic unit of political organisation and primary location of political agency. These arguments do not entail the view that the state is disappearing, obsolete or no longer important; only that it is transforming.

This line of argument does not go far enough, however, and cannot because it is methodologically limited. The idea of a global proto-state must be made recognisable, if we are to recognise what agency means in the contemporary world, but the debate has two major flaws. First, the idea is bound to be partial unless it radically reconceptualises the state-international organisation relationship. Shaw (1994a, 1997) and Murphy (1994) do deal explicitly with the relations between states and international regional and global organisations, but without disturbing 'state' and 'international organisation' as different categories of actor. Secondly, the overwhelming tendency (except for Gill) is to maintain the differentiation between political and economic power, by constructing a global state as a purely or mainly political construct, distinct from but embedded in a separated global economy.

The second condition is new non-territorial dimensions of capital accumulation, in particular of production, distribution and consumption, along with non-territorial forms of the firm and labour. This has received more extended discussion (and for longer) than the issue of global governance, and is less contested. Even critics of the globalisation thesis will concede that there is something close to a global – at least an international – economy (Strange 1996; Hirst and Thompson 1996; Palan, Abbot and Deans 1996). This focus has emerged prominently in international relations and international political economy since the 1970s, and more recently in heavily contested forms within international business studies (Dicken 1992; Dunning 1993; Dunning and Hamdani 1997; El Kahal 1994, 1998). Work in both disciplines is comprehensive and empirically rich, but it is also, mostly, richly orthodox and non-radical, especially in business studies.

There are important exceptions on the barely tolerated margins of international political economy (Cox 1981, 1983, 1987, 1995; Gill and Law 1988, 1989; Gill 1994, 1995; Tooze 1987, 1988, 1997; Murphy and Tooze 1996; Saurin 1996). However, the established orthodoxy mimics the categorical dichotomy found in writings on global governance and the state. Whereas the latter privileges 'the political', international political economy privileges 'the economic'; both separate economics from politics. Until this mutually sustaining separation is overturned, both attempts will remain conceptually and practically limited, not only in explaining their separate explicit foci, but also concerning the causal relations of globalisation in general.

The third condition is new non-territorial forms of social and cultural identity, i.e. a global proto-civil society. This focus – especially concerning 'new' social movements and civil society – has been developed initially outside international relations and only recently has it been pushed into the discipline. Causal relations between 'new' social movements/civil society and the establishment of hegemony within globalisation are often misrecognised (Lipschutz 1992; Shaw 1994a, b, Stammers in this volume) by the way in which the former are constructed as a sphere of activity. Consequently, writers misrecognise the extent to which a new non-territorial form, global civil society, is causally necessary to realise globalisation in general and dominant agency within it.

The fourth condition is a transcendental form of academic (especially social-scientific) knowledge, which is capable of universalisation – in the sense of a dominant view about what constitutes the basis of maximally reliable knowledge. Hegemony within theory is a central, but almost invisible, element within the concrete practices that constitute global hegemony and agency. The issue of the relationship between academic theory and social practice, and more generally about subject–object relations, is more than just a matter of epistemological discussion. There is little explicit work on this within international relations (or any other social science), and what there is, is highly marginalised.

Some theories are consciously developed and articulated in order to reproduce specific social practices and some scholars move directly into the sphere of policy-making. However, it is not these explicit and purposive relations but the indirect, heavily obscured and explicitly – even if sincerely – denied relations between theory and practice which are most significant. All social theory embodies such indirect relationships but their nature and role within analysis varies significantly. It is upon this variation that the distinction between problem-solving (conservative) and radical (emancipatory) theory depends (Cox 1981; MacLean 1981a; Krippendorf 1982).

Within international relations Peterson (1992), Saurin (1995, 1996), Smith, S. (1995, 1996), Youngs (1996), Tooze (1987, 1988) and Murphy and Tooze (1996) have tried to deal with this problem explicitly. It is not surprising that this effort is marginalised; dealing with the theory/practice relation in other than a positivist manner is complex and difficult. The issue is unfamiliar and the vocabulary of mainstream international relations inadequate to the task. The resolution of the theory/practice relationship is seen as a technical-methodological rather than a conceptual problem.

To expose the fallacy of the assumed severe separation of theory from practice simultaneously exposes the causal relationship between academic production and social power. This in turn invalidates the core identity of the social scientist, rooted in reason and the assumed value-free impartiality of social scientific knowledge, honed and stiffened through the long history of modernity. Of course modern social science is not lacking in dispute or debate, and some disciplines – e.g. international relations, sociology – appear more contested than others – e.g. economics, business studies. However, debates take the form of a bounded or limited heterodoxy, allowable if they do not disturb the boundaries of what is taken for granted conceptually and substantively within each discipline.

The claim concerning intimate causal relations between knowledge and power is not simply about those agents in the world – Microsoft or the International Monetary Fund, for example – who have appropriated both the artefacts of knowledge production and decision-making power about what counts as relevant knowledge (Strange 1988). It is also a claim that academic practice, capable of universalisation as though wholly separated from the interests of any particular agents, was necessary to enable a complex global expert-knowledge system to be established.

It is one thing for agents participating in international relations directly – politicians, bankers, refugees or sex-tourist workers – to claim privileged access to knowing what 'is' the case ('reality') as distinct from what 'ought' to be the case in international relations. If this was the only context of such claims, all could be characterised as partisan, partial or wholly self-interested, and resolution of disputes would depend upon capabilities or access to power. This is not only inefficient but also incompatible with hegemonic power; it situates power as external to the everyday distinction between 'is' and 'ought'. It is quite another thing that academic practice hinges upon the security of reproducing objectivity and impartiality through the logical distinction between 'is' and 'ought' in the world. This allows some of the everyday struggles appropriating the 'is' of social practice to be legitimated by recourse to an apparently disinterested, impartial set of expert knowledges.

This indirect relation involving academic practice falsely situates the technical distinction between 'is' and 'ought' as external to everyday conditions of power. However, to the extent that academic practitioners, dominant and subordinated agents all take this impartiality for granted, the necessary partiality of orthodox social science and its links with distributive authority within international relations becomes hidden. This distinction between is and ought is at the centre of both academic and social practice, disciplining emancipatory academic projects and social practices alike. And this is a large part of what hegemony means in practice. In this sense, a globalised form of social science is a historically necessary constituent of global hegemony.

The condition of globalised academic knowledge is not however synonymous with a global world view or discourse, which is the final major condition of globalisation and global hegemony. This has received very little attention within international relations. Global discourse is close to the conception of world view developed by Gramsci, but I extend it in three important respects. First, I place it within Marx's idea (1973: 100–8) of the totality as a meta-methodology; global discourse comes to mean the total ensemble of phenomena in and through which the social production of meaning in habitualised forms takes place. Central to understanding this process is the deconstruction of philosophy, from an academic, meta-physical discourse outside society towards its real character as philosophy in society (Gramsci 1971: 161, 32, 34, 36; Mészaros 1986: 14; MacLean, 1999: 23–4, 28–30). Secondly, I highlight the element, essential to Gramsci, of establishing hegemonic leadership, namely intellectual and moral consent. Thirdly, I argue that Gramsci was mistaken to suppose (see Bocock 1986: 68–70) that intellectual, moral and philosophical leadership within hegemony could not, even in principle, be based on science.

The global world view has a different causal status from the first four conditions. It is the core unobservable element which ties other apparently discrete elements of globalisation into a coherent structural totality, enabling global hegemony to be enacted. The establishment of global discourse was not inevitable, although within modernity (understood as the gradual establishment and expansion of the capitalist mode of production and social relations) it was always immanent. The social reproduction of the Structure II elements of globalisation – private property, heterodoxy defined as difference, the use of force, gender, time and space and technical-rational knowledge – was not straightforward or smoothly accomplished, and they are still not completely fixed or at rest. They have the quality of continuously tendential movements, always emerging initially in particular places and representative of particularistic interests. They were always and still are subject to countervailing forces; the social process through which they become transformed into apparently objective universals is complex, contested and conflict-ridden (MacLean 1988b).

International relations history is not smooth, inevitable or evolutionary. However, the core elements of globalisation have become more taken-for-granted and elusive in their causal powers, exactly because they have become distanciated in time and space – no longer linked in the same way to specific places. Consequently, the identification of possible countervailing forces or counter-hegemonic practices is more complex and problematic than before. This makes the question of agency and its relationship with civil society both more ambiguous – because civil society is normally implicated in dominant agency – and more important – because civil society is not normally the terrain of potential radical agency and contestation.

In identifying the conditions of globalisation, I have not forgotten information and communications technologies, upon which many studies have placed great causal reliance. These cannot be conceptualised as purely technological effects of other spheres of apparently non-technological social practices, but neither do they have independent causal status. Rather, these technologies constitute a continuously necessary element of social organisation, the causal weight of which varies historically. In the contemporary world, the role of information and communication technology is embedded in and across the conditions above. Indeed political, economic and ethical agency has itself become technological practice.

The five historical conditions necessary to establish globalisation as a causal structure have not been established coevally. They represent different historical velocities but not wholly separate histories. For example, the mobility of capital was capable of being realised much earlier than the mobility of the sovereign state form or of labour. The sovereign state cannot be mobile in the sense of transcending territorial boundaries, only in the sense of being replicated in other territorial places. There cannot be a global sovereign state, but this does not mean there cannot be a global state form.

Similarly, labour is not and cannot be mobile in the same way as capital. Capital early developed many abstract forms such as promissory notes, credit and exchange-value. Labour on the other hand has only a singular, subordinated abstract form, its capacity for surplus-value within objectified labour, ironically termed labour-power. Labour has always been capable of geographical movement, but the distinctive mobility of labour-power is in its capacity to be in or out of employment. This is simultaneously its core weakness against capital, and its latent counter-hegemonic strength. But this latent agency was more capable of being articulated when capital formation and accumulation was predominantly national; it is more heavily enclosed in contemporary conditions than ever before. Labour can only organise itself transnationally, but it is at the same time subject to global organisation. These differences in what it means to be mobile affect what forms of agency can be realised and by what kinds of agents.

Reconciling polity, economy and civil society in establishing and maintaining the globalisation of capitalist social relations has been a lumpy, uneven process. However, recent developments indicate that a new global form of hegemony, although inchoate, has been established. This renders globalisation less rudimentary than it was prior to the 1990s. Several significant developments cannot be accounted for separately or in their relations; globalisation needs to be developed as a causal concept, not left as a descriptive term, as something to be explained.

The first recent development is the widespread rejection and reversal of Marxism/socialism as both intellectual system and basis for political and economic organisation. This refers to not only the former Soviet Union and Communist political economies of east-central Europe, but also Tanzania, Angola, Jamaica, Nicaragua and Syria, and the partial privatisation and marketisation of the economy in China (Biersteker 1992). As interesting is the gradual transformation of forms of socialism developed in the advanced political economies of Western Europe after the Second World War. The ending of the Cold War has also produced a recasting of 'international security' and global threats (Kostakos *et al.* 1991).

The second development is the transformation of the content of the North–South division in international relations, partly but not wholly as a consequence of the ending of the Cold War. Most significant is the apparently increased passivity of underdeveloped political economies, with the decline of large-scale demands for structural change in the global political economy. In the 1970s, huge, potentially counter-hegemonic demands were articulated in rapid succession through international organisations, including those for a New International Economic Order, a New International Information Order and an International Seabed Authority. None was realised, although minor concessions were made by the advanced political economies. Since the early 1980s, no such concerted demands have emerged from underdeveloped political economies. Specific threats to stability, such as the attempts by Mexico and Argentina unilaterally to renege on their international debts, were closed down. The end of the Cold War meant that the core rationale for extended demand cooperation between subordinated political economies, together with their leverage in the context of Cold War rivalry, disappeared. In addition, former

Communist states have become major competitors for aid from public international organisations and private foreign direct investment.

The evidence of underdeveloped political economies' activities in the global political economy since the late 1980s and their authoritative role in restructuring local political and economic organisation, points to a significant transformation in policy-making. Apparently individual cases can be coherently evaluated as variants of a generic neo-liberal project – a qualitatively different level of disciplining and normalising authority in the world. This has been enacted mostly not through overt coercion but by means of informed consent on the part of subordinated actors. Within this process the bases for the articulation of radical alternative policies have not just been contained or removed from the international agenda – they have been removed from thought. The central motifs inscribed in this disciplinary transformation are privatisation, deregulation, trade liberalisation and formal democratisation. The latter represents the classic liberal privileging of legal, political and electoral forms which are together assumed 'to guarantee a free space for civil society' (Meiksins Wood 1995: 247). The advanced political economies – principally through the Organisation for Economic Cooperation and Development and their global managerial alliance as the Group of 8 – are central actors in defining the broad parameters of transformation. However, so far as agency more generally is concerned, a great amount of the substantial policy-making involved has become increasingly mediated through global and regional international organisations. The tailored structural adjustment programmes of the International Monetary Fund and their convergence with World Bank policy-making are striking examples, as is the ready acceptance by subordinated political-economies of unequal conditions within the Trade-Related Intellectual Property Measures, and Trade-Related Investment Measures, negotiated within the final stages of the Uruguay Round of the General Agreement on Trades and Tariffs (1986–1993), which represent a 'devastating political change which increases inequalities in the international system quite markedly' (Farrands 1996: 183).

Such policies do not enhance the long-term development prospects of subordinated political economies – indeed, they deepen and exacerbate their subordination (Biersteker 1990, 1992; Williams 1994). Nevertheless, they have been more or less 'freely' chosen by sovereign governments. In terms of Lukes' three dimensions of power, such evidence points to the misrecognition of their real interests by the majority of state actors on a global scale. Thus within globalisation, generic agency has increased its tendential character towards dominant agency – and this means that the prospects for radical agency within a global civil society are more limited and co-opted than before.

The third development is that international organisation, in its global, regional and non-governmental forms, appears to be performing an increasingly significant and comprehensive amount of decisive agency. This seems fairly obvious in the activities of the International Monetary Fund and

World Bank. However, the extent of this global organisation of social life is obscured by the way in which the international relations discipline privileges the neo-realist conception of the state, most recently transformed through the 'neo-institutionalist' turn of authoritative figures like Keohane (1989) and Goldstein and Keohane (1993), and more generally in American international political economy. It is also obscured by the significant increase in the number of new states since 1989. The core assumption – that states increasingly choose to articulate their separate and competing interests through cooperation within international and regional formal organisations – cannot be sustained. It represents an attempt to shore up earlier formulations of complex interdependence. Contemporary international relations are much more complex than this epistemologically- and ontologically-challenged neo-realist conception can comprehend. To suppose that states have simply changed the way they advance their separate interests through international organisation is extremely simplistic. This neo-institutionalist view simultaneously removes from discussion ideas about the transformation not only of the state, but also of international organisation, and the possibility of causal linkages between these two sets of transformation.

International organisation represents the central device through which globalisation has been realised and dominant agency revitalised. However, the key to exposing these complex transformations requires a thorough-going reconceptualisation of the state-international organisation relation. Private sites of agency – multinational corporations, global firms, non-governmental agencies and some new social movements – while not formally members of intergovernmental global and regional organisations are nevertheless increasingly formally and internally involved in their decision-making and policy implementation. These private sites no longer perform agency simply through traditional means of lobbying and pressure-group activity (El Kahal 1995; Lee 1996; Emadi-Coffin 1996; Willetts 1996; Nelson 1996). Correspondingly, international public organisations and states are increasingly becoming privatised. Within states the traditional form of privatisation, the transfer or sale of publicly owned assets to private individual or corporate ownership, is almost everywhere a central policy (Letwin 1988; El Kahal 1996; Hoopes 1997). Within both states and international public organisations, the application of private-sector management and budgetary techniques to the public sphere predominates (Dowding 1995; El Kahal 1996; Clegg *et al.* 1996; Easton 1997; Kickert, Klijn and Koppenjan 1997). International public organisations and states are increasingly sub-contracting elements of public policy-formation and especially implementation to private local and global firms, and to private non-governmental international organisations. Health, security, environment, transport, education and international aid are prominent examples of this tendency. More surprising perhaps is the sub-contracting by the European Union of the evaluating and auditing of levels of formal democratisation in former Communist states. Recent examples include the contract obtained by a consortium of Sussex academics and a private research company to audit local democratisation in locations in Romania, Poland and Bulgaria during 1997–98; and the contract awarded to the major global consultancy and accounting firm, Sykes Waterhouse Coopers, to audit levels of democratisation in localities in Hungary in 1998 (Katona 1998).

All this implies that the traditional separation of states from international organisations, with the latter categorised as non-state actors and states placed outside the process of international organisation of social relations, is positively misleading. It implies also that the categorical separation of states from firms is misleading. Furthermore, these rapid transformations imply a fundamental historical change in the context and form of the relationship between public and private spheres (including civil society) within globalisation. To understand these changes, we must reinstate the concept of the formalisation of social life as a generic and also now global concept. We must move from orthodox questions about what named states, firms, international and non-governmental organisations – constructed as distinctive, separated sites of action – do or do not do *in* the world, to questions about the history, nature and form of organisation *of* the world, and to questions about agency rather than only about observable activity. In this way the possibilities for radical agency can be constructed in a normative, yet not philosophically idealist form.

Individual states, international organisations, firms, social movements or cities can be conceptualised as specific and specialised forms which are both a cause and an effect of the global organisation of social life. To analyse the global proto-state does not mean that international organisations have come to dominate states. For all the empirical examples which appear to show this, there are as many which show the opposite. The implied question here – are states or international organisations the more powerful actors? – is exactly like the old question – are states or multinational corporations the more powerful actors? Neither can ever be resolved on empirical grounds; both are misconceived. States, international organisations and firms are all implicated in a new, historically specific form of global organisation. The different forms mediate aspects of specialisation and maintain the appearance of heterodoxy and difference as natural, which are essential for the reproduction of global hegemony through global governance.

The fourth development is that business activity in general has become globalised. The work of dependency theorists and world-systems theorists focused early attention upon the idea of a world economy. Many proponents of globalisation also suppose that it can be categorically – as distinct from historically – differentiated across economic, political, cultural and other dimensions so as to imply that the economic is more globalised than others (Dicken 1992; Dunning 1993; Shaw 1994a; Waters 1995; Cerny 1995; Taylor 1996b). It is mistaken to construct such differentiations on the basis of separated sectoral histories, when they are better seen as a function of differentiated velocities within a singular time-space context.

The global firm is qualitatively different from the multinational firm; it is nationality-less, non-territorial (in the sense of the still predominant division between 'home state' and 'host state') and capable of moving production, market, capital and headquarters sites almost at will. Global firms imply a global division of labour, involving a shift from geographical patterns of specialisation. Global firms do not occupy non-territorial space in their day-to-day activities; all activity must necessarily take place in some geographical place. However, the causal liabilities of global firms can no longer be territorially defined, but occupy a new placeless meta-theoretical space. We can no longer conceptualise different forms of business – small, medium, large, multinational – in terms of the assumed distinction of domestic and international. All firms have become globalised in the sense of their causal content. However, this does not mean that the state form is now obsolete (Levitt 1983; Ohmae 1990, 1995), merely that relations between states and firms are transformed.

Within the global political economy, service industries – finance, insurance, banking and leisure – have become the central sectoral component in capital accumulation, displacing secondary industrial manufacturing from the role it occupied from the early nineteenth to the late twentieth century. This has implications for transformations within both advanced and underdeveloped political economies, including the apparently paradoxical 'Asian miracle' followed so closely by the 'Asian crisis', and intensive changes in global patterns of employment and unemployment.

The fifth major development is that new transnational forms of political and social movements have emerged, together with new transnational non-governmental organisations. Willetts (1996: 71 and footnote 95) reports 1,521 such bodies registered in 1993 with approved observer status at the Economic and Social Council of the United Nations. These cover both established issues (labour, disarmament, health and poverty) and apparently new concerns (ethnic minorities, human rights, child rights, environmental issues and consumer rights).

Finally, the exponential rate of developments in new information and communications technology cuts across all the others. Specific information and communication technologies are a necessary condition of globalisation, but globalisation – especially of production, distribution and consumption – is a necessary condition of research and these developments in technology. The relationship, as in previous historical (particularly modern) forms of connection between technology and society, is one of reciprocal causality. However, given the centrality of the service sector within global capital accumulation, information and communication technology is qualitatively more important in reproducing a global political economy than it was in earlier national or local forms.

What pulls these apparently diverse, historically differentiated developments into a coherent and hegemonic totality is neither clear nor straightforward. But the mechanism cannot be derived directly from empirical manifestations of globalisation. The question now is what do these developments – and those relationships between them capable of observation – together presuppose for their existence and appearance? My answer is that a global discourse or world view, capable of providing a basis for hegemonic leadership and intellectual and moral consent, and through which the social production of meaning (in habitualised, or taken-for-granted ways) on a global scale could take place, has recently developed.

In setting out what this consists of, my argument starts from ideas about the technical rationalisation of society (Weber 1964); the ideological content of technical rationality and its relation to political domination (Marcuse 1964, 1968) and rational society and depoliticisation (Habermas 1977). However, it extends beyond these arguments which are confined to national contexts and do not consider how these tendencies might be constituted in international or global form.

The accomplishment of establishing scientific-technical rationality as a global discourse has been as complex as it has been spectacular, not the least because such a transformation was never inevitable within capitalist social relations or modernity. The historically specific new resolution of the agent-structure relation necessary for this world-view has involved purposeful – yet not purposive – behaviour by a variety of actors. Although global discourse continues the privileging of certain interests over others, it is a largely unintended consequence of particular habitualised practices of agents, under conditions intersubjectively constructed as objective and external to them. For the historical conditions of globalisation and global hegemony to be drawn into a coherent global discourse, a fundamental transformation of the content and relations of the public and private realms of social life has been a central requirement.

By means of an unspoken, unarranged alliance between academic, economic and political production, the traditional content of initially Western political theory and practice has been evacuated and reformed. Rationality was already established as the unassailable basis of the categorical separation of economics from politics and ethics, earlier in the history of modernity. At first sight it seems that an economistic, expert-knowledge-based system of rational-technical politics, has developed so that politics and economics, public and private domains, have become indistinguishable.

However politics is not being *replaced* by economics within globalisation, it is being *reinvented* within the deep structure of globalisation. Beck's (1977) prescription for the emancipatory reinvention of politics from below is unsustainable; the reinvention of politics has already become inscribed within hegemony and is not waiting realisation outside the latter. The globalisation of capitalist social relations still requires the reproduction of separated politics and economics in some believable form – in particular the characterisation of politics and ethics as distinctively value-laden, ideologically based practices.

This is necessary to maintain the apparent impartiality, ahistoricicity and universalisability of economic science. In addition, capital accumulation requires that its social costs – education, health, legislation, welfare and security – are not wholly born by capitalist enterprises, and this is entirely consistent with expanded forms of privatisation and sub-contracting.

It might be argued (Ohmae 1990, 1995) that the globalisation of production, markets and consumption would be rendered more efficient and uncontested if the state and politics were reconstructed as purely economic institutions. But this view is entirely simplistic; if the institutions and practices of economy were to be saddled with the tasks of coercion and consent as well as of capital accumulation, the partiality of global capitalism would be revealed, its objectivity called into question. The globalisation of social relations has required the construction of a global proto-state, not over and above sovereign territorial states but enclosing them, and a global proto-civil society similarly endowed. Neither of these new forms are extensions outwards, or new non-territorial forms of, the sovereign state and national civil society. They are completely and historically new forms, not intended to replace traditional forms of statehood or civil society. Rather, they have to subject these traditional formations to new kinds of disciplinary and normalising surveillance at the global level, without disrupting their characterisation as manifestations of difference and heterodoxy.

This process is extremely complex and almost impossible to specify clearly. However, this analysis means that globalisation is a qualitatively different and historically very recent condition in the world, not capable of being traced back into earlier periods of imperialism and the gradual internationalisation of social relations, except by means of a quite unwarranted analytical imputation back into history.

In the global 'reinvention of politics', it could be argued that politics and ethics have acquired a new significance in dominant agency. To become concrete, globalisation has had to appropriate and re-colonise the very heart of separated politics; the normative discourse and practices of government, citizenship, rights and obligations. 'Timeless' liberal political and ethical concepts have had to be socially maintained but with a reinvented historical content, in which they are able to represent themselves socially as rational-technical (pseudo-scientific) concepts. This movement is clearly identifiable across the trinity of contemporary political theory, political science and political practice.

As Howard Williams (1996) argues, there is a new 'flowering of political theory. ... After its apparent demise in the 1950s, political theory has made a remarkable leap to prominence. ... The focus of this recent writing has remained as ever upon the relationship between the individual and the state.' Williams contends however that 'The individualist, voluntarist assumptions of [contemporary] political theory would seem to be out of touch with the realities of international relations where choice seems at best to be severely limited.' He asserts, 'But political theory will not do as it stands. We cannot I think use a solely nation-state-centred theory to look at a world which is becoming rapidly less nation-state centred.' (1996: 146, 147). Williams is right about this, but misses the point of his own objection. This form of political theory, based as it is to greater or lesser extent upon utilitarian rational-choice assumptions, is exactly the kind of theory required to reproduce – even if unintentionally – the relative invisibility of globalisation and global hegemony. To this extent, the possibility of a critical account of the globalisation of political theory, and the latter's reductionist formulation of inequality and injustice, is pushed out of contemplation. Similarly, political science is dominated today by public administration studies and the application of models, developed strictly within management science, to political issues, also articulated fully and clearly on the basis of rational-choice assumptions. Finally, there can be little doubt either that political practices, at local and global level, manifest an embedded alliance in the shift towards non-political politics, that is towards the so-called modernisation of politics within the advanced political economies (Blair 1998; Giddens 1994, 1998).

Together, this army of rational-choice theorists and practitioners both contribute to and are an effect of global hegemony. The reinvention of liberal political and ethical concepts is a quite stunning feat of social reproduction. It has not been a matter of replacing a historical normative discourse with an ahistorical scientific discourse, constructed as non-normative or non-ideological. Instead, it has required the social transformation of the very basis for what can be intelligibly said to constitute normative discourse itself.

This argument does not belie the intimate, necessary relationship within modernity between liberal political and economic theory and reason constructed as science. It postulates, however, that technical-instrumental reason, previously embedded within science but continuously transferred to society through technology, has become the ordering framework for all political decision-making. Previously, technical-instrumental reason encountered politics in a relation of categorical difference or opposition, which helped to make sense of both science and politics. The outcome of this reinvention is not that politics, states, parties or governments disappear or become anachronistic. Rather, it is that the historic separations of politics and ethics from economics, governance from wealth creation, citizenship from production and consumption – in short, the politician and the citizen from the business person and the administrator – is apparently maintained as a new technical division of the public sphere from the private sphere.

However, within this new historical division, scientific-technical reason transgresses its boundaries. It is no longer located only with the 'is' construction of social reality, and thus seen only as the maximally reliable basis for determining the optimum *means* for achieving the separated political and ethical *ends* of society. In addition, it has now come to appropriate the basis also for establishing what can be objectively articulated as constituting the proper ends of society. The goals of society, local and global, become constructed through an apparently non-normative discourse, in the sense of constructing criteria for deciding what opportunities or goals are technically and objectively feasible or available for society in the first place.

In this way the core concepts of liberal political theory can be re-located as a global philosophical and moral view, without complete severance from their originally national locations. Their new form divests them, however, of a central part of their history – their capacity (in principle at least) to stand as a conceptual and practical basis for radical, alternative and potentially counter-hegemonic practices. In their earlier historical forms, reason and the practices it implied were necessarily partial and continuously debatable – exactly because they could not be finally decided upon objectively, nor subjected to the discipline of scientific-rational principles. In global discourse, the central concerns of normative decision-making have been transformed: equality of health care has become quality; democratic participation as dissidence has become the consumption of political goods and services and the celebration of difference; justice has become the evaluation of returns in relation to individual inputs; obligation and duty have become reconstructed as performance contracts; education as cumulative knowledge and critical subversive thought has become education as training and transferable measurable skills. In all, planning for social need has become a need for social planning and continuous audit.

To the extent that this core of a global world view has become established, it completes the Gramscian triangle. To the transnational, managerial, global but diffused proto-state, and a global political economy of fragmented production, consumption, market and labour sites, is added a global proto-civil society of informed rational consent. It completes the formation of a properly global hegemony and represents the increased marginalisation of normative projects – at least in their classic form as potentially emancipatory projects based on the possibility of enhancing equality of access to decision-making and goods, redistributive justice in the world or even basic human needs. Emancipatory agency is more enclosed in the conditions of globalisation than ever before, even though the observable range of individuated choices about politics has been expanded. The objectification of difference has allowed a perverse form of political equality to emerge; the equality of all voices whatever they have to say. This is perverse because the assumed equality of difference renders the conditions of inequality even more invisible than in earlier historical periods. It replaces dissidence with difference, when it is difference that must be disrupted.

The social relations and forces of production realised through generic agency's relation with the global polity-economy-civil society axis are undoubtedly a triumph for capital. But this is to concede the reproduction of inequality and exploitation as necessary and natural. The critical analysis of agency reveals that these conditions are not objective; they have become objectified through specific constraints upon agency, academic and non-academic. There is, then, a clear new space for emancipatory agency in the world, but it does not exist in the form of a practical political and economic space waiting to be filled. It has to be created conceptually first, and subsequently enacted. The only possible emancipatory agency now available – which can disrupt generic agency within globalisation – is that which overturns the core structural elements of global hegemony, namely private property, heterodoxy defined as difference, gender subordination, force, time and space and technical-rational reason. And this means that any project in the late modern world, to be emancipatory, has to be revolutionary.

BIBLIOGRAPHY

Abrams, P. (1982) *Historical Sociology*, New York: Cornell University Press.

Alan, J. (1995) *Dialogy o Obcanske spolecnosti*, Prague: Sociologicke nakladatelstvi.

Albo, G., Langille, D. and Panitch, L. (eds) (1993) *A Different Kind of State? Popular Power and Democratic Administration*, Oxford: Oxford University Press.

Albrow, M. (1996) *The Global Age*, Cambridge: Polity Press.

Alger, C.F. (1994) 'Citizens and the UN System in a Changing World', in Y. Sakamoto (ed.) *Global Transformation: Challenges to the State System*, Tokyo: United Nations University Press.

Almond, G. (1988) 'The Return to the State', *American Political Science Review*, 82, 3: 853–901.

____ (1989) 'The International-National Connection', *British Journal of Political Science*, 19, 1: 237–59.

____ (1996) 'Political Science: The History of the Discipline', in R. Goodin and H-D. Klingemann (eds) *A New Handbook of Political Science*, Oxford: Oxford University Press.

Amin, A. (ed.) (1994) *Post-Fordism: A Reader*, Oxford: Blackwell.

Amin, A. and Palan, R. (2000) 'Post-rationalist IPE', in *The Routledge Encyclopedia in International Political Economy*, London: Routledge.

Amin, A. and Thrift, N. (1994) *Globalization, Institutions and Regional Development in Europe*, Oxford: Oxford University Press.

Amin, A., Palan, R. and Taylor, P. (1994) 'Forum for Heterodox International Political Economy', *Review of International Political Economy*, 1, 1: 1–12.

Anderson, B. (1991) *Imagined Communities: Reflections on the Origin and Spread of Nationalism*, London: Verso.

Anderson, C.J. (1995) 'Economic Uncertainty and European Solidarity Revisited: Trends in Public Support for European Integration', in C. Rhodes and S. Mazey (eds) *The State of the Union. Volume 3: Building a European Polity?*, Harlow: Longman.

Anderson, C.J. and Kaltenthaler, K.C. (1996) 'The Dynamics of Public Opinion Toward European Integration, 1973–1993', *European Journal of International Relations*, 2, 2: 175–99.

Anderson, K. and Blackhurst, R. (1993) *Regional Integration and the Global Trading System*, London: Wheatsheaf.

Anderson, P. (1998) *The Origins of Postmodernity*, London: Verso.

Aron, R. (1967) *Eighteen Lectures on Industrial Society*, London: Weidenfeld.
Ash, T.G. (1990) *We The People*, Cambridge: Granta Books.
Ashley, R.K. (1988) 'Untying the Sovereign State: A Double Reading of the Anarchy Problematique', *Millennium*, 17, 2: 227–62.
____ (1996) 'The Achievements of Post-Structuralism', in S. Smith, K. Booth and M. Zalewski (eds) *International Theory: Positivism and Beyond*, Cambridge: Cambridge University Press.
Axelrod, R. (1970) *Conflict of Interest*, Chicago: Markham.
Axelrod, R. and Keohane, R. (1993) 'Achieving Cooperation Under Anarchy: Strategies and Institutions', in D. Baldwin (ed.) *Neorealism and Neoliberalism: The Contemporary Debate*, New York: Columbia University Press.
Bachrach, P. and Baratz, M. (1970) *Power and Poverty: Theory and Practice*, Oxford: Oxford University Press.
Bairoch, P. (1996) 'Globalization – Myths and Realities: One Century of External Trade and Foreign Investment', in R. Boyer and D. Drache (eds) *States Against Markets: The Limits of Globalization*, London: Routledge.
Bakker, I. and Miller, R. (1996) 'Escape from Fordism: The Emergence of Alternative Forms of State Administration and Output', in R. Boyer and D. Drache (eds) *States Against Markets: The Limits of Globalization*, London: Routledge.
Baldwin, R.A. (1997) 'The Causes of Regionalism', *The World Economy*, 20, 7: 865–88.
Barber, B.R. (1989) 'Liberal Democracy and the Costs of Consent', in N. Rosenblum (ed.) *Liberalism and the Moral Life*, Cambridge: Harvard University Press.
Barry, B. (1973) *A Liberal Theory of Justice,* Oxford: Oxford University Press.
____ (1982) 'Humanity and Justice in a Global Perspective', in J.R. Pennock and J.W. Chapman (eds) *Nomos XXIV: Ethics, Economics and the Law*, New York: New York University Press.
____ (1995) *A Treatise on Social Justice. Volume 2: Justice as Impartiality*, Oxford: Oxford University Press.
Bartky, S.L. (1995) 'Agency: What's the Problem', in J.K. Gardiner (ed.) *Provoking Agents: Gender and Agency in Theory and Practice*, Urbana: University of Illinois Press.
Bates, R. (1990) 'Macroeconomic Economy in the Field of Development', in J.E. Alt and K. Shepsle (eds) *Perspectives on Positive Economy*, Cambridge: Cambridge University Press.
Baylis, J. and Smith, S. (eds) (1997) *The Globalization of World Politics*, Oxford: Oxford University Press.
Beck, U. (1977) *The Reinvention of Politics*, trans. M. Ritter, Cambridge: Polity Press.
____ (1992) *Risk Society*, London: Sage.
Beitz, C.R. (1979) *Political Theory and International Relations*, Princeton: Princeton University Press.
____ (1983) 'Cosmopolitan Ideals and National Sentiment', *Journal of Philosophy*, 80, 10: 591–600.
____ (1985) 'Justice and International Relations', in C.R. Beitz, M. Cohen, T. Scanlon and A.J. Simmons (eds) *International Ethics: A Philosophy and Public Affairs Reader*, Princeton: Princeton University Press.
____ (1991) 'Sovereignty and Morality in International Affairs', in D. Held (ed.) *Political Theory Today*, Cambridge: Polity Press.

Bell, D. (1974) *The Coming of Post-Industrial Society*, London: Heinemann.
Belohradsky, V. (1991) *Prirozeny svet jako politicky problem*, Prague: Orientace.
____ (1992) *Kapitalismus a obcanske ctnosti*, Prague: Ceskoslovensky spisovatel.
Benveniste, G. (1972) *The Politics of Expertise*, London: Glendessary Press.
Berger, S. and Dore, R. (eds) (1997) *National Diversity and Global Capitalism*, New York: Cornell University Press.
Bergsten, C.F. (1997) 'Open Regionalism', *The World Economy*, 20, 5: 545–65.
Beuchler, S.M. (1995) 'New Social Movement Theories', in *Sociological Quarterly*, 36, 3: 441–64.
Bhaskar, R. (1978) *A Realist Theory of Science*, Brighton: Harvester Press.
____ (1986) *Scientific Realism and Human Emancipation*, London: Verso.
____ (1989) *Reclaiming Reality*, London: Verso.
____ (1991) *Philosophy and the Idea of Freedom*, Oxford: Blackwell.
Biersteker, T. (1990) 'Reducing the Role of the State in the Economy: A Conceptual Exploration of IMF and World Bank Prescriptions', *International Studies Quarterly*, 34, 2: 477–92.
____ (1992) 'The Triumph of Neo-Classical Economics in the Developing World: Policy Convergence and Bases of Governance in the International Economic Order', in J. Rosenau and E-O. Czempiel (eds) *Governance Without Government: Order and Change in World Politics*, Cambridge: Cambridge University Press.
____ (1998) 'Globalization and the Modes of Operation of Major Institutional Actors', *Oxford Development Studies*, 26, 1: 15–31.
Blackhurst, R. (1997) 'The WTO and the Global Economy', *The World Economy*, 20, 5: 527–44.
Blair, A. (1998) *The Third Way: New Politics for the New Century*, London: Fabian Society.
Bocock, R. (1986) *Hegemony*, London: Ellis Horwood and Tavistock Publications.
Bourdieu, P. (1977) *Outline of a Theory of Practice*, Cambridge: Cambridge University Press.
Brams, S.J. (1985) *Superpower Games: Applying Game Theory to Superpower Conflict*, New Haven: Yale University Press.
Brandt, W., *et al.* (1980) *North–South: A Programme for Survival*, London: Pan.
Braudel, F. (1979) *Civilization and Capitalism 15th–18th Century*. New York: Harper & Row.
Brown, C. (1992) *International Relations Theory: New Normative Approaches*, Hemel Hempstead: Harvester Wheatsheaf.
____ (1995) 'International Political Theory and the Idea of World Community', in K. Booth and S. Smith (eds) *International Relations Theory Today*, Cambridge: Polity Press.
____ (1997) 'Theories of International Justice', *British Journal of Political Science*, 27, 4: 273–97.
Brown, S. (1988) 'Feminism, International Theory, and International Relations of Gender Inequality', *Millennium*, 17, 3: 461–75.
Brzezinski, Z. and Huntington, S. (1964) *Political Power: USA–USSR*, London: Chatto.
Bull, H. (1977) *The Anarchical Society: A Study of Order in World Politics*, London: Macmillan.

Burchill, S. (1996) 'Liberal Internationalism', in S. Burchill and A. Linklater (eds) *Theories of International Relations*, London: Macmillan.

Burn, G. (1997) 'The State, the City and the Euromarkets', paper presented to the *British International Studies Association Annual Conference*, 15–17 December, Leeds University.

Burnell, P.J. (1986) *Economic Nationalism in the Third World*, Brighton: Wheatsheaf.

Burtless, G. (1998) *Globaphobia: Confronting Fears about Open Trade*, Washington: Brookings Institution.

Buzan, B. (1995) 'The Level of Analysis Problem in International Relations Reconsidered', in K. Booth and S. Smith (eds) *International Relations Theory Today*, Cambridge: Polity Press.

Buzan, B., Jones, C. and Little, R. (1993) *The Logic of Anarchy*, New York: Columbia University Press.

Cable, V. and Henderson, D. (1994) *Trade Blocs? The Future of Regional Integration*, London: Royal Institute of International Affairs.

Calhoun, C. (1993) 'New Social Movements of the Early Nineteenth Century', *Social Science History*, 17: 385–427.

Cameron, A. (1997) 'One World Divisible: The Global, The State and Social Exclusion', paper presented at the *British International Studies Association Annual Conference*, 15–17 December, Leeds University.

Cameron, D. (1978) 'The Expansion of the Public Economy: A Comparative Analysis', *American Political Science Review*, 72, 4: 1243–61.

Cameron, R. (1989) *A Concise Economic History of the World: From Paleolithic Times to the Present*, New York: Oxford University Press.

Campbell, D. (1993) *Politics Without Principle: Sovereignty, Ethics and the Narratives of the Gulf War*, Boulder: Lynne Rienner.

Campbell, T. (1987) *The Earliest Printed Maps, 1472–1500*, London: British Library.

Carlsnaes, W. (1992) 'The Agency-Structure Problem in Foreign Policy Analysis', *International Studies Quarterly*, 36, 4: 245–70.

Carlsson, I. *et al.* (1995) *Our Global Neighbourhood*, Oxford: Oxford University Press.

Carroll, W.K. and Ratner, R. (1994) 'Between Leninism and Radical Pluralism: Gramscian Reflections on Counter-Hegemony and the New Social Movements', *Critical Sociology*, 20, 2: 1–24.

Carter, G. (ed.) (1966) *National Unity and Regionalism in Eight African States*, New York: Cornell University Press.

Castaneda, G. (1994) *Utopia Unarmed*, New York: Vintage Books.

Castells, M. (1989) *The Informational City: Information, Technology, Economic Restructuring, and the Urban-Regional Process*, Oxford: Blackwell.

____ (1996) *The Information Age: Economy, Society and Culture. Volume 1: The Rise of the Network Society*, Oxford: Blackwell.

Castoriadis, C. (1987) *The Imaginary Constitution of Society* [1975], Cambridge: MIT Press.

Cerny, P.G. (1990) *The Changing Architecture of Politics: Structure, Agency and the Future of the State*, London: Sage.

____ (1995) 'Globalization and the Changing Logic of Collective Action', *International Organization*, 49, 4: 595–625.

Cervenka, Z. (1977) *The Unfinished Quest for Unity: Africa and the OAU*, London: Friedmann.

Chase-Dunn, C.K. (1989) *Global Formation: Structures of the World Economy*, Oxford: Blackwell.

Cisarovska, B., Drapala, M., Precan, V. and Vancura, J. (eds) (1997) *Charta 77 ocima soucasniku*, Prague: Ustav pro soudobe dejiny Akademie Ved Ceske Republiky.

Clasen, J., Gould, A. and Vincent, J. (1998) *Voices Within and Without: Responses to Long-term Unemployment in Germany, Sweden and Britain*, Bristol: Policy Press.

Claude, I. (1965) *Swords into Plowshares*, London: University of London Press.

Clegg, S.R., Hardy, C. and Nord, W. (eds) (1996) *Handbook of Organization Studies*, London: Sage.

Cohen J. and Arato, A. (1992) *Civil Society and Political Theory*, Cambridge: MIT Press.

Commission on Global Governance (1995) *Our Global Neighbourhood*, New York: Oxford University Press.

Cooper, R. (1986) 'Worldwide Regional Integration: Is there an Optimal Size of the Integrated Area?', in R. Cooper (ed.) *Economic Policy in an Interdependent World*, Massachussetts: MIT Press.

Cox, R. (1981) 'Social Forces, States and World Orders: Beyond International Relations Theory', *Millennium*, 10, 2: 126–55.

____ (1983) 'Gramsci, Hegemony and International Relations: An Essay in Method', *Millennium* 12, 2: 162–75.

____ (1987) *Production, Power and World Order*, New York: Columbia University Press.

____ (1995) 'Critical Political Economy', in B. Hettne (ed.) *International Political Economy: Understanding Global Disorder*, London: Zed Books.

Crane, G.T. (1998) 'Economic Nationalism: Bringing the Nation Back In', *Millennium*, 27, 1: 55–76.

Curtain, P. (1969) *The Atlantic Slave Trade*, Madison: University of Wisconsin Press.

Curzon Price, V. (1981) 'Recessions and the World Economic Order', in S. Strange and R. Tooze (eds) *The International Politics of Surplus Capacity*, London: George Allen & Unwin.

Cutler, A.C. (1995) 'Global Capitalism and Liberal Myth: Dispute Settlement in Private International Trade Relations', *Millennium*, 24, 3: 377–97.

Dahrendorf, R. (1991) *Uvahy o revoluci v Evrope*, Prague: Evropsky kulturni klub.

____ (1997) *After 1989: Morals, Revolution and Civil Society*, London: Macmillan.

Dalby, S. (1990) *Creating the Second Cold War: The Discourse of Politics*, London: Pinter.

____ (1996) 'Crossing Disciplinary Boundaries: Political Geography and International Relations after the Cold War', in E. Koffman and G. Youngs (eds) *Globalization: Theory and Practice*, London: Pinter.

Dalton, R.J. and Keuchler, M. (eds) (1990) *Challenging the Political Order*, Cambridge: Polity Press.

D'Anieri, P., Ernst, C. and Kier, E. (1990) 'New Social Movements in Historical Perspective', in *Comparative Politics*, 22, 4: 445–58.

Dearlove, J. (1989) 'Neo-Classical Politics', *Review of Political Economy*, 1, 2: 208–37.

Dearlove, J. and Saunders, P. (1984) *Introduction to British Politics*, Cambridge: Polity.

De Bassompierre, G. (1988) *Changing the Guard in Brussels: An Insider's View of the EC Presidency,* New York: Praeger.

Dell, S. (1963) *Trade Blocs and Common Markets*, London: Constable.

Der Derian, J. (1987) *On Diplomacy: A Genealogy of Western Estrangement*, Oxford: Blackwell.

____ (1990) 'The (S)pace of International Relations: Simulation, Surveillance, and Speed', *International Studies Quarterly*, 34, 3: 295–310.

____ (1992) *Antidiplomacy: Spies, Terror, Speed and War*, Cambridge, Mass: Blackwell.

Deutsch, K. (1957) *Political Community and the North Atlantic Area*, Princeton: Princeton University Press.

Dicken, P. (1992) *Global Shift: The Internationalization of Economic Activity*, London: Paul Chapman.

Dinan, D. (1998) *Ever Closer Union*, London: Macmillan.

Dodd, N. (1994) *The Sociology of Money*, Cambridge: Polity Press.

____ (1995) 'Money and the Nation-State: Contested Boundaries of Monetary Sovereignty in Geopolitics', *International Sociology*, 10, 2: 139–54.

Donaldson, T. (1992) 'Kant's Global Rationalism', in T. Nardin and D.R. Mapel (eds) *Traditions of International Ethics*, Cambridge: Cambridge University Press.

Donelan, M. (1990) *Elements of International Political Theory*, Oxford: Clarendon Press.

Dowding, K. (1995) 'Model or Metaphor? A Critical Review of the Policy Network Approach', *Political Studies*, 43, 1: 136–58.

Dryzek, J. and Leonard, S. (1988) 'History and Discipline in Political Science', *American Political Science Review*, 82, 4: 1245–60.

Dunne, T. (1997) 'Liberalism', in J. Baylis and S. Smith (eds) *The Globalization of International Politics*, Oxford: Oxford University Press.

Dunning, J. (1993) *The Globalization of Business*, London: Routledge.

Dunning, J. and Hamdani, K. (eds) (1997) *The New Globalism and Developing Countries*, Tokyo: United Nations University Press.

Earnshaw, D. and Judge D. (1995) 'Early Days: the European Parliament, Co-decision and European Union Legislative Process Post-Maastricht' *Journal of European Public Policy*, 2, 4: 624–49.

Easton, D. (1953) *The Political System*, Chicago: The University of Chicago Press.

____ (1991) 'Political Science in the United States: Past and Present', in D. Easton, J. Gunnell and L. Graziano (eds) *The Development of Political Science*, London: Routledge.

____ (1997) 'The Future of the Post-Behavioural Phase in Political Science', in K.R. Monroe (ed.) *Contemporary Empirical Political Theory*, Berkeley: University of California Press.

El Kahal, S. (1994) *Introduction to International Business*, London: McGraw-Hill.

____ (1995) 'The Global Political Economy, Politicization and Consensus in International Organization: The Case of UNESCO', unpublished D.Phil. Thesis, University of Sussex.

____ (1996) 'International Business: The Global Political Economy and Eastern Europe', in B. Einhorn, M. Kaldor and Z. Kavan (eds) *Citizenship and Democratic Control in Contemporary Europe*, Cheltenham: Edward Elgar.

____ (1998) *Doing Business in Europe*, London: McGraw-Hill.

Emadi-Coffin, B. (1996) 'The Multinational Corporation and the State: International Regulation and the Establishment of Enterprise Zones and Export Processing Zones', unpublished D.Phil. Thesis, University of Sussex.

Enloe, C. (1989) *Bananas, Beaches and Bases: Making Feminist Sense of International Relations*, London: Pandora.

Eschle, C. (1999) 'Globalizing Civil Society? Social Movements and the Challenge of Global Politics from Below', in P. Hamel, H. Lustiger-Thaler and S. Roseneil (eds) *Global Flows: New Frameworks for Collective Action*, Basingstoke: Macmillan.

Escobar, A. and Alvarez, S. (eds) (1992) *The Making of Social Movements in Latin America*, Boulder: Westview Press.

European Bank for Reconstruction and Development (1997) *Transition Report*, London: European Bank for Reconstruction and Development.

European Commission (1993) *Employment, Growth and Competitiveness*, Commission for European Communities, Brussels. Online. Available HTTP: http://europa.eu.int/en/record/white/c93700/ch2a_1.html

Evans, P. (1978) *Dependent Development*, Princeton: Princeton University Press.

____ (1995) *Embedded Autonomy*, Princeton: Princeton University Press.

____ (1997) 'The Eclipse of the State: Reflections on Stateness in an Era of Globalization', *World Politics*, 50, 1: 62–87.

Evans, P., Jacobson, H. and Putnam, R. (1993) *Double Edged Diplomacy: International Bargaining and Domestic Politics*, London: University of California Press.

Evans, P., Rueschemeyer, D. and Skocpol, T. (eds) (1985) *Bringing the State Back In*, Cambridge: Cambridge University Press.

Farr, J. and Seidelman R. (eds) (1993) *Discipline and History: Political Science in the U.S.*, Ann Arbor: University of Michigan Press.

Farrands, C. (1996) 'The Globalization of Knowledge and the Politics of Global Intellectual Property: Power, Governance and Technology', in E. Koffman and G. Youngs (eds) *Globalization: Theory and Practice*, London: Pinter.

Ferguson, Y.H. and Mansbach, R.W. (1989) *The State, Conceptual Chaos and the Future of International Relations*, Boulder: Lynne Rienner.

Fernandez-Jilberto, A.E. and Mommen, A. (1997) 'Globalization versus Regionalization', in A.E. Fernandez-Jilberto and A. Mommen (eds) *Regionalism and Globalization in the Modern World Economy*, London: Routledge.

Financial Times (1997) 'Africa Faces a Crisis of Governance', 26 June: p. 4.

Fiorina, M. (1995) 'Rational Choice, Empirical Contributions and the Scientific Enterprise', *Critical Review*, 9: 71–84.

Fordham, B. (1998) 'Economic Interests, Party and Ideology in Early Cold War Era U.S. Foreign Policy', *International Organization*, 52, 2: 359–96.

Foucault, M. (1980) *Power/Knowledge: Selected Interviews and Other Writings, 1972–1977*, Brighton: Harvester.

____ (1982) 'The Subject and Power', in H. Dreyfus and P. Rabinow (eds) *Michel Foucault: Beyond Structuralism and Hermeneutics*, Chicago: University of Chicago Press.

IV Sjezd Svazu ceskoslovenskych spisovatelu (1967), Prague: Ceskoslovensky spisovatel.

Franklin, M., Marsh, M. and McLaren, L. (1994) 'Uncorking the Bottle: Popular Opposition to European Unification in the Wake of Maastricht', *Journal of Common Market Studies*, 32, 4: 455–72.

Franklin, M., van der Eijk, C. and Marsh, M. (1995) 'Referendum Outcomes and Trust in Government: Public Support for Europe in the Wake of Maastricht', *West European Politics*, 18, 3: 101–17.

Frieden, J.A. (1991) 'Invested Interests: The Politics of National Economic Policies in a World of Global Finance', *International Organization*, 45, 4: 425–52.

Fukuyama, F. (1992) *The End of History and the Last Man*, New York: Basic Books.

Gabel, M. and Palmer, H.D. (1995) 'Understanding Variation in Public Support for European Integration', *European Journal of Political Research*, 27, 1: 3–19.

Galbraith, J.K. (1967) *The New Industrial State*, London: Hamilton.

Gamble, A. (1990) 'Theories of British Politics', *Political Studies*, 38, 3: 404–20.

Gamble, A. and Payne, A. (eds) (1996) *Regionalism and World Order*, Basingstoke: Macmillan.

Gamble, C. (1994) *Timewalkers: The Prehistory of Global Colonization*, London: Sutton.

Garcia, S. (ed.) (1993) *European Identity and the Search for Legitimacy*, London: Pinter.

Garrett, G. (1998) 'Shrinking States? Globalization and National Autonomy in the OECD', *Oxford Development Studies*, 26, 1: 71–97.

Gellner, E. (1983) *Nations and Nationalism*, Oxford: Blackwell.

Giddens, A. (1985) *The Nation State and Violence*, Cambridge: Polity Press.

____ (1990) *The Consequences of Modernity*, Cambridge: Polity Press.

____ (1991) *Modernity and Self-identity*, Cambridge: Polity Press.

____ (1994) *Beyond Left and Right*, Cambridge: Polity Press.

____ (1998) *The Third Way*, Cambridge: Polity Press.

Gill, S. (1990) *American Hegemony and the Trilateral Commission*, Cambridge: Cambridge University Press.

____ (1992) 'The Emerging World Order and European Change: The Political Economy of European Union' in R. Miliband and L. Panitch (eds) (1992) *New World Order: Socialist Register 1992*, London: Merlin Press.

____ (1994) 'Structural Change and the Global Political Economy: Globalizing Elites and the Emerging World Order', in Y. Sakamoto (ed.) *Global Transformation: Challenges to the State System*, Tokyo: United Nations University Press.

____ (1995) 'The Global Panoptican: The Neo-Liberal State, Economic Life and Democratic Surveillance', *Alternatives*, 20, 2: 1–49.

____ (ed.) (1996) *Globalization, Democratization and Multilateralism*, Basingstoke: Macmillan.

Gill, S. and Law, D. (1988) *The Global Political Economy*, London: Harvester Wheatsheaf.

____ (1989) 'Global Hegemony and the Structural Power of Capital', *International Studies Quarterly*, 33, 3: 475–99.

Gilpin, R. (1987) *The Political Economy of International Relations*, Princeton: Princeton University Press.

Goldblatt, D., Held, D., McGrew, A. and Perraton, J. (1997) 'Economic Globalization and the Nation-State: Shifting Balances of Power', *Alternatives*, 22, 2: 269–86.

Goldstein, J. and Keohane, R. (eds) (1993) *Ideas and Foreign Policy*, Ithaca: Cornell University Press.

Goodin, R. and Klingemann, H-D. (1996) 'Political Science: The Discipline', in R. Goodin and H-D. Klingemann (eds) *A New Handbook of Political Science*, Oxford: Oxford University Press.

Gosovic, B. and Ruggie, J. (1976) 'On the Creation of a New International Economic Order', *International Organization*, 30, 2: 309–46.

Gourevitch, P. (1978) 'The Second Image Reversed: The International Sources of Domestic Politics', *International Organization*, 32, 4: 881–912.

____ (1986) *Politics in Hard Times*, New York: Cornell University Press.

Gramsci, A. (1971) *Selections from Prison Notebooks*, trans. Quentin Hoare and Geoffrey Nowell Smith, London: Lawrence and Wishart.

Grant, R. and Newland, K. (1991) *Gender and International Relations*, Milton Keynes: Open University Press.

Gray, J. (1998) *False Dawn: The Delusions of Global Capitalism*, London: Granta Publications.

Grieco, J.M. (1995) 'Anarchy and the Limits of Cooperation: A Realist Critique of the Newest Liberal Institutionalism', in C. Kegley, Jr. (ed.) *Controversies in International Relations Theory: Realism and Neoliberalism*, New York: St. Martin's Press.

Gual, J. (ed.) (1996) *The Social Challenge of Job Creation: Combating Unemployment in Europe*, Cheltenham: Edward Elgar.

Gunnell, J. (1991) 'The Historiography of American Political Science', in D. Easton, J. Gunnell and L. Graziano (eds) *The Development of Political Science*, London: Routledge.

Haas, E. (1964) *Beyond the Nation State*, Stanford: Stanford University Press.

____ (1976) 'Turbulent Fields and the Theory of Regional Integration', *International Organization*, 30, 2: 173–212.

Haas, E. and Schmitter, P. (1965) *The Politics of Economics in Latin American Regionalism*, Denver: University of Denver.

Haas, P. (1998) 'Compliance with European Union Directives: Insights from International Relations and Comparative Politics', *Journal of European Public Policy*, 5, 1: 17–37.

Habermas, J. (1977) *Towards a Rational Society*, trans. J. Shapiro, London: Heinemann.

____ (1989) *The Structural Transformation of the Public Sphere*, trans. Thomas Burger with Friedrich Lawrence, Cambridge M.A.: MIT Press.

Halliday, F. (1999) *Revolution in International Relations*, London: Macmillan.

Halliday, F. and Rosenberg, J. (1998) 'Interview with Kenneth Waltz', *Review of International Studies*, 24, 3: 371–86.

Hancock, D. (1995) *Citizens of the World: London Merchants and the Integration of the British Atlantic Community, 1735–1785*, Cambridge: Cambridge University Press.

Harvey, D. (1989) *The Condition of Postmodernity: An Enquiry into the Conditions of Cultural Change*, Oxford: Blackwell.

Havel, V. (1985) 'The Anatomy of Reticence', in *Living in Truth* [1989], London: Faber and Faber.

____ (1989) *Living in Truth*, J. Vladislav (ed.), London: Faber and Faber.
____ (1992a) *Summer Meditations*, London: Faber and Faber.
____ (1992b) *Vazeni obcane*, Prague: Lidove noviny.
Havel, V., *et al.* (1985) *The Power of the Powerless*, J. Keane (ed.), London: Palach Press.
Hayes-Renshaw, F. and Wallace, H. (1997) *The Council of Ministers*, Basingstoke: Macmillan.
Heater, D. (1992) *The Idea of European Unity*, Leicester: Leicester University Press.
Heidegger, M. (1950) 'The Thing', in *Poetry, Language, Thought* [1971], New York: Harper & Row.
Held, D. (1991a) 'Democracy and Globalization', *Alternatives*, 16: 201–8.
____ (1991b) 'Democracy, the Nation-State and the Global System', in D. Held (ed.) *Political Theory Today*, Cambridge: Polity Press.
____ (1995) *Democracy and the Global Order*, Cambridge: Polity Press.
Helleiner, E. (1994) *States and the Reemergence of Global Finance: From Bretton Woods to the 1990s*, Ithaca: Cornell University Press.
Henderson, W. (1959) *The Zollverein*, London: Cass.
____ (1962) *Genesis of the Common Market*, London: Cass.
Hinsley, F.H. (1963) *Power and the Pursuit of Peace: Theory and Practice in the History of Relations Between States*, Cambridge: Cambridge University Press.
Hirschman, A. (1970) 'The Search for Paradigms as a Hindrance to Understanding', *World Politics*, 22: 330–43.
Hirst, P. (1991) 'The State, Civil Society and the Collapse of Soviet Communism', *Economy and Society*, 20, 2: 217–41.
Hirst, P. and Thompson, G. (1996) *Globalization in Question: The International Economy and the Possibilities of Governance*, Cambridge: Polity Press.
Hix, S. (1994) 'Approaches to the Study of the European Community: The Challenge to Comparative Politics', *West European Politics*, 17, 1: 1–30.
____ (1998) 'The Study of the European Union II: The "New Governance" Agenda and its Rival', *Journal of European Public Policy*, 5, 1: 38–65.
Hobsbawm, E. (1968) *The Age of Revolution*, London: Fontana.
Hobson, J. and Weiss, L. (1995) *States and Economic Development*, Cambridge: Polity Press.
Hoekman, N. and Sauve, P. (1994) 'Regional and Multilateral Liberalization of Service Markets: Complements or Substitutes?', *Journal of Common Market Studies*, 32, 3 (September 1994): 283–317.
Hoffman, J. (1995) *Beyond the State*, Cambridge: Polity Press.
Hoffmann, S. (1966) 'Obstinate or Obsolete? The Fate of the Nation-State and the Case of Western Europe', *Daedalus*, 95, 3: 862–915.
____ (1981) *Duties Beyond Borders: On the Limits and Possibilities of Ethical International Politics*, Syracuse: Syracuse University Press.
____ (1995) 'The Crisis of Liberal Internationalism', *Foreign Policy*, 98: 159–79.
Holland, S. (1980) *Uncommon Market*, London: Macmillan.
Hollingsworth, J., Schmitter, P. and Streeck, W. (1994) 'Capitalism, Sectors, Institutions and Performance', in J. Hollingsworth, P. Schmitter and W. Streeck (eds) *Governing Capitalist Economies*, Oxford: Oxford University Press.
Hollis, M. and Smith, S. (1991) 'Beware of Gurus: Structure and Action in International Relations', *Review of International Studies*, 17, 4: 393–410.

____ (1994) 'Two Stories about Structure and Agency', *Review of International Studies*, 20, 3: 214–51.

____ (1996) 'A Response: Why Epistemology Matters in International Theory', *Review of International Studies*, 22, 1: 111–16.

Hoopes, S. (1997) *Oil Privatization, Public Choice and International Forces*, Basingstoke, Macmillan.

Hoopes, S. and Nicholson, M. (1997) 'Individual Preferences and Group Decision-Making', paper presented at the *American Political Science Association Conference*, 28 August–1 September, Washington, D.C.

Hopkins, T.K. and Wallerstein, I. (eds) (1996) *The Age of Transition: Trajectory of the World-System, 1945–2025*, London: Zed.

Horkheimer, M. (1972) 'Traditional and Critical Theory', in M. Horkheimer, *Critical Theory: Selected Essays*, trans. M. O'Connell, New York: Herder and Herder.

Horsman, M. and Marshall, A. (1994) *After the Nation-State: Citizens, Tribalism and the New World Order*, London: HarperCollins.

Hoskyns, C. (1994) 'Gender Issues in International Relations: The Case of the European Commuity', *Review of International Studies*, 20, 3: 225–39.

Huntington, S. (1988) 'One Soul at a Time: Political Science and Political Reform', *American Political Science Review*, 82, 1: 3–10.

Husak, P. (1997) *Budovani kapitalismu v Cechach*, Prague: Volvox Globator.

Hyde, F. and Hyde, E. (1975) *Cunard and the North Atlantic, 1840–1973*, London: Macmillan.

Ikenberry, G.J. (1989) 'Rethinking the Origins of American Hegemony', *Political Science Quarterly*, 104, 3: 375–400.

ISA Consult, Sussex European Institute, GJW Europe (1997) *Report on the Evaluation of the PHARE and TACIS Democracy Programme, 1992–1997*, Brighton and Hamburg: European Union Commission.

Jabri, V. and Chan, S. (1996) 'The Ontologist Always Rings Twice: Two More Stories about Structure and Agency in Response to Hollis and Smith', *Review of International Studies*, 22, 1: 107–10.

Jackson, R. (1990) *Quasi-States: Sovereignty, International Relations and the Third World*, Cambridge: Cambridge University Press.

____ (1996) 'Is There a Classical International Theory?', in S. Smith, K. Booth, and M. Zalewski (eds) *International Theory: Positivism and Beyond*, Cambridge: Cambridge University Press.

Jacobs, J. (1985) *Cities and the Wealth of Nations*, New York: Vintage.

Janos, A. (1997) 'Paradigms Revisited: Protectionism, Globality, and Postmodernity in Comparative Politics', *World Politics*, 50, 1: 118–49.

Jessop, R. (1990) *State Theory: Putting Capitalist States in their Place*, Cambridge: Cambridge University Press.

____ (1993) 'Towards a Schumpeterian Workfare State? Preliminary Remarks on Post-Fordist Political Economy', *Studies in Political Economy*, 40: 7–39.

Jicinsky, Z. (1995) *Charta 77 a pravni stat*, Prague: Doplnek.

John, P. (1994) 'Central-Local Relations in the 1980s and 1990s: Toward a Policy Learning Approach', *Local Government Studies*, 20, 3: 412–36.

Kahler, M. (1990) 'Orthodoxy and its Alternatives', in J. Nelson (ed.) *Economic Crisis and Policy Choice: The Politics of Adjustment in the Third World*, Princeton:

Princeton University Press.
Kaldor, M. (ed.) (1991) *Europe from Below*, London: Verso.
____ (1996) 'New and Old Wars: Organized Violence in a Global Era', in R. Caplan and J. Feffer (eds) *Europe's New Nationalisms*, Cambridge: Cambridge University Press.
____ (1999) 'Transnational Civil Society', in T. Dunne and N.J. Wheeler (eds) *Human Rights in Global Politics*, Cambridge: Cambridge University Press.
Kaldor, M., Holden, G. and Falk, R. (eds) (1989) *The New Detente*, London: Verso.
Kaldor, M. and Vashee, B. (eds) (1997) *New Wars*, London: Cassell.
Kant, I. (1929) *Critique of Pure Reason*, trans. N. Kemp Smith, London: Macmillan.
____ (1971) *Political Writings*, trans. H. Reiss, Cambridge: Cambridge University Press.
____ (1991) *The Moral Law: Groundwork of the Metaphysics of Morals*, trans. H.J. Paton, London: Routledge.
Kaplan, M. (1957) *System and Process in International Politics*, New York: Wiley.
Kasse, M. and Newton, K. (eds) (1995) *Beliefs in Government*, Oxford: Oxford University Press.
Katona, A. (1998) 'The Globalization of Consultancy', unpublished M.A. dissertation, University of Sussex.
Kavan, Z. (1996) 'Democracy and Nationalism', in B. Einhorn, M. Kaldor and Z. Kavan (eds) *Citizenship and Democratic Control in Contemporary Europe*, Cheltenham: Edward Elgar.
Kavan, Z. and Palous, M. (1999) 'Democracy in the Czech Republic', in M. Kaldor and I. Vejvoda (eds) *Democratization in Central and Eastern Europe*, London: Cassell.
Keane, J. (ed.) (1988) *Civil Society and the State*, London: Verso.
Kegley Jr., C.W. (1995) 'The Neoliberal Challenge to Realist Theories of World Politics: An Introduction', in C.W. Kegley, Jr. (ed.) *Controversies in International Relations Theory: Realism and Neoliberalism*, New York: St. Martin's Press.
Kegley Jr., C.W. and Hermann, M.G. (1998) 'The Interventionist Rationale: Promoting the Democratic Peace', unpublished paper prepared for the 39th meeting of the *International Studies Association*, Minneapolis.
Keohane, R. (1981) 'The Theory of Hegemonic Stability and Changes in International Economic Regimes, 1967–77', in O. Holsti, R. Silverson and A. George (eds) *Change in the International System*, Boulder: Westview Press.
____ (1982) 'The Crisis of Embedded Liberalism', in J. Goldthorpe (ed.) *Order and Conflict in Contemporary Capitalism*, Oxford: Clarendon Press.
____ (1984) *After Hegemony: Cooperation and Discord in the World Political Economy*, Princeton: Princeton University Press.
____ (1989) *International Institutions and State Power: Essays in International Relations Theory*, Boulder: Westview Press.
____ (1990) 'International Liberalism Reconsidered', in J. Dunn (ed.) *The Economic Limits to Modern Politics*, Cambridge: Cambridge University Press.
Keohane, R. and Milner H. (eds) (1996) *Internationalization and Domestic Politics*, Cambridge: Cambridge University Press.
Keohane, R. and Nye, J. (eds) (1972) *Transnational Relations and World Politics*, Cambridge: Harvard University Press.
____ (1973) *Transnational Relations and World Politics*, Cambridge: Harvard Centre for International Affairs.

____ (1977) *Power and Interdependence*, Boston: Little, Brown.

Kerr, C. (1962) *Industrialism and Industrial Man*, London: Heinemann.

Kickert, W.J.M., Klijn, E.H. and Koppenjan, J.F.M. (eds) (1997) *Managing Complex Networks: Strategies for the Public Sector*, London: Sage.

Kindleberger, C. (1969) *American Business Abroad*, New Haven: Yale University Press.

King, A. (1975) 'Overload: Problems of Governing in the 1970s', *Political Studies*, 23, 2–3: 284–96.

Kirchner, E. (1992) *Decision-Making in the European Community: The Council Presidency and European Integration*, Manchester: Manchester University Press.

Klaus, V. (1991a) *O tvar zitrka*, Prague: Prazska Imaginace.

____ (1991b) *Nemam rad katastroficke scenare*, Ostrava: Sagit.

____ (1994) *Ceska cesta*, Prague: Profile.

____ (1997) *Obhajoba zapomenutych myslenek*, Prague: Academia.

Klein, B. (1988) 'Hegemony and Strategic Culture: American Power Projection and Alliance Defence Politics', *Review of International Studies*, 14, 2: 133–49.

Kohak, E. (1993) *Jan Patocka*, Prague: H&H.

Konrad, G. (1984) *Anti-Politics*, London: Quartet Books.

Kostakos, G., Groom, A.J.R., Morphet, S. and Taylor, P. (1991) 'Britain and the New UN Agenda: Towards Global Riot Control?', *Review of International Studies*, 17, 1: 95–105.

Krasner, S. (1978) *Defending the National Interest*, Princeton: Princeton University Press.

____ (ed.) (1983) *International Regimes*, Ithaca: Cornell University Press.

____ (1985) *Structural Conflict: The Third World against Global Liberalism*, Berkeley: University of California Press.

Krause, J. (1995) 'The International Dimensions of Gender Inequality and Feminist Politics', in J. Macmillan and A. Linklater (eds) *Boundaries in Question: New Directions in International Relations*, London: Pinter.

Krippendorf, E. (1982) *International Relations as a Social Science*, Brighton: Harvester Press.

Krueger, A. (1974) 'The Political Economy of the Rent Seeking Society', *American Economic Review*, 64, 3: 291–303.

Laffran, B. (1997) 'From Policy Entrepreneur to Policy Manager: The Challenge Facing the European Commission', *Journal of European Public Policy*, 4, 3: 422–38.

Lapid, Y. (1989) 'The Third Debate: On the Prospects of International Theory in a Post-Positivist Era', *International Studies Quarterly*, 33, 3: 235–54.

Lash, S. and Urry, J. (1994) *Economies of Signs and Space*, London: Sage.

Lawrence, R. (1996) *Regionalism, Multilateralism and Deeper Integration*, Washington: Brookings Institute.

Laxer, G. (1995) 'Social Solidarity, Democracy and Global Capitalism', *Canadian Review of Sociology*, 32, 3: 287–313.

Layard, R. (1996) 'Preventing Long-Term Unemployment: An Economic Analysis', in J. Gual (ed.) *The Social Challenge of Job Creation*, Cheltenham: Edward Elgar.

Lee, K. (1996) *Global Telecommunications Regulation: A Political Economy Perspective*, London: Pinter.

Leonard, D. and Straus S. (1997) 'Putting Your Company's Whole Brain to Work', *Harvard Business Review*, 4: 111–21.

Letwin, O. (1988) *Privatizing the World*, London: Cassell.

Levitas, R. (1996) 'The Concept of Social Exclusion and the New Durkheimian Hegemony', *Critical Social Policy*, 46, 16: 5–20.

Levitt, T. (1983) 'The Globalization of Markets', *Harvard Business Review*, 83, 3: 92–102.

Lijphart, A. (ed.) (1992) *Parliamentary versus Presidential Government*, Oxford: Oxford University Press.

Lipset, S.M. and Rokkan, S. (1968) 'Cleavage Structures, Party Systems and Voter Alignments', in S.M. Lipset and S. Rokkan (eds) *Party Systems and Voter Alignments: Cross National Perspectives*, New York: The Free Press.

Lipshutz, R. (1992) 'Reconstructing World Politics: The Emergence of Global Civil Society', *Millennium*, 21, 3: 389–420.

Lovett, A. (1996) 'The United States and the Schuman Plan: A Study in French Diplomacy 1950–52', *Historical Journal*, 39, 2: 425–55.

Luard, E. (1990) *The Globalization of Politics: The Changed Focus of Political Action in the Modern World*, London: Macmillan.

____ (1992) 'Human Rights and Foreign Policy', in R.P. Claude and B.H. Weston (eds) *Human Rights in the World Community*, Philadelphia: University of Pennsylvania Press.

Ludlow, P. (1993) 'The UK Presidency: A View from Brussels', *Journal of Common Market Studies*, 31, 2: 246–60.

Lukes, S. (1974) *Power: A Radical View*, London: Macmillan.

Lynn-Jones, S.M. (1998) 'Why the United States Should Spread Democracy', *BCSIA Discussion Paper 98-01*, Kennedy School of Government, Harvard University.

McGowan, F. (1994) 'What is the Alternative? The Labour Party Ownership and Competition', in M. Bishop, J. Kay and C. Mayer (eds) *Privatisation and Economic Performance*, Oxford: Clarendon Press.

____ (1999) *European Integration and Disembedded Liberalism*, Brighton: University of Sussex, mimeo.

McGowan, F. and Seabright, P. (1995) 'Regulation in the European Community and its Impact on the UK', in M. Bishop, J. Kay and C. Mayer (eds) *The Regulatory Challenge*, Oxford: Clarendon Press.

McGowan, F. and Wallace, H. (1996) 'Towards a European Regulatory State', *Journal of European Public Policy*, 3, 4: 560–76.

McGrew, A. (ed.) (1997) *The Transformation of Democracy*, Cambridge: Polity Press.

McGrew, A.G. and Lewis, P., *et al.* (1992) *Global Politics: Globalization and the Nation-State*, Cambridge: Polity Press.

McKay, D. (1996) *Rush to Union: Understanding the Federal Bargain*, Oxford: Clarendon Press.

McLuhan, M. (1964) *Understanding Media*, London: Routledge.

McMichael, P. (1996) *Development and Social Change: A Global Perspective*, Thousand Oaks: Pine Forge Press.

Machlup, F. (1977) *A History of Thought on Economic Integration*, London: Macmillan.

MacLean, J. (1981a) 'Political Theory, International Theory and Problems of Ideology', *Millennium*, 10, 2: 102–25.

____ (1981b) 'Marxist Epistemology, Explanations of Change, and the Study of International Relations', in R.J. Jones and B. Buzan (eds) *Change and the Study of*

International Relations, London: Pinter.
____ (1988a) 'Marxism and International Relations: A Strange Case of Mutual Neglect', *Millennium*, 17, 2: 295–319.
____ (1988b) 'Belief Systems and Ideology in International Relations: A Critical Approach', in R. Little and S. Smith (eds) *Belief Systems and International Relations*, Oxford: Blackwell.
____ (1996) 'The Ideology of the End of Marxism/End of Socialism Thesis: A Critical Global Perspective', in B. Einhorn, M. Kaldor and Z. Kavan (eds) *Citizenship and Democratic Control in Contemporary Europe*, Cheltenham: Edward Elgar.
____ (1999) 'Philosophical Roots of Globalization: Philosophical Routes to Globalization', in R. Germain (ed.) *Globalization and its Critics: Perspectives from Political Economy*, Basingstoke: Macmillan.
Maiguascha, B. (1994) 'The Transnational Indigenous Movement in a Changing World Order', in Y. Sakamoto (ed.) *Global Transformation: Challenges to the State System*, Tokyo: United Nations University Press.
Majone, G. (1994) 'The Rise of the Regulatory State in Europe', *West European Politics*, 17, 3: 77–101.
Mann, M. (1993) *The Sources of Social Power. Volume 2*, Cambridge: Cambridge University Press.
____ (1997) 'Has Globalization Ended the Rise and Rise of the Nation-State?', *Review of International Political Economy*, 4, 3: 472–96.
Manzo, K. (1992) 'Global Power and South African Politics: A Foucauldian Analysis', *Alternatives*, 17, 1: 23–66.
March, J.C. and Olsen, J.P. (1984) 'The New Institutionalism: Organizational Factors in Political Life', *American Political Science Review*, 78, 3: 734–49.
____ (1989) *Rediscovering Institutions: The Organizational Basis of Politics*, New York: Free Press.
Marcuse, H. (1964) *One Dimensional Man*, London: Routledge and Kegan Paul.
____ (1968) *Negations: Essays in Critical Theory*, London: Allen Lane.
Marks, G., Hooghe, L. and Blank, K. (1996) 'European Integration from the 1980s: State-Centric versus Multi-Level Governance', *Journal of Common Market Studies*, 34, 3: 341–78.
Marks, G., Scharpf, F.W., Schmitter, P. and Streek, W. (1996) *Governance in the European Union*, London: Sage.
Marquand, D. (1997) *Coping with Capitalism*, London: Polity Press.
Martin, R. (1994) 'Stateless Monies, Global Financial Integration and National Economic Autonomy: The End of Geography?', in S. Corbridge, R. Martin and N. Thrift (eds) *Money, Power and Space*, Oxford: Blackwell.
Marx, K. (1973) *Grundrisse*, trans. M. Nicholaus, Harmondsworth: Penguin Books.
Marx, K. and Engels, F. (1998) *The Communist Manifesto* [1848], London: Verso.
Maturana, H.R. and Varela, F.J. (1980) 'Autopoiesis and Cognition: The Realization of the Living', *Boston Studies in the Philosophy of Science*, 42.
Meehan, E. (1993) *Citizenship and the European Community*, London: Sage.
Meiksins Wood, E. (1995) *Democracy Against Capitalism*, Cambridge: Cambridge University Press.
Melo, J. and Panagariya, A. (eds) (1993) *New Dimensions in Regional Integration*, Cambridge: Cambridge University Press.

Melucci, A. (1989) *Nomads of the Present: Social Movements and Individual Needs in Contemporary Society*, London: Hutchinson Radius.

Meny, Y. and Knapp, A. (1998) *Government and Politics in Western Europe*, Oxford: Oxford University Press.

Mészaros, I. (1986) *Philosophy, Ideology and Social Science*, Brighton: Wheatsheaf Books.

Meynaud (1964) *La Technocratie: Mythe ou Realité?*, Paris: Payot.

Michnik, A. (1985) *Letters from Prison and other Essays*, Berkeley: University of California Press.

Mills, C.W. (1956) *The Power Elite*, Oxford: Oxford University Press.

Milner, H. (1988) *Resisting Protectionism: Global Industries and the Politics of International Trade*, Princeton: Princeton University Press.

Milward, A. (1995) 'The Springs of Integration', *Journal of European Integration History*, 1, 1.

Mittelman, J. (1996) 'The Dynamics of Globalization', in J. Mittelman (ed.) *Globalization: Critical Reflections*, Boulder: Rienner.

____ (ed.) (1996) *Globalization: Critical Reflections*, Boulder: Rienner.

Moravscik, A. (1991) 'Negotiating the Single Act', *International Organization*, 45, 1: 19–56.

____ (1993) 'Preferences and Power in the European Community: A Liberal Intergovernmentalist Approach', *Journal of Common Market Studies*, 31, 4: 473–524.

Mosca, G. (1939) *The Ruling Class*, New York: McGraw Hill.

Moses, J. (1994) 'Abdication from National Policy Autonomy: What's Left to Leave?', *Politics and Society*, 22, 2: 125–48.

Murphy, C. (1994) *International Organization and Industrial Change*, Cambridge: Polity Press.

Murphy, C. and Tooze, R. (1996) 'The Epistemology of Poverty and the Poverty of Epistemology in IPE: Mystery, Blindness and Invisibility', *Millennium*, 25, 3: 681–707.

Nelson, P.J. (1996) 'Internationalizing Economic and Environmental Policy: Transnational NGO Networks and the World Bank's Expanding Influence', *Millennium*, 25, 3: 605–33.

Neunreither, K.H. (1994) 'The Democratic Deficit of the European Union', *Government and Opposition*, 29, 3: 299–319.

Nicolaides, P. (1988) *Liberalizing Service Trade*, London: Royal Institute of International Affairs.

Notermans, T. (1993) 'The Abdication from National Policy Autonomy', *Politics and Society*, 21, 2: 133–68.

Nugent, N. (1995) 'The Leadership Capacity of the European Commission', *Journal of European Public Policy*, 2, 4: 603–23.

Nye, J. (1966) *Pan-Africanism and East African Integration*, Cambridge: Harvard University Press.

____ (1968) *International Regionalism*, Boston: Little, Brown.

OED (1989) *The Oxford English Dictionary*, 2nd edn, Oxford: Clarendon Press.

Ohmae, K. (1990) *The Borderless World: Power and Strategy in the Inter-linked Economy*, London: Collins.

____ (1993) 'The Rise of the Region State', *Foreign Affairs*, 72, 2: 76–87.
____ (1995) *The End of the Nation-State: The Rise of Regional Economies*, London: HarperCollins.
Olson, M. (1965) *The Logic of Collective Action*, Cambridge: Harvard University Press.
____ (1982) *The Rise and Decline of Nations*, New Haven: Yale University Press.
O'Neill, O. (1988) 'Ethical Reasoning and Ideological Pluralism', *Ethics*, 98: 705–22.
____ (1991) 'Transnational Justice', in D. Held (ed.) *Political Theory Today*, Cambridge: Polity Press.
____ (1992) 'Justice, Gender and Boundaries', in R. Attfield and B. Wilkins (eds) *International Justice and the Third World*, London: Routledge.
____ (1995) 'Moral Standing and State Boundaries', *Christopher Thorne Memorial Lecture*, 5 December, University of Sussex, Brighton.
____ (1996) *Towards Justice and Virtue: A Constructive Account of Practical Reasoning*, Cambridge: Cambridge University Press.
Ostrom, E. (1990) *Governing the Commons: The Evolution of Institutions*, Cambridge: Cambridge University Press.
____ (1998) 'A Behavioural Approach to the Rational Choice Theory of Collective Action', *American Political Science Review*, 92, 1: 1–22.
Otto, D. (1996) 'Nongovernmental Organizations in the UN System: The Emerging Role of International Civil Society', *Human Rights Quarterly*, 18, 1: 107–41.
Paarlberg, R. (1997) 'Agricultural Policy Reform and the Uruguay Round: Synergistic Linkage in a Two-Level Game?', *International Organization*, 51, 3: 413–44
Pakkasvirti, J. (1996) 'Nationalism and Continentalism in Latin America', *Institute of Development Studies Working Paper 14/96*, University of Helsinki.
Palan, R. (1997) 'Offshore and the Symbiotic Theory of the State and Globalization', paper presented at the *British International Studies Association Annual Conference*, 15–17 December, Leeds University.
____ (1998) 'Having Your Cake While Eating It: How and Why the State System Created Offshore', *International Studies Quarterly*, 42, 3: 625–44.
Palan, R., Abbott, J. and Deans, P. (1996) *State Strategies in the Global Political Economy*, London: Pinter.
Parsons, T. (1952) *The Social System*, New York: Tavistock Publications.
Patterson, L-A. (1997) 'Agricultural Policy Reform in the European Community: A Three-Level Game Analysis', *International Organization*, 51, 1: 135–72.
Payne, A. and Gamble, A. (1996) 'Introduction: The Political Economy of Regionalism and World Order', in A. Gamble and A. Payne (eds) *Regionalism and World Order*, Basingstoke: Macmillan.
Peck, J. (1998) 'From Federal Welfare to Local Workfare? Remaking Canada's Work-Welfare Regime', in A. Herod, G.Ó Tuathail and S. Roberts (eds) *An Unruly World? Globalization, Governance and Geography*, London: Routledge.
Pehe, J. (1994) 'Civil Society at Issue in the Czech Republic', *RFE/RL Research Report*, 19 August, 3, 32.
Peters, B.G. (1992) 'Bureaucratic Politics and the Institutions of the European Community', in A.M. Sbragia (ed.) *Euro-Politics: Institutions and Policymaking in the 'New' European Community*, Washington: Brookings Institute.
____ (1994) 'Agenda-Setting in the European Community', *Journal of European Public Policy*, 1, 1: 19–26.

Peterson, V.S. (1992) 'Transgressing Boundaries: Theories of Knowledge, Gender and International Relations', *Millennium*, 21, 2: 183–206.

Peterson, V.S. and Runyan, A. (1993) *Global Gender Issues*, Boulder: Westview Press.

Pieterse, J-N. (1996) 'The Development of Development Theory: Towards Critical Globalism', *Review of International Political Economy*, 3, 4: 541–64.

Pinder, J. (1968) 'Positive Integration and Negative Integration', *World Today*, 24, 3: 88–110.

Plotke, D. (1990) 'What's So New About New Social Movements?', *Socialist Review*, 20, 1: 81–102.

Pogge, T.W. (1987) *Realizing Rawls*, Ithaca: Cornell University Press.

Polanyi, K. (1944) *The Great Transformation*, Boston: Beacon Press.

Pollard, S. (1974) *European Economic Integration, 1815–1970*, London: Thames and Hudson.

Putnam, R. (1988) 'Diplomacy and Domestic Politics: the Logic of Two-Level Games', *International Organization*, 43, 2: 427–60.

Rawls, J. (1971) *A Theory of Justice*, Cambridge: Harvard University Press.

____ (1980) 'Kantian Constructivism in Moral Theory', in *Journal of Philosophy*, 77, 9: 515–72.

____ (1993a) 'The Law of Peoples', in S. Shute and S. Hurley (eds) *On Human Rights: The Oxford Amnesty Lectures, 1993*, New York: Basic Books.

____ (1993b) *Political Liberalism*, New York: Columbia University Press.

Reif, K. and Schmitt, H. (1980) 'Nine Second-Order National Elections: A Conceptual Framework for the Analysis of European Election Results', *European Journal of Political Research*, 8, 1: 3–44.

Reiser, O.L. and Davies, B. (1944) *Planetary Democracy: An Introduction to Scientific Humanism and Applied Semantics*, New York: Creative Age.

Remmer, K. (1997) 'Theoretical Decay and Theoretical Development: The Resurgence of Institutional Analysis', *World Politics*, 50, 1: 34–61.

Richta, R., a kolektiv (1969) *Civilizace na rozcesti*, Prague: Svoboda.

Riddell Dixon, E. (1995) 'Social Movements and the United Nations', *International Social Science Journal*, 144: 289–303.

Riggs, F. (1994) 'Conceptual Homogenization of a Heterogeneous Field: Presidentialism in Comparative Perspective', in M. Dogan and A. Kazancigil (eds) *Comparing Nations: Concepts, Strategies, Substance*, Oxford: Blackwell.

Risse-Kappen, T. (1996) 'Exploring the Nature of the Beast: International Relations Theory and Comparative Policy Analysis Meet the European Union', *Journal of Common Market Studies*, 34, 1: 53–80.

Roberts, S. (1994) 'Fictitious Capital, Fictitious Spaces: the Geography of Offshore Financial Flows', in S. Corbridge, R. Martin and N. Thrift (eds) *Money, Power and Space*, Oxford: Blackwell.

Robertson, R. (1992) *Globalization: Social Theory and Global Culture*, London: Sage.

____ (1995) 'Glocalization: Time-Space and Homogeneity-Heterogeneity', in M. Featherstone, S. Lash and R. Robertson (eds) *Global Modernities*, London: Sage.

Robinson, F. (1996) 'Rethinking Ethics in an Era of Globalization', *Sussex Papers in International Relations 2/96*, University of Sussex, Brighton.

Robinson, W. (1996) *Promoting Polyarchy*, Cambridge: Cambridge University Press.

Rodrik, D. (1997) 'Paradoxes of the Successful State', *European Economic Review*, 41, 3–5: 411–42.

Rorty, R. (1989) *Contingency, Irony and Solidarity*. Cambridge: Cambridge University Press.

Rosenau, J. and Czempiel, E-O. (1992) *Governance Without Government: Order and Change in World Politics*, Cambridge: Cambridge University Press.

Rosenberg, J. (1994) *The Empire of Civil Society: A Critique of the Realist Theory of International Relations*, London: Verso.

____ (1996) 'Isaac Deutscher and the Lost History of International Relations', *New Left Review*, 215: 3–15.

Rosenthal, J.H. (1995) 'Rethinking the Moral Dimensions of Foreign Policy', in C.W. Kegley, Jr. (ed.) *Controversies in International Relations Theory: Realism and the Neoliberal Challenge*, New York: St. Martin's Press.

Ross, G. (1998) 'European Integration and Globalization', in R. Axtmann (ed.) *Globalization and Europe*, London: Pinter.

Rostow, W.W. (1971) *The Stages of Economic Growth: A Non-Communist Manifesto*, Cambridge: Cambridge University Press.

Ruggie, J.G. (1982) 'International Regimes, Transactions and Change: Embedded Liberalism in the Post-war Economic Order', *International Organization*, 36, 2: 379–416.

____ (1993a) 'Territoriality and Beyond: Problematizing Modernity in International Relations', *International Organization*, 47, 4: 139–74.

____ (1993b) *Multilateralism Matters*, New York: Columbia University Press.

____ (1995) 'At Home Abroad, Abroad at Home: International Liberalization and Domestic Stability in the New World Economy', *Millenium*, 24, 3: 507–26.

____ (1996) *Winning the Peace: American and World Order in a New Era*, New York: Columbia University Press.

Sandholtz, W. and Zysman, J. (1989) '1992: Recasting the European Bargain', *World Politics*, 42, 1: 95–128.

Saurin, J. (1995) 'The End of International Relations? The State and International Theory in the Age of Globalization', in J. Macmillan and A. Linklater (eds) *Boundaries in Question: New Directions in International Relations*, London: Pinter.

____ (1996) 'Globalization, Poverty and the Promises of Modernity', *Millennium*, 25, 3: 657–80.

Sayer, A. (1992) *Method in Social Science*, London: Routledge.

Sbragia, A.M. (1992) 'Thinking about the European Future: The Uses of Comparison', in A.M. Sbragia (ed.) *Euro-Politics: Institutions and Policymaking in the 'New' European Community*, Washington: Brookings Institution.

Scanlon, T.M. (1982) 'Contractualism and Utilitarianism', in A. Sen and B. Williams (eds) *Utilitarianism and Beyond*, Cambridge: Cambridge University Press.

Schmitter, P.C. (1996) 'Some Alternative Futures for the European Polity and their Implications for European Public Policy', in Y. Mény, P. Muller and J-L. Quermonne (eds) *Adjusting to Europe: the Impact of the European Union on National Institutions and Policies*, London: Routledge.

Scholte, J.A. (1993) *International Relations of Social Change*, Buckingham: Open University Press.

____ (1996a) 'The Geography of Collective Identities in a Globalizing World', *Review of International Political Economy* 3, 4: 565–607.

____ (1996b) 'Globalization and Collective Identities', in J. Krause and N. Renwick (eds) *Identities in International Relations*, Basingstoke: Macmillan.

____ (1997) 'Global Capitalism and the State', *International Affairs*, 73, 3: 427–52.

____ (1999) 'Globalization and Governance', in P. Hanafin (ed.) *Identity, Rights and Constitutional Transformation*, Aldershot: Ashgate.

____ (forthcoming) *Globalization: A Critical Introduction*, London: Macmillan.

Scott, A. (1992) 'Political Culture and Social Movements', in J. Allen, P. Braham and P. Lewis (eds) *Political and Economic Forms of Modernity*, Cambridge: Polity Press.

Sedelmeier, U. (1998) 'The European Union's Association Policy Towards the Countries of Central and Eastern Europe: Policy Paradigms and Collective Identities in a Composite Policy', unpublished D.Phil. Thesis, Sussex European Institute, University of Sussex.

Seers, D. (ed.) (1981) *Dependency Theory: a Critical Reassessment*, London: Pinter.

Seidler, V.J. (1986) *Kant, Respect and Injustice: The Limits of Liberal Moral Theory*, London: Routledge.

Shakespeare, W. (1979) *A Midsummer Night's Dream* [1595–6], London: Methuen.

Shaw, M. (1994a) *Global Society and International Relations*, Cambridge: Polity Press.

____ (1994b) 'Civil Society and Global Politics: Beyond a Social Movements Approach', *Millennium*, 23, 3: 647–67.

____ (1996) *Civil Society and Media in Global Politics*, London: Pinter.

____ (1997) 'The State of Globalization: Towards a Theory of State Transformation', *Review of International Political Economy*, 4, 3: 497–513.

Shklar, J.N. (1984) *Ordinary Vices*, Cambridge: Harvard University Press.

Simecka, M. (1979) *Obnoveni poradku*, Koln: Index.

Simmel, G. (1997) *The Philosophy of Money*, London: Routledge.

Simpson, J.H. (1996) 'The Great Reversal: Selves, Communities and the Global System', *Sociology of Religion*, 57, 2: 115–25.

Singer, J.D. (1960) 'International Conflict: Three Levels of Analysis', *World Politics*, 12, 3: 453–61.

Sklair, L. (1995) 'Social Movements and Global Capitalism', *Sociology*, 29, 3: 495–512.

Skocpol, T. (1979) *States and Social Revolutions*, Cambridge: Cambridge University Press.

Smith, A. (1992) 'National Identity and the Idea of European Unity', *International Affairs*, 68, 1: 55–76.

Smith, M.J. (1992) 'Liberalism and International Reform', in T. Nardin and D.R. Mapel (eds) *Traditions of International Ethics*, Cambridge: Cambridge University Press.

Smith, R.M. (1996) 'The Unfinished Tasks of Liberalism', in B. Yack (ed.) *Liberalism Without Illusions: Essays on Liberal Theory and the Political Vision of Judith N. Shklar*, Chicago: University of Chicago Press.

Smith, S. (1995) 'The Self-Images of a Discipline: A Genealogy of International Relations Theory', in K. Booth and S. Smith (eds) *International Relations Theory Today*, Cambridge: Polity Press.

____ (1996) 'Positivism and Beyond', in S. Smith, K. Booth, and M. Zalewski (eds) *International Theory: Positivism and Beyond*, Cambridge: Cambridge University Press.

Smith, S., Booth, K. and Zalewski, M. (eds) (1996) *International Theory: Positivism and Beyond*, Cambridge: Cambridge University Press.

Snyder, G. and Deising, P. (1977) *Conflict Among Nations: Bargaining, Decision Making, and System Structure in International Crises*, Princeton: Princeton University Press.

Stammers, N. (1999) 'Shadows from the East: The End of New Social Movements?', *Papers in Social Theory 3*, Coventry: Warwick Social Theory Centre and Sussex Centre for Critical Social Theory.

Steans, J. (1998) *Gender and International Relations*, Cambridge: Polity Press.

Stoker, G. (1991) *The Politics of Local Government*, London: Macmillan.

____ (1995) 'Introduction', in D. Marsh and G. Stoker (eds) *Theory and Methods in Political Science*, London: Macmillan.

Strange, S. (1988) *States and Markets*, London: Pinter.

____ (1996) *The Retreat of the State*, Cambridge: Cambridge University Press.

Strange, S. and Tooze, R. (eds) (1981) *The International Politics of Surplus Capacity*, London: George Allen & Unwin.

Strauss, J. (1963) *Men and Decisions*, London: Macmillan.

Sylvester, C. (1993) *Feminist Theory and International Relations in a Postmodern Era*, Cambridge: Cambridge University Press.

Taggart, P. (1996) *The New Populism and the New Politics*, London: Macmillan.

____ (1998) 'A Touchstone of Dissent: Euroscepticism in Contemporary Western European Party Systems', *European Journal of Political Research*, 33, 3: 363–88.

Tarrow, S. (1994) *Power in Movement*, Cambridge: Cambridge University Press.

Taylor, C. (1995) 'Cross-Purposes: The Liberal-Communitarian Debate', in *Philosophical Arguments*, Cambridge: Harvard University Press.

Taylor, P. (1982) 'Intergovernmentalism in the European Communities in the 1970s', *International Organization*, 36, 4: 741–66.

____ (1996a) 'Embedded Statism and the Social Sciences: Opening up to New Spaces', *Environment and Planning A*, 28, 11: 1917–28.

____ (1996b) 'The Modern Multiplicity of States', in E. Kofman and G. Youngs (eds) *Globalization: Theory and Practice*, London: Pinter.

Teubner, G. (ed.) (1997) *Global Law Without a State*, Aldershot: Dartmouth.

Thomas, C. and Wilkin, P. (eds) (1996) *Globalization and the South*, Basingstoke: Macmillan.

Tooze, R. (1987) 'International Political Economy and International Relations: From "Enfant Terrible" to Child Prodigy or Just a Cuckoo in the Nest?', *Millennium*, 16, 2: 349–51.

____ (1988) 'The Unwritten Preface: "International Political Economy" and Epistemology', *Millennium*, 17, 2: 285–93.

____ (1997) 'International Political Economy in an Age of Globalization', in J. Baylis and S. Smith (eds) *The Globalization of World Politics*, Oxford: Oxford Univerity Press.

Tooze, R. and Murphy, C. (1996) 'The Epistemology of Poverty and the Poverty of Epistemology in IPE: Mystery, Blindness and Invisibility', *Millennium*, 25, 3: 681–707.

Touraine, A. (1977) *The Self-Production of Society*, Chicago: University of Chicago Press.

____ (1981) *The Voice and the Eye: An Analysis of Social Movements*, Cambridge: Cambridge University Press.
____ (1987) *The Workers' Movement*, Cambridge: Cambridge University Press.
____ (1997) *What Is Democracy?*, Boulder: Westview Press.
____ (1998) 'Can We Live Together Equal and Different?', in R. Fine, W. Outhwaite and P. Wagner (eds) *Papers in Social Theory I*, Coventry: University of Warwick.
Trebilcock, M.J. and Howse, R. (1995) *The Regulation of International Trade*, London: Routledge.
Tsebelis, G. (1994) 'The Power of the European Parliament as a Conditional Agenda-Setter', *American Political Science Review*, 88, 1: 128–42.
Tucker, K. (1991) 'How New are the New Social Movements?', *Theory, Culture and Society*, 8, 2: 75–98.
Tussie, D. (1998) 'Globalization and World Trade: From Multilateralism to Regionalism', *Oxford Development Studies*, 26, 1: 33–45.
UIA (1997) *Yearbook of International Organizations, 1997/98. Volume I*, Munich: Saur and the Union of International Associations.
UNCTAD (1994) *World Investment Report, 1994*, New York: United Nations.
____ (1997) *World Investment Report, 1997*, New York: United Nations.
Van den Anker, C. (1993) 'North-South: Development and Agency from an Impartial Perspective', Nottingham: Political Studies Association.
____ (1995) 'The Moral Problem of Global Inequality', in J. Lovenduski and J. Stanyer (eds) *Contemporary Political Studies*, York: Political Studies Association.
____ (forthcoming) *Justice in One World*.
Van der Eijk, C. and Franklin, M.N. (1996) *Choosing Europe: The European Electorate and National Politics in the Face of Union*, Ann Arbor: Michigan University Press.
van der Pijl, K. (1984) *The Making of an Atlantic Ruling Class*, London: Verso.
Vejvoda, I. (1995) 'The Exit from Totalitarianism in East Central Europe and Globalization', St. Paul: Macalester International.
Viner, J. (1950) *The Customs Union Issue*, New York: Carnegie Institute.
Vogel, S. (1997) 'International Games with National Rules: How Regulation Shapes Competition in "Global" Markets', *Journal of Public Policy*, 17, 2: 169–93.
Wade, R. (1990) *Governing the Market*, Princeton: Princeton University Press.
____ (1996) 'Globalization and Its Limits: Reports of the Death of the National Economy Are Greatly Exaggerated', in S. Berger and R. Dore (eds) *National Diversity and Global Capitalism*, Ithaca: Cornell University Press.
Walker, R.B.J. (1988) *One World, Many Worlds: Struggles for a Just World Peace*, Boulder: Lynne Rienner.
____ (1993) *Inside/Outside: International Relations as Political Theory*, Cambridge: Cambridge University Press.
Wallace, H. (1985) 'The Presidency of the Council of Ministers of the European Communities: A Comparative Perspective', in C. O'Nullain (ed.) *The Presidency of the European Council of Ministers*, London: Croom Helm.
____ (1996) 'Politics and Policy in the EU: The Challenge to Governance', in H. Wallace and W. Wallace (eds) *Policy-Making in the European Union*, 3rd edn, Oxford: Oxford University Press.
____ (1997) *One Europe or Several*, mimeo.

Wallace, H. and Wallace, W. (eds) (1996) *Policy-Making in the European Union*, 3rd edn, Oxford: Oxford University Press.

Wallace, H., Wallace, W. and Webb, C. (1983) *Policy-Making in the European Communities*, Oxford: Oxford University Press.

Wallace, W. (1994) 'The Nation State: Rescue or Retreat', *Political Studies*, 42: 52–76.

Wallace, W. and Smith, J. (1995) 'Democracy or Technocracy? European Integration and the Problem of Popular Consent', *West European Politics*, 18, 3: 137–57.

Wallerstein, I. (1979) *The Capitalist World-Economy*, Cambridge: Cambridge University Press.

____ (1986) 'Societal Development Or Development of the World-System?' *International Sociology* 1, 1: 3–17.

____ (1991) *Unthinking Social Science: The Limits of Nineteenth-Century Paradigms*, Cambridge: Polity Press.

____ (1995) *After Liberalism*, New York: The New Press.

Waltz, K.N. (1959) *Man, the State and War*, New York: Columbia University Press.

____ (1970) 'The Myth of National Interdependence', in C. Kindleberger (ed.) *The International Corporation*, Cambridge: MIT Press.

____ (1979) *Theory of International Politics*, Reading, M.A.: Addison-Wesley.

Walzer, M. (1985) *Spheres of Justice: A Defence of Pluralism and Equality*, Oxford: Basil Blackwell.

____ (1996) 'On Negative Politics', in B. Yack (ed.) *Liberalism Without Illusions: Essays on Liberal Theory and the Political Vision of Judith N. Shklar*, Chicago: University of Chicago Press.

Waters, M. (1995) *Globalization*, London: Routledge.

Weber, C. (1995) *Simulating Sovereignty*, Cambridge: Cambridge University Press.

Weber, M. (1964) *The Theory of Social and Economic Organization*, trans. A. Henderson and T. Parsons, New York: The Free Press.

Webster (1961) *Webster's Third New International Dictionary of the English Language, Unabridged*, Springfield: Merriam.

Weiler, J.H.H. (1995) 'After Maastricht: Community Legitimacy in Post-1992 Europe', in W.J. Adams (ed.) *Singular Europe*, Ann Arbor: Michigan University Press.

Weiss, L. (1998) *The Myth of the Powerless State*, Cambridge: Polity Press.

Wendt, A. (1987) 'The Agent-Structure Problem in International Relations Theory', *International Organization*, 41, 3: 335–70.

____ (1992) 'Levels of Analysis vs. Agents and Structures: Part III', *Review of International Studies*, 18, 2: 181–5.

Wheaton, B. and Kavan, Z. (1992) *The Velvet Revolution*, Boulder: Westview Press.

Whitfield, P. (1994) *The Image of the World: Twenty Centuries of World Maps*, London: British Library.

Wiener, J. (1999) *Globalization and the Harmonization of Laws*, London: Cassell.

Wilke, M. and Wallace, H. (1990) 'Subsidiarity: Approaches to Power Sharing in the European Community', Royal Institute of International Affairs Discussion Paper no. 27, London: RIIA.

Willetts, P. (1996) 'From Stockholm to Rio and Beyond: the Impact of the Environmental Movement as the UN Consultative Arrangements for NGOs', *Review of International Studies*, 22, 1: 57–80.

Williams, H. (1992) *International Relations in Political Theory*, Milton Keynes: Open University Press.

____ (1996) *International Relations and the Limits of Political Theory*, Basingstoke: Macmillan.

Williams, J. (1996) 'Nothing Succeeds Like Success?: Legitimacy and International Relations', in B. Holden (ed.) *The Ethical Dimensions of Global Change*, London: Macmillan.

Williams, M. (1994) *International Economic Organizations and the Third World*, London: Harvester Wheatsheaf.

Williams, S. (1990) 'Sovereignty and Accountability in the European Community', *Political Quarterly*, 61, 3: 299–317.

Williamson, J.G. (1994) *The Political Economy of Policy Reform*, Washington: Institute for International Economics.

____ (1996) 'Globalization, Convergence and History', *Journal of Economic History*, 56, 2: 277–306.

Winters, L.A. (1997) 'What can European Experience Teach Developing Countries about Integration', *The World Economy*, 20, 7: 889–912.

World Bank (1997) *World Development Report*, New York: Oxford University Press.

Wurzel, R.K.W. (1996) 'The Role of the EU Presidency in the Environmental Field: Does it Make a Difference which Member-State Runs the Presidency?', *Journal of European Public Policy*, 3, 2: 272–91.

Young, O. (1989) *International Cooperation*, Ithaca: Cornell University Press.

Youngs, G. (1996) 'Dangers of Discourse: The Case of Globalization', in E. Kofman and G. Youngs (eds) *Globalization: Theory and Practice*, London: Pinter.

Yurdesev, A. (1993) 'Level of Analysis and Unit of Analysis: A Case for Distinction', *Millennium*, 22, 1: 77–88.

Zak, V. (1997) *Rizika mobilizacni politiky*, Prague: Cesky spisovatel.

Znoj, M. (ed.) (1995) *Nase soucasne spory o liberalismus*, Prague: Centrum liberalnich studii.

INDEX